Writing Timbuktu

THE BOOK IN WEST AFRICAN HISTORY

SHAMIL JEPPIE

PRINCETON UNIVERSITY PRESS
PRINCETON & OXFORD

Published by Princeton University Press
41 William Street, Princeton, New Jersey 08540
99 Banbury Road, Oxford OX2 6JX

press.princeton.edu

GPSR Authorized Representative: Easy Access System Europe - Mustamäe tee 50, 10621 Tallinn, Estonia, gpsr.requests@easproject.com

ISBN 9780691273853
ISBN (e-book) 9780691273846

Library of Congress Control Number: 2025936707

British Library Cataloging-in-Publication Data is available
Editorial: Priya Nelson and Emma Wagh
Production Editorial: Sara Lerner
Jacket Design: Katie Osborne
Production: Erin Suydam
Publicity: Alyssa Sanford and Carmen Jimenez
Copyeditor: Lachlan Brooks
Indexer: Rita Sephton

Jacket Credit: horst friedrichs / Alamy Stock Photo

This book has been composed in Minion3

Printed in the United States of America

10 9 8 7 6 5 4 3 2 1

WRITING TIMBUKTU

To the memory of my parents

Ayesha Sampson (1929–2006) and Moegsien Jeppie (1928–2006)

أنا أقل عشيرتي كتبا نهبت له ستة عشر مائة مجلد

I had the smallest library of any of my kin, and they seized 1,600 volumes.

—AHMAD BABA

. . . in la dicta ciptà se spacciano assai libri in mercantia, li quali vanno da la Barbaria tutti scriti di mano e quilli che portano libri guadagnano più in libri chín lo resto de tutti le mercantie.

. . . in this city many books are sold, coming from Barbary, written by hand and the trade in books are more profitable than any other goods.

—GIOVANNI LEONE AFRICANO,
LA COSMOGRAPHIA DE L'AFFRICA

CONTENTS

List of Illustrations xi

Acknowledgments xiii

Note on Transliteration xvii

Key Dates xix

List of Authors Discussed xxiii

Titles of Key Manuscripts Mentioned xxv

Glossary xxix

Introduction: Books and Rebels in the Desert 1

1 Discovering Books in the Desert 27

2 The Education of Ahmad Baba, 1556–91 49

3 Exile in Marrakesh 65

4 Ahmad Baba's Later Years in Timbuktu, 1608–27 85

5 The Rise of Shinqit 98

6 The Kunta Writers: From Tuwat to Timbuktu and Beyond 114

7 The Collector of Timbuktu: Ahmad Bularraf 137

8 Manuscript, Print, and Memory 155

Epilogue 175

Notes 179

Bibliography 195

Index 205

LIST OF ILLUSTRATIONS

1. Map 11
2. Epigraphy, earliest evidence of writing 12
3. *Catalan Atlas* of Abraham Cresques (fourteenth century) 31
4. Heinrich Barth, View of Timbuktu (1853) 40
5. "Notice" from Felix Du Bois, *Tombouctou la mystérieuse* (1897) 44
6. "Déchiffrement de manuscrits chez les puels de say," in G. de Gironcourt, *Missions de Gironcourt en Afrique occidentale* (1920) 48
7. *Jalb al-ni'ma* by Ahmad Baba 56
8. Image of Marrakesh, "Vue de Merrakech" or "El Badi Palace" by Adriaen Matham (1640) 72
9. *Kifāyat al-muḥtāj* by Ahmad Baba 77
10. *Tuḥfat al-fuḍalā* by Ahmad Baba 80
11. René Caillié, View of Timbuktu (1830) 116
12. *al-Ṭarā'if wa'l-talā'id* by Sidi Muhammad al-Kunti 123
13. *al-Risāla al-ghallāwiyya* by Sidi Muhammad al-Kunti (older *and* newer copy) 124
14. *Izālat al-rayb* by Ahmad Bularraf 150
15. Group photograph of 1956 Congress of Black Writers and Artists, Paris 166
16. "Homme et femme toucouleurs: Marabout faisant un grigri," in P. D. Boilat, *Illustrations de esquisses sénégalaises, physionomie du pays, peuplades, commerce, religions, passé et avenir, récits et légendes* (1853) 169

ACKNOWLEDGMENTS

BORN, RAISED, and having lived most of my life in a peninsula on the southern tip of Africa, a future immersed in the distant, dry, and desert northern parts of the continent was improbable. The impulse to write about it probably lies deeper in the past than I had realized. I first learned the outlines of the history of West Africa, the Maghreb, and the world around Timbuktu in the early 1980s in a small seminar class led by the late Neville Alexander, linguist, historian, and anti-racist intellectual and activist. At the time it was still rare to study African history in a country where the official syllabi taught that history began in Europe and only Europeans in Africa had a past. With few exceptions, no African history was taught even at university level. It was then inconceivable that two decades later, I would be part of a project initiated by then–president of South Africa, Thabo Mbeki, to revitalize the archives thousands of kilometers away, in Timbuktu, Mali, in a collaborative project between the national archives of South Africa and Mali. Mbeki appointed a Minister in his office, the late Dr. Essop Pahad, to oversee the project. In the intervening years—between first hearing about the Songhai and Gao and going to the Niger River Bend in the first years of the millennium—my knowledge and ability to write about that region caught up with my curiosity.

I was fortunate to learn a huge amount from many people during the writing of this book, most importantly from scholars in the region. My work was made possible by their interest. I should like to acknowledge most warmly Mohamed Diagayete, Abdul Kader Haidara, Cheikh Hammou, Seydou Traore, and Dr. Mahmoud Zouber, as well as many others whom I got to know over the years, and who allowed me to work with their materials and taught me so much about the intricacies of the writing culture of the region. Dr. Diagayete, in his position as director of the main manuscript archives in Timbuktu also kindly granted me permission to use images of the manuscripts in his care. During my first trip to Timbuktu, I was fortunate to be accompanied by Graham Dominy and Alexio Motsi to look at the collections and see them from the perspective of the archivist and conservator.

Among the specialists on the region who were most supportive of my work were the late John Hunwick, Charles C. Stewart, Louis Brenner, and Paulo F. de Moraes Farias. Paulo responded immediately and dug out his original photographs of the inscriptions I use in the book. No writing on the area is possible without reference to their outstanding scholarship. They have set high standards. For a view from the eastern parts of the continent I benefitted from the expertise and marvelous stories of the late Sean O'Fahey. The thorough commentary of the anonymous readers kept me on my feet—or rather, on my seat!

Mohamed Nouhi welcomed me in Agadir and then supplied me with pages of comments (twice) on two chapters. Mohamed Elemine in Nouakchott responded promptly to requests for details on scholars and sources. Seyni Moumouni and his colleagues welcomed me in Niamey. Fatima Harrak, Rahal Boubrik, and Hamidi Belaid, and many others in Rabat were quick to respond to requests for information and books; Hamidi was a patient and cheerful calligraphy instructor. More recently, the Académie Royaume du Maroc has welcomed me and its officers effortlessly facilitated my visits to Rabat. There I am able to regularly meet my collaborator on a previous book, Souleymane Bachir Diagne, whose conversation is always insightful.

For reading various parts of the manuscript I want to thank Louis Brenner, Dmitry Bondarev, Islam Dayeh, Adrien Delmas, Mohamed Elemine, Aslam Farouk-Ali, Baz Lecocq, Paul Naylor, and Mauro Nobili. Aslam and I went on a road trip—an adventure—to Guelmim, which, apart from historical fiction, always comes up in our conversation. Needless to say, I probably missed a number of comments and questions by these generous readers.

Students and researchers at the Tombo*uct*ou Manuscripts Project at the University of Cape Town were and are in many ways my teachers. I benefitted from working with them and advising their research projects, and we were able to bring a small part of the Sahara and the Sahel to Cape Town: Saniyakubu Adam, Saarah Jappie, Hassen Kawo, Shahid Mathee, Abigail Moffett, Susanna Molins-Lliteras, Ebrahim Moos, and Samaila Suleiman. Ebrahim kindly assisted with translations and transliterations, and could find classical Arabic references in an instant! More recently, Osas Asemota has assisted with keeping some order in my office and Grace Brain with checking endless bibliographic details and keeping the text readable for a nonspecialist.

The Tombo*uct*ou Manuscripts Project at the University of Cape Town received funding from the Ford Foundation and the Gerda Henkel Stiftung, and most recently I had a grant from the National Institute for the Humanities and Social

Sciences. To bring colleagues from West Africa to Cape Town, to work in collections in various parts of the continent and Europe, and to support doctoral students and postdoctoral research would not have been possible without such generous funding over the years.

At the University of Cape Town, the humanities deans and heads of my department supported my work, along with my colleagues in the department. The librarians at the African Studies Library, Inter-Library Loans, and the humanities librarians have always been responsive and efficient. There was constant engagement especially from my colleagues Bodhi Kar and Nigel Penn. During our time at the Institute for Humanities in Africa (Huma), Deborah Posel was a keen interlocutor and provided my project and visitors with ample office space. Andrea Brigaglia has been a wonderful friend and travel companion, letting me enjoy the benefits of his intimate knowledge of Kano and Kaduna, Napoli and Palermo. Among the administrative staff for many years Rifqah Kahn was a stalwart of the project, going far beyond the call of duty. And finally, Colleen Petersen has in recent years kept me administratively on my feet.

During the height of the COVID-19 pandemic, in late 2020–21, I enjoyed more silence than I had contemplated at the Wissenschaftskolleg zu Berlin, and I was able to rely on the exceptional library team to work with materials I would have had great difficulty accessing otherwise. I would like to thank the director, Barbara Stollberg-Rilinger, Daniel Schönpflug, Katarina Wiedermann, and Vera Pfeffer, among the many others at the institute. Sonja Assal's interview led to conversations about book and intellectual history. Among the Fellows, Alex Bevilacqua, Ève Chiapello, Angela Creager, Merve Emre, Jaeeun Kim, and many others that year offered me lots to think and talk about. Daniel Schönpflug convened a group who wanted to produce scholarly work in accessible prose, and so I found myself in the company of evolutionary biologists and an astronomer: so to Madeleine Beekman, Hakan Ceylan, Anna Frebel, Benjamin Oldroyd, here is my contribution; and the running remains wicked!

Over the years, many colleagues arranged for me to give talks about my work. They are too many to mention but among them are Olly Akkerman, Anne Bang, Alex Bevilacqua, Ann Blair, Rens Bod, Dmitry Bondarev, Mirjam De Bruijn, Leon Buskens, Tony Crooks, Michael Friedrich, Alesandro Gori, Georges Khalil, Kai Kresse, Premesh Lalu, Peter Miller, Mahmood Mamdani, Yoichi Mine, Yoko Nagahara, Sheldon Pollock, Christelle Rabier, Umar Ryad, Ebrima Sall, Carlo Taviani, Li Weijian, and Stephanie Zehnle. Most recently, Avinoam Shalem and Director Alina Payne of the I Tatti Centre for the Study of Italian

Renaissance invited me to the exceptional environment in the hills above Florence, where I also relied on a great library and was stimulated by a wonderful and diverse group of fellows.

When it came to finding a publisher, my former supervisor, the late Bob Tignor and Mahmoud Mamdani suggested Princeton, and Jeremy Adelman made the introductions. At the press, the professionalism and support has been exceptional. I am immensely grateful to Priya Nelson for her time and support from the proposal onward, and to Emma Wagh and Sara Lerner for their patience and attention to detail, and all the others who worked on the book at PUP. The maps were made by Ralph Schroder and Siddique Motala, who quietly tolerated my indecision about which places to mark and connect.

Thanks to friends and colleagues in Cape Town who heard some of the same stories many times over, smiled at endless excuses, and allowed my evasions: Armien Abrahams, Nadia Abrahams, Ebrahiem Bardien, Eugene Cairncross, Wahbie Long, Nazeem Mahatey (with whom I hitchhiked from Bamako to Djenne and back when that was still possible), Eddie Maloka, Shuaib Manjra, Ashraf Mohamed, Ebrahim Moosa, Rashied Omar, Abdul Aleem Somers, Waheed Sookool, and Abdul Kader Tayob. Neville, Bridget, Bradley, and Brian at the Cape Carpentry Collective have been trying to teach me the basics of a craft while listening to my updates on publishing; I now recognize that art comes out of craft.

Over the years my family has supported me with their interest in my work and my general well-being, which I deeply appreciate: Nazley, Ebrahim, Phaldie, Zahrah, Shamilah, and Ghalib, along with the larger extended family: Abdurrahman (Lago), Surour, Shamilah, Salih and Siham, Ramzi, Thameen, Suhair and Matthew, Daleel and Merve, Zulfiq and Leila, Nadier, Lamine, and Hanan. You will hear less about "the book" from now on.

Finally, for the many years of absentmindedness and playing too much Ali Farka Touré or Tinariwen, and warmly entertaining guests from across West Africa and the globe, this book would not have been possible without the presence, sacrifices, and urging of Gigi (Gadija), Mazin, and Haytham. My deepest gratitude to you.

NOTE ON TRANSLITERATION

A GREAT many choices have to be made when representing names of people, places, books originally written in the Arabic script; and the challenges are multiplied when they are not Arabic. Fortunately, some conventions have developed in scholarly communities. But I have tried to keep things simple. I have kept diacritics to a minimum. Following a strict system of transcribing the name Ahmad Baba, it should appear as Aḥmad Bābā; likewise Ahmad Bularraf should be written Aḥmad Bulʿarrāf. In the interest of accessibility to the nonspecialist reader, I keep spellings as unencumbered by additional diacritical markings as possible. Place names have been kept as they appear most commonly in widely used maps. In general, the system of the *International Journal of Middle East Studies* has been used. When manuscripts were dated, they followed the Hijri calendar, and I have followed the conversion to the Common Era as used as the catalogs in which they are mentioned, or I have used the "date converter" from muslimphilosophy.com.

KEY DATES

c. 1100: Timbuktu is founded by the Tuareg Imashagan, known as Kel Tamasheq. One popular local story is that the town was named after a woman who discovered a well. Her name was Buktu and thus *Tin Buktu* ("well of Buktu") was born.

1307: Mansa Musa becomes ruler of Mali and extends the reach of his realm; the state of Mali is at its height under him.

1324: Kankan/Mansa Musa goes on pilgrimage to Mecca and arrives in Cairo with vast quantities of gold, which cause the gold market to collapse. And so starts the Bilad al-Sudan's fame. The ruler stops in Timbuktu on his return and is so impressed with the settlement that he appoints Andalusian architect Abu Ishaq al-Sahili to design the city's first mosque, the Jingere-Ber (grand mosque).

1353: Ibn Battuta, the North African globetrotter, arrives in Timbuktu.

1375: Abraham Cresques, cartographer from Mallorca (Spain), first reports the name "Timbuktu," in the form of "Tenbuch," in his well-known *Catalan Atlas* made for the King of Aragon. The map displays the region of northwest Africa with a large image of Mansa Musa sitting on his throne holding a big gold nugget.

c. 1400: State of Mali begins to decline.

1461–62: Death of Sidi Yahya, a scholar from North Africa, who settled in Timbuktu and became the imam of one of the most important mosques of the city, named after him.

1465: Sonni Ali establishes Songhay state.

1493–1528: Under Askiya Muhammad, new ruler of the Songhay, Timbuktu becomes an important center of Islamic scholarship and the Songhay realm continues to expand.

1506: The Andalusian, Hasan al-Wazzan, also known as Leo Africanus, goes to Timbuktu on a diplomatic mission for the Sultan of Fez and writes his famous impression of the city.

1548: Death of Mahmud bin 'Umar bin Muhammad Aqit, first known imam of the Sankoré Mosque.

1556: Birth of Ahmad Baba, one of the most famous scholars from Timbuktu.

1591: Army of Sultan Mansur of Marrakesh conquers and destroys the Songhay power at Gao.

1593: Ahmad Baba is exiled to Marrakesh.

1607: Ahmad Baba returns to Timbuktu and spends the rest of his life in the city devoted to teaching and writing.

1655–56: This is the last date mentioned in the *Tārīkh al-Sūdān* by 'Abd al-Rahman al-Sa'di, describing the events, rulers, and scholars of the region.

1660: The Armạ, descendants of the Moroccan invaders, sever their loyalty to Morocco and begin to rule the area from Timbuktu.

1700s: Establishment of the Bambara kingdom of Segou, which eventually extends influence to Timbuktu in about 1800.

Nineteenth century: Period of Fulbe jihads aiming to revivify the practice of Islam and establish states in the region. The main leaders were 'Uthman bin Fudi (d. 1817), who established the Sokoto state in contemporary northern Nigeria; Ahmad Lobbo (d. 1845), founder of the state of Masina based in the central region of Mali; and 'Umar Tal (d. 1864), leader of the so-called "Toucouleur [Tukulor] Empire" extending from present-day eastern Senegal to central Mali.

1811: Death of Shaykh Sidi al-Mukhtar al-Kunti. The Kunta were a powerful scholarly family linked to the Qadiriyya *tariqa.*

1818–19: Muhammad al-Kunti, son of Shaykh Sidi al-Mukhtar al-Kunti, settles in Timbuktu.

1826: Gordon Laing, a Scottish explorer, was the first European to reach Timbuktu via the desert, and was killed on his way back to Europe.

1828: The French explorer René Caillié visits the city of Timbuktu and is the first European to arrive back to Europe alive; he goes on to publish his diary.

1853: Heinrich Barth spends seven months in Timbuktu during his trip throughout West Africa; he is threatened by Ahmad bin Ahmad Lobbo but saved by Ahmad al-Bakkay, the Kunta leader of the city.

1893–94: Timbuktu is conquered by the French.

1897: After visiting Timbuktu in 1895, *Le Figaro* journalist Félix Du Bois publishes the bestseller *Tombouctou la mystérieuse*, soon translated into English as *Timbuktu the Mysterious.*

1898–1900: Octave Houdas, the French orientalist, edits and translates into French al-Sa'di's *Tārīkh al-Sūdān.*

1904: Ahmad Bularraf, the legendary copyist and collector, settles in Timbuktu.

1912–13: Houdas and Maurice Delafosse edit and translate into French the Timbuktu chronicle, the *Tārīkh al-fattāsh.*

1950s: Arguments are made by the Tuareg scholar Muhammad Mahmoud Ould Cheikh, so-called "Qadi of Timbuktu," to establish a pro-French Tuareg state in the Sahara.

1961: Formation of the Republic of Mali with Modibo Keita as first President.

1963: First rebellion against independent Mali in the north.

1968–91: Dictatorship of Musa Traoré in Mali.

1970: Establishment of Ahmed Baba Institute (Cedrab) in Timbuktu by UNESCO to preserve intellectual legacy of region.

1970s: Drought in the Sahel.

1977: Mahmoud Zouber's biography of Ahmad Baba, *Aḥmad Bābā de Tombouctou: Sa vie et son oeuvre* (Paris: G. P. Maisonneuve et Larose), is published.

1990s: Publication of the first catalogs of Timbuktu manuscripts by the Al-Furqan Foundation in London.

1990–93: Tamasheq Rebellion in the north of Mali.

1996: Peace Accords between Bamako-centered state and Tuareg rebels in the north of Mali.

2000s: Establishment of first private libraries of Timbuktu, such as the Mamma Haidara and the Fondo Kati libraries. More private collections are organized.

2001: South African President Thabo Mbeki travels to Mali and goes to Timbuktu. Birth of the SA-Mali Project to help preserve the manuscripts of Timbuktu.

2003: John Hunwick publishes volume 4 of the *Arabic Literature of Africa* (*ALA*) series, *The Writings of Western Sudanic Africa* (Leiden: Brill), a compendium of known works and authors of the region. (Volume 5, *The Writings of Mauritania and the Western Sahara*, appears in 2015.)

2009: Inauguration of the South African–sponsored new building of the Ahmed Baba Institute located opposite the Sankoré Mosque.

January 2012: Beginning of the crisis in Mali.

LIST OF AUTHORS DISCUSSED

IN BROADLY chronological order by century.

Sixteenth to seventeenth centuries

Leo Africanus (Ḥasan al-Wazzān) (d. 1554)
Aḥmad bin Aḥmad bin 'Umar bin Muḥammad 'Umar bin 'Ali bin Yaḥyā (d. 1583)
Muḥammad Baghayogho al-Wangarī (d. 1593)
Aḥmad Bābā (d. 1627)
Aḥmad bin Qāsim al-Ḥajarī (d. after 1640)
'Abd al-Raḥmān al-Sa'dī (d. 1655/56)

Eighteenth to nineteenth centuries

Muḥammad al-Yadālī (d. 1752)
Sīdī al-Mukhtār al-Kuntī (d. 1811)
Sīdī Muḥammad al-Khalīfah (d. 1826)
Al-Ḥājj 'Umar Tāl (d. 1864)
Aḥmad al-Bakkāy (d. 1865)

Nineteenth to twentieth centuries

Muḥammad Yaḥya Sālim al-Wallātī al-Yūnusī (d. 1912)
Mūsā Kamara (d. 1943/1945)
Aḥmad Bul'arrāf (d. 1955)
Boubou Hama (d. 1982)
Aḥmadou Hampâté Bâ (d. 1991)
Aḥmad Baber al-Arawānī (d. 1997)

European writers / travelers (nineteenth century)

René Caillié (d. 1838)
Heinrich Barth (d. 1865)
Felix Du Bois (d. 1945)

TITLES OF KEY MANUSCRIPTS MENTIONED

DETAILS ABOUT manuscript locations can be found in John O. Hunwick, comp., *Arabic Literature of Africa*, vol. 4, *The Writings of Western Sudanic Africa* (Leiden: Brill, 2003), and Charles C. Stewart, comp., *Arabic Literature of Africa*, vol. 5, *The Writings of Mauritania and the Western Sahara* (Leiden: Brill, 2015). For manuscripts by Baba, see also Mahmoud Zouber, *Ahmad Baba de Tombouctou: Sa vie et son oeuvre* (Paris: G. P. Maisonneuve et Larose, 1977).

'Ayn al-'iṣāba fī ḥukm al-ṭāba (Hitting the mark regarding the ruling of tobacco) by Aḥmad Bābā

Bayān mā waqa'a baynanā wa bayna Amīr Māsīna (The explanation of what happened between us and the leader of the Māsīna) by 'Umar ibn Sa'īd al-Fūtī Ṭāl

Bayān wujūb al-hijra 'alā l'ibād (The explanation on the obligation of migration on the servants [of God]) by 'Uthmān ibn Fūdī

Dīwān al-mulūk fī salāṭīn al-Sūdān (The records of the kings regarding the rulers of the Sudan) attributed to al-Mukhtār al-Kabīr ibn Aḥmad ibn Abī Bakr al-Kuntī

Diyā' al-hukkām fī mā lahum wa 'alayhim min aḥkām (Illuminating the path of rulers: The rules that are in their favor or against them) by 'Abdullāh b. Muḥammad Fūdī

Diyā' al-Sultān (The illumination of the Sultan) by 'Abdullāh b. Muḥammad Fūdī

Fatḥ al-Shakūr fī ma'rifat a'yān 'ulamā al-Takrūr (The opening of the Praised in knowing the scholars of Takrūr) by Muḥammad b. Abī Bakr al-Bartīlī

Ghāyat al-amal fī tafḍīl al-nīyya 'alā l'amal (The object of hope in explaining the superiority of intention) by Aḥmad Bābā

Infāq al-maysūr fī tārīkh bilād al-Takrūr (Easy expenditure in understanding the history of the lands of Takrūr) by Muḥammad Bello b.'Uthmān ibn Fūdī

Izālat al-rayb wal-shakk wal-tafrīṭ fī dhikr al-muʾallifīn min ahl al-Takrūr wal-saḥrāʾ wa ahl Shinqīṭ (Removing the doubt, skepticism, and negligence regarding the authors of Takrūr, the Sahara, and Shinqīṭ) by Aḥmad Bulʿarrāf

Jalb al-niʿma wa dafʿ al-niqma bi mujānabat al-wulāt al-ẓalama (Acquiring blessings and repelling affliction by avoiding unjust rulers) by Aḥmad Bābā

Jawāb ʿan thalātha asʾila (The response to three questions) by Aḥmad Bābā

Jawāhir al-maʿānī (The jewels of all meanings) by ʿAlī Ḥarāzim Barāda

Kifāyat al-muḥtāj li maʿrifa man laysa fi al-Dībāj (The adequate supplement for those who want to know which scholars do not appear in the Dībāj) by Aḥmad Bābā

al-Laʾālī al-sundusiyya fīl-faḍāʾil al-sanūsiyya (The silk pearls in extolling the virtues of the Sanūsiyya) by Aḥmad Bābā

al-Lamʿ fīlʾishāra li-ḥukm al-tibgh (The shimmering light regarding the ruling on tobacco) by Aḥmad Bābā

al-Lumʿa fī ajwibat al-asʾilat al-arbaʿa (The gleaming light in response to the four questions) by Aḥmad Bābā

Mā rawāhu al-ruwāt (What the narrators narrated) by Aḥmad Bābā

Minan al-Rabb al-Jalīl bi bayān muhimmāt Khalīl (The gifts of the majestic Lord in explaining important aspects of Khalil) by Aḥmad Bābā

al-Minna fī iʿtiqād ahl al-sunna (The divine gift in explaining the beliefs of the people of tradition) by Sīdī al-Mukhtār al-Kuntī

Miʿrāj al-ṣuʿūd ilā nayl ḥukm mujallab al-Sūd (The ascent toward grasping the law concerning transported Blacks) by Aḥmad Bābā

Nayl al-ibtihāj bi-taṭrīz al-dībāj (Achievement of joy in embellishing the Dībāj) by Aḥmad Bābā

Rimāḥ ḥizb al-Raḥīmʿalā nuḥūr ḥizb al-rajīṃ (The spears of the merciful party on the throats of the accursed party) by ʿUmar ibn Saʿīd al-Fūtī

al-Risāla al-ghallāwiyya (The ghallāwī epistle) by Sīdī Muḥammad al-Kuntī

al-Saʿāda al-abadiyya fīl-taʿrīf bi-ʿulamāʾ Timbuktu (The eternal bliss in introducing the scholars of Timbuktu) by Aḥmad Bābīr al-ʿArawānī

Tadhkirat al-nisyān fī akhbār mulūk al-Sūdān (A reminder to the forgetful regarding the history of the kings of the Sudan). Anonymous

al-Ṭarāʾif waʾl-talāʾid min karāmāt al-shaykhayn al-wālida wal-wālid (The exquisite and rare narrations on the miracles of the mother and father) by Sīdī Muḥammad al-Kuntī

Tārīkh al-fattāsh fī dhikr al-mulūk wa akhbār al-juyūsh wa akābir al-nās (The chronicle of the investigator regarding the history of the kings, the armies, and other notables) attributed to Maḥmūd Ka'tī

Tārīkh al-Sūdān (Chronicle of the Land of the Blacks) by 'Abd al-Raḥmān al-Sa'dī

Ṭarīq al-janna fī fawā'id kitāb al-minna (The road to paradise regarding the benefits of Kitab al-Minna) by Aḥmad Bul'arrāf

Tuḥfat al-fuḍalā bi ba'ḍ fadā'il al-'ulamā (Gift to the virtuous in explaining the excellence of scholars) by Aḥmad Bābā

al-Wasīṭ fī tarājim 'udabā Shinqīṭ (The mediator on the writers of Shinqit) by Aḥmad ibn al-Amīn al-Shinqīṭī

Zuhūr al-basātīn fī tārīkh al-sawādīn (Flowering gardens in [describing] the history of the Blacks) by Mūsā Aḥmad Kāmara

GLOSSARY

Arshif: A term for archive used in some Arabic works instead of "khizanah" (see below). Derived from the French and English archive.

Ansar Dine: Also Ansar al-Din or "Helpers of the Faith." The organization of ethno-nationalists in northern Mali that was said to be linked to Al-Qaeda. They led an assault on and occupation of Timbuktu.

Berber: A term with origins outside north Africa that become generalized in discussions of the people who would call themselves Amazigh or identify with one of its various subgroups across the Sahara.

Fatwa: A legal opinion by an expert in Islamic law, often in the form of a response to a legal question.

Hawsawi: From the Hausa language. Used to describe a style of calligraphy in West African manuscripts.

Ijaza: An authorization to teach, given to students after they have mastered a text.

Kel Tamasheq: The Tamasheq people.

Khizana: Storeroom. A term often used for a collection of manuscripts. Another term for "arshif."

Kitab: Literally, "a book." Often used in titles of scholarly works.

Kunta: Used to refer to the Kunta clan that played a major role in Sahara in the nineteenth century.

Maghribi: Used to refer to a script widely used in North Africa, especially in Morocco, which was also known as *al-Maghrib al-Aqsa* (the furthest West).

Makhtutat: Arabic term used for manuscripts (sing. Mukhtuta; pl. Makhtutat).

Maktaba: Library.

Mali: The name of the political formation that was at its height in the fourteenth century. The Republic of Mali was formed in 1960 after independence from France.

Mufti: Scholar with the learning and experience to give fatwas. A mufti could also play the role of *qadi* (judge) (see below).

Naskhi: A style of calligraphy widely used in the Middle East. Hardly ever present in the manuscript collections of West Africa.

Qadi: Judge.

Riq'a: A style of calligraphy that emerged in Istanbul and was used in the Ottoman Empire as an everyday, administrative script.

Risala: Letter, epistle. Used in titles of shorter works.

Sahel: Refers to the lands on the edge of the Sahara.

Salafi: In West Africa, used to refer to those who are critical of Sufism or popular religious practices; often used as a pejorative term.

Sudani: Style of calligraphy. Often used as a collective term for the calligraphy of all the manuscripts of West Africa.

Sufi/Sufism: From the Arabic *tasawwuf* referring to scholars and movements in West Africa that stressed uses of unique liturgies and that grew into movements with mass following.

Suqi: Style of calligraphy in manuscripts that probably originated in the area around Essuki (Essouk), north of Timbuktu.

Tamashek: A variety of the Berber language spoken in northern Mali.

Tifinagh: A script used to write in the Tamashek language. No manuscripts in this script in the known collections.

Tikna: A grouping of families and clans with an extensive trading network in southern Morocco and adjoining territories. Ahmad Bularraf's family was part of this network.

Acronyms

Cedrab: Centre de Documentation et Recherche Ahmed Baba

Iheri-Ab: Institut des Hautes Etudes et de Recherche Islamique Ahmed Baba

MNLA: Mouvement National de Libération de l'Azawad

Introduction

BOOKS AND REBELS IN THE DESERT

FROM AROUND late march 2012, reports about events in the Sahara Desert gave Timbuktu a prominence that the town had not enjoyed for more than a century, since the late nineteenth-century European imperial conquests of Africa. If you had only heard about the place but never thought about its actual existence, Timbuktu was now a contemporary reality, a regular item on international television news channels and websites. Like other African towns, Timbuktu would make the global news only because of a natural disaster or man-made crisis such as a civil war. This town on the edge of the desert, with sand always blowing and settling into everything, reached international headlines because of the impact of events that originated far to its north, beyond the borders of Mali, in countries that do not even share a border with this landlocked West African country. The popular uprisings of the Arab Spring started in Tunisia in December 2010, spreading eastward, firstly to Egypt and then to neighboring Libya and beyond North Africa to other Arabic-speaking countries. Sustained protests in Libya grew into an armed insurrection against the Libyan regime of Colonel Muammar Gaddafi. He responded not by fleeing the country, like the ruler of Tunisia, but by threatening more violence against the protesters. Malians were following these events on their transistor radios, mobile phones, and grainy television screens. Timbuktu's inhabitants also listened and watched, but they never felt that they would become part of the news, that their lives would be affected by these events. Then, in March 2011, NATO-led aerial attacks sped up the fall of the Libyan regime and ultimately the killing of Gaddafi in August 2011. Especially from the early 1980s, Gaddafi had fostered and equipped rebel movements from African countries, including Mali, such as the groups from north of Timbuktu in the vast Azawad region. They identified themselves as *Kel Tamasheq*, or Tuareg nationalists. They had been engaged in cycles of insurgency and extended peace talks with the central government since soon after independence in 1960; the first armed rebellion began in 1963, the second in 1990, and the third in 2006.[1] Another insurgency unfolded in 2011, as a consequence of the Arab Spring, and this new insurgency swept through large swathes of northern Mali. With the fall of the Gaddafi regime and the breakup of his army, the exiled Tuareg rebels fled southward with large caches of weapons, driving 4×4s fitted with rocket-launchers, through the Libyan desert, across Algeria, and back to their homeland in Mali where they picked up eager young recruits. They arrived in northern Mali, not for new rounds of talks with the government, but ready to fight, to seize territory, and to proclaim their own state. They would soon declare the establishment of the Republic of Azawad, the region of the country they believed belonged to them.

In 2012, the *Oxford English Dictionary* voted "omnishambles" its word of the year. Mali, at the time seen as West Africa's model democracy by some Western think-tanks, became a case of omnishambles.[2] Years of corruption by twice-elected President Amadou Toumani Touré were revealed, Malian soldiers refused to fight insurgents, and the political elite in Bamako were in complete disarray, unable to address any of the mounting challenges in the country. From every perspective, the situation was a shambles: from the rebel massacre of soldiers at Menaka, to a battle in Aguelhok in the far north of the country at the start of 2012, to a coup d'etat led by a mid-ranking officer, then numerous changes at the presidential office, to a military command wracked by corruption while ordinary soldiers went without pay. These poorly equipped soldiers had, over years of neglect, lost any sense of duty and, when they had to face small bands of well-armed rebels, they simply fled. More and more territory fell effortlessly to the rebels of the MNLA (Le Mouvement national pour la Liberation de l'Azawad, or the National Movement for the Liberation of Azawad).

The fall of Timbuktu was a matter of time. It came right at the end of March 2012. Many people simply fled the town, fearing what might happen next, and those who remained lived in fear. A handful of adventurous, unemployed youth joined or attempted to join the rebels, out of curiosity or to survive the new political reality. Timbuktu was a symbolic and strategic location. For centuries, victorious warring parties in the larger region had seen the town as a necessary location to control. Timbuktu was born as a trading settlement, probably at the end of the eleventh century, and since that time has always attracted merchants crossing the Sahara with their diverse wares. It was a gateway to northern Africa and provided access to the Niger River for traders coming south. For the contemporary rebels, taking Timbuktu meant an important town was under their rule. The capture also offered instant global media coverage. They already had nominal control over large swathes of the desert and settlements that were unknown, even to most Malians. Taking Timbuktu was a prize worth all their effort and sacrifices. They entered the precincts of the town without a battle.

After the shock of the fall of Timbuktu, there was not much to report, and Timbuktu fell off the news cycle. Mali was not a priority of the major international broadcasters, except in some of the French-language media, since it was a former French colony. The Arab Spring was still unfolding in hotspots like Egypt and Syria and there were many other tragedies and wars to cover. Meanwhile, the rebels faced a divided population, some fearful, others welcoming them. The rebels who captured Timbuktu had splintered from an older Tuareg nationalist movement that stressed ethnic solidarity. The groups called Tuareg are historically nomads whose language is commonly called Berber. The splinter group, Ansar Dine ("supporters of the religion"), stressed religious identity. They proclaimed themselves Muslims first and only incidentally invoked any ethnic or linguistic identity, such as Tamasheq or Berber. They stressed their adherence to a literalist interpretation of the Quran, believed that they could create some kind of theocratic state in the Sahara, and were also bent on driving out any Muslims who visited grave sites of holy men, which they viewed as a pagan practice. The Ansar Dine linked this kind of activity to the practices of Sufis, who had in recent years built up a large following in the larger West African Muslim communities. The rebels, in turn, were labelled by their detractors as Salafi and Saudi-influenced, and not rooted in Africa.

One of the popular expressions in the town is that "Timbuktu is the city of 333 saints," because of the long history of numerous pious individuals who inspired the town's population. The tombs of the saints are regarded with reverence and as historic monuments by the locals, even by those who had little time for them. Disregarding the local respect and reverence for the holy men, the rebels soon set about knocking down, with hammers and hoes, the tombs of these Timbuktu saints. The Ansar Dine rebels believed the tombs were un-Islamic. Moreover, attacking the tombs demonstrated their capacity, as well-armed men, to do whatever they wanted irrespective of local sentiment.

The Ansar Dine's fighters took over key government buildings, including the town's newest major modern architectural addition, the archive-library that had opened in early 2009. This two-story facility stood opposite the famous, centuries-old Sankoré Mosque, a UNESCO World Heritage Site. The new building's reception hall and public spaces have high ceilings with handcrafted brass chandeliers made in Morocco. It was, at the time, fully furnished with the required workbenches for conservators, desks for librarians and administrators, ample reading room space, living quarters for visiting researchers, and a large auditorium. An underground vault, with extra-thick walls for storing the book and manuscript collections, would keep the items at a stable temperature in the event of power-outages switching off the air-conditioning. The government administrative buildings, spread through the town, are shabby and rather neglected relative to this new structure. When their eyes fell on the newest building in town, designed with touches of the regional Sudanic style, the rebels saw the spot for their headquarters. They could not refuse the seduction of an attractive modern building.

The new archive-library is a replacement for the older, original archive built in the early 1970s, called the Centre de Documentation et Recherche Ahmed Baba (Cedrab), which English-speakers simply called the Ahmed Baba Centre.[3] That is an unremarkable labyrinth of low, single-story buildings, which could be mistaken for an old primary school building organized around a courtyard. Its form gives no indication of its function. Furthermore, it was located in a neighborhood on the edge of the town, not close to any historic structure such as the iconic fourteenth-century Sankoré Mosque. By the time of the rebel occupation, Timbuktu thus had two archival-library buildings—the original, older one, and the new, recently constructed showpiece—and while most of the staff were placed in the new one, it was still in preparation for full operation. Conservators were making covers for each manuscript and the administrative staff were moving between the two buildings. The older one still held the bulk of the manuscript collections, which had to be moved, in the near future, to the new building that the Ansar Dine were occupying.

There are a number of families in the town who have manuscript collections of their own.[4] Since the late 1990s, charismatic representatives of two families have managed to raise funds from international cultural foundations to support the construction of buildings to house their collections. Mali attracted international aid, and independent cultural initiatives, such as the family manuscript collections, were among the projects that aid agencies supported. Other families with smaller collections, perhaps a few trunks or just a shelf or two, simply kept their materials at home. An association of these private family archives had been established in the early 2000s but not all families joined this body. Unlike the archive-library in the new building, that operated under the regulations of the Ministry of Culture in the capital, the association of private archives was not restricted in how it worked or raised funds. When the rebels settled into the archive-library, they restricted access to the building, and there was a fear that the materials that had already been moved there would be neglected, mishandled, or possibly disappear.

The rebels had no interest in the original archive-library, where nearly all the materials were still stored. Meanwhile, the leadership of the association of private family collections began planning to secure their materials and move them surreptitiously to safety, in case the manuscripts were laid upon by the rebels. Why the rebels would have involved themselves with these families and their manuscripts has never been clear. There appears to have been no immediate threat to the private manuscript collections. There were probably rumors in town, after the occupation of the main archive-library building, that the rebels would search homes for valuables, and the two private libraries with their sponsored computers, cameras, and conservation equipment might have attracted attention. Would the rebels occupy these private libraries and lay claim to the manuscripts? There was never any such attempt; the occupiers had other concerns. Attacking tombs with hoes and hammers did not mean manuscripts would be torn up or burned. Yet the owners of the private libraries locked up their homes, hid parts of their collections as best they could, and left town with their most valuable manuscripts. Hiding materials and moving them elsewhere were ways of preserving manuscripts from the many earlier episodes of conflict in and around Timbuktu. Manuscripts, and entire collections, were always mobile, as the following chapters illustrate.

I was in regular contact with colleagues in Timbuktu throughout this period. Hearing the news about the occupation of the new archival building, I was worried that the manuscripts would be forgotten and neglected. If a battle should take place around the building, a fire could destroy the entire collection, as has happened with other libraries in war zones around in the world throughout the twentieth century. In all the major wars and civil conflicts of modern times, libraries have been direct or indirect objects of destruction. Less dramatically, the desert sand and dust, termites and other insects, and the occasional seasonal rain that takes everyone by surprise, which had caused damage in the past, could easily return if there were no daily inspections of the stores where the materials were meant to be kept securely. Furthermore, in the rush to move the manuscripts, it would be easy to mishandle them. Meanwhile, efforts to quietly move some or all of the manuscripts out of Timbuktu and to the capital had begun. The organizers of the moving project would later tell stories of packing tin crates, filled with manuscripts, onto donkey-carts in the dark of night and then leading the carts to Kabara, a small port on the Niger River, about fifteen kilometers (nine miles or so) away. There, the crates were transferred onto awaiting *pinasses*, traditional riverboats, to cross the river, where taxis were waiting to take the manuscript-filled crates. After a short stretch of driving through the bush, the vehicles would turn onto the country's longest tarred road, all the way to the capital. Apartments in quiet residential neighborhoods on the outskirts of the capital were turned into storage houses for these tin crates of manuscripts. Eventually, in this way, the collections from the old archive-library building, the original Cedrab storerooms, also arrived in the capital, Bamako.

Unable to deal with the multiple challenges the rebels posed as they took more territory, the political elite in Bamako decided to do the unthinkable. The Republic of Mali had a history of representing itself as a genuinely independent, postcolonial state.[5] But now, after fifty years of independence from France, the ex-colonial power was called in to save the country from further collapse. To maintain the territorial integrity of the country, the French soldiers landed in the northern regions to deal with a situation the Malian military was incapable of handling. At the end of January 2013, the rebels were driven from Timbuktu by the French military in Operation Serval. The rebels fled into the desert, possibly a tactical retreat into terrain they knew so well. A few days later, on February 2, the president of Mali's former colonial ruler triumphantly landed in the town. French President Hollande and his Malian counterpart, acting head of state Dioncounda Traore, declared Timbuktu "liberated." The rumors and blurry images of rebels destroying the mud-brick tombs of local saints became enduring emblems of those tumultuous times in Mali. Even more startling were the images of the remains of old manuscript books they had set on fire. Fanatics bent on destruction.

What was reported, on the day the rebels fled and the first news crew entered the archive-library, was that thousands of manuscripts had been set on fire and destroyed. About a week later another news source reported the story of the undercover transfer of the manuscripts out of town. But the image of books burning had already been broadcast and repeated relentlessly (and somehow it persists, more than a decade later). The new reportage was about the movement of the book collections, undertaken right under the noses of the rebels. A fresh image was circulated: many hundreds, perhaps thousands, of tin crates filled with manuscripts leaving Timbuktu on donkey-carts, then crossing the Niger River in complete darkness to the awaiting taxis on the opposite bank, then transported onward to safety in the capital. The booklovers of Timbuktu had risked their lives, fooled the rebels, and saved their heritage. All done before the rebels were even expelled.

Through most of the period of the rebel occupation and lockdown, during which time ordinary folk stayed indoors, I was able to get updates on the situation from a few colleagues in Timbuktu. Some had arrived in Timbuktu only recently to work at the Ahmed Baba Centre, because they had the linguistic skills to work with the manuscripts: they were able to read and classify the materials. They were the researchers who were preparing catalogs of the manuscripts. A few of them had higher degrees and even doctorates from universities in North Africa. When the rebels took over the town, some of them left with their families, to Bamako and then to their villages or hometowns. There was an exodus from the town by bus and boat. Other colleagues stayed on, making use of the closure of institutions to concentrate on reading manuscripts, making copies, or writing their own texts. One of them managed to leave the town to conduct research for work he was copying and editing; a few managed to go in and out, bringing out parts of their manuscript collections and computer hard drives to the relative safety of the capital. Rebel access patrols appear to have been rather lax.

I was also able to stay in touch with those who had relocated to Bamako. Telecommunication lines with Timbuktu broke down after the occupation; electricity supply was uneven, and then the state cut the internet connectivity, except for specific hours on some days. Despite these impediments, however, I was able to put together stories from people in Bamako who got news regularly from within Timbuktu.

No library or archive was attacked and razed to the ground and no manuscripts were willfully destroyed as the French marched into Timbuktu and the rebels fled, as was reported by Sky News, Reuters, and other news sources. There was a need for a compelling story to broadcast to the world as Timbuktu was retaken without a fight; a bonfire of local, valued, old, handwritten books was to be the story of Timbuktu. However, manuscripts were moved out of the town. What percentage moved *during* the occupation and what *after* the rebels fled Timbuktu is unclear. This is a significant distinction to make but it is now a theoretical concern, because a large amount of material eventually was moved to the capital, where it remains in storage. In order to keep the integrity of their collections, the owners probably decided *after* the end of the conflict that it was better to keep their collections together in the same place. So, they were taken to the capital. This mobility of the materials is not new. Timbuktu has always been one node in a larger setting of nomadic movement. Scholars and their manuscript books moved around and over long distances, as will become clear in the following chapters. Historically, scholars, teachers, and students were not only found in the settlements and towns of the Sahara and the adjacent territories to the south (the area often referred to as the Sahel) but also in the nomadic encampments that were highly mobile. Book learning, especially in the territories to the west of Timbuktu, in what is today southwestern Mauritania, flourished from the late seventeenth century among sedentary *and* among some nomadic groups. In the history of the wider region, there is a long history of manuscripts moving around. Books always moved with their authors and owners. Books were borrowed and copied, then returned to their owners.[6] Throughout the following chapters, the history of the mobility of scholars, books, and other objects will become clearer. But Bamako, the capital, created by the French, was never a center of scholarship or the production of texts. There was scholarly activity there, but it began only in the post–World War II period (see chapter 8).

Manuscripts, Books

Up until very recently, the small cohort of scholars concerned with the Sahara and Sahel, and who used written historical evidence, referenced these manuscripts, and still fewer scholars—philologists, specialists concerned with the study of texts—actually worked closely on specific manuscripts from the collections held in the state archive-library, the Ahmed Baba Centre (Cedrab). There is a long tradition of specialist scholarship published in academic journals and by academic publishers that relied on the written culture of the larger region.[7] There were occasional brief articles in popular magazines that included images of the manuscripts. However, Timbuktu and other settlements in the larger region were never seen as part of the global history of books. When I searched the words "Timbuktu" and "books" together in the catalogs of major libraries in Europe in the early 2000s, I got no results, except in the catalog of the British Library where I came across a California publisher of poetry called Timbuktu Books, whose works were all unrelated to West Africa. African history and book history were not subjects that intersected. According to the dominant view, Africa was never supposed to have writing, until the coming of colonialism. This was explicitly articulated by the philosopher G.W.F. Hegel in the early nineteenth century and repeated by the English historian Hugh Trevor-Roper in the 1960s. What is remarkable is that recent works that claim global coverage of books and libraries have completely ignored this West African book culture. The footage of thousands of books going up in flames, and then the images of tin crates filled with manuscripts, were captivating, especially to Europeans with memories of a long continental past of book and library destruction well into the twentieth century. Now, out of this once-mythical place, there were real books, tangible objects, things that can be held and touched, read and moved. Not books of the imagination: texts organized not as ancient scrolls, but as codices made of paper held between leather covers. Objects that looked familiar, resembling the book in Europe from the medieval or early modern periods. Does it take such a crisis, and the confusing media reportage of books first presented as destroyed then revealed to have been saved by moving them hundreds of kilometers, to bring attention to a long-established book culture in the interior of Africa, one that predates the arrival there of European explorers, late nineteenth-century colonialism, and the spread of the printing press on the continent?

By the end of the rebel occupation, and in the reportage immediately afterward, local tour guides, who spoke some French and English but who had no knowledge of the collections, gave foreign journalists exaggerated figures about the numbers of manuscripts destroyed or the drama of how they were moved out of town—sometimes incorporating both contradictory stories at the same time. Hundreds of manuscripts turned into thousands, then turned into hundreds of thousands; manuscripts that were always organized as codices sometimes became scrolls in these presentations. One or two well-heeled collection owners, who in recent years had emerged as brokers between the family collections and the outside world and had a more detailed knowledge of the materials, did not dispel the myths about the figures and contents. Later, they continued to embellish the numbers.

The town of Timbuktu became the sole focus in the reportage of a writing culture that is, in fact, present in numerous surrounding towns and settlements across a much larger desert space. Timbuktu was indeed a significant place for scholars but not the only locus of literacy. At the time of the crisis, the focus on Timbuktu was, in a way, understandable, but the coverage never changed and did not touch on the much more expansive extent of libraries across the region. Other settlements across the desert had open-air classes to teach basic literacy. Their authors' works were copied and circulated. Timbuktu, like so many other towns, had its period of ascendancy and then of decline. In the following chapters, I introduce the history of scholars and collectors in Timbuktu and in connected settlements, their major writers and copyists, and the titles of manuscript books written by scholars in the region. I introduce some specific manuscripts in greater detail. The material—economic and political—and intellectual contexts of which they were once part will be elucidated along the way. In most cases, an actual text can be closely described but the context of its production is often difficult to identify with any detail. What motivated writers living often precarious lives to write the works that they did, and *when* they did? Who were these authors and what were their arguments? How did various manuscript collections grow, change and move, or stay in the same place?

The evidence for writing in the region goes back to tombstones with Arabic inscriptions that date to the early eleventh century.[8] Before there is a history of writing on paper or parchment, there is a history of writing on stone. The earliest evidence of writing in the larger region around Timbuktu is not on paper but on stone and rock, going as far back as 1011 CE (fig. 1 shows a map of the region). There are over four hundred, probably reaching closer to a thousand, extant inscriptions that record the names and dates of the death of men and women with high social status. Among them could be the rulers or elites of the time. While the Arabic calligraphy of the inscriptions is not the most striking or polished by the standards of similar inscriptions elsewhere, or later writing in the region, its syntax is clear, classical Arabic that includes many local, non-Arabic first names. The accompanying images of the inscriptions on tombstones together with line drawings of the script (figs. 2a–d) are from the early twelfth century—one for a man described as a king, the other for a woman described as a queen.

There is a gap in the documentation between the period of the later inscriptions of the early 1400s and the evidence from the manuscripts of the sixteenth century. In manuscripts produced much later there are references to texts between these periods but no actual material remains of either original works or copies that were made later. Thus, literacy and literature go back well before the sixteenth century. The handwritten works that were passed down to succeeding generations, or were mentioned but have left no trace, are the products of a writing culture that developed in the desert. It is impossible to speculate about rates of literacy but judging from the range of writing and confident expression in prose and poetry, there was definitely a deeply embedded literate culture by the time a figure like Ahmad Baba (discussed in detail in chapters 2 to 4) started writing in the late 1500s. Writing was used to record prayers for common use, to make amulets and charms, and inscribe tombstones. There were preachers or teachers who used their writing skills for purposes of magic and healing and not for scholarship. This book focuses on the works of scholars who wrote mainly serious works to prove their capacities to their peers, to expound theological and legal opinions, and to engage in arguments with each other. The book spans the period from the fifteenth-century arrival in Timbuktu of the ancestors of the town's preeminent scholar, Ahmad Baba, until the time of the energetic manuscript collector and trader, Ahmad Bularraf, in the first half of the twentieth century. In between them, writers from within and outside Timbuktu will be introduced.

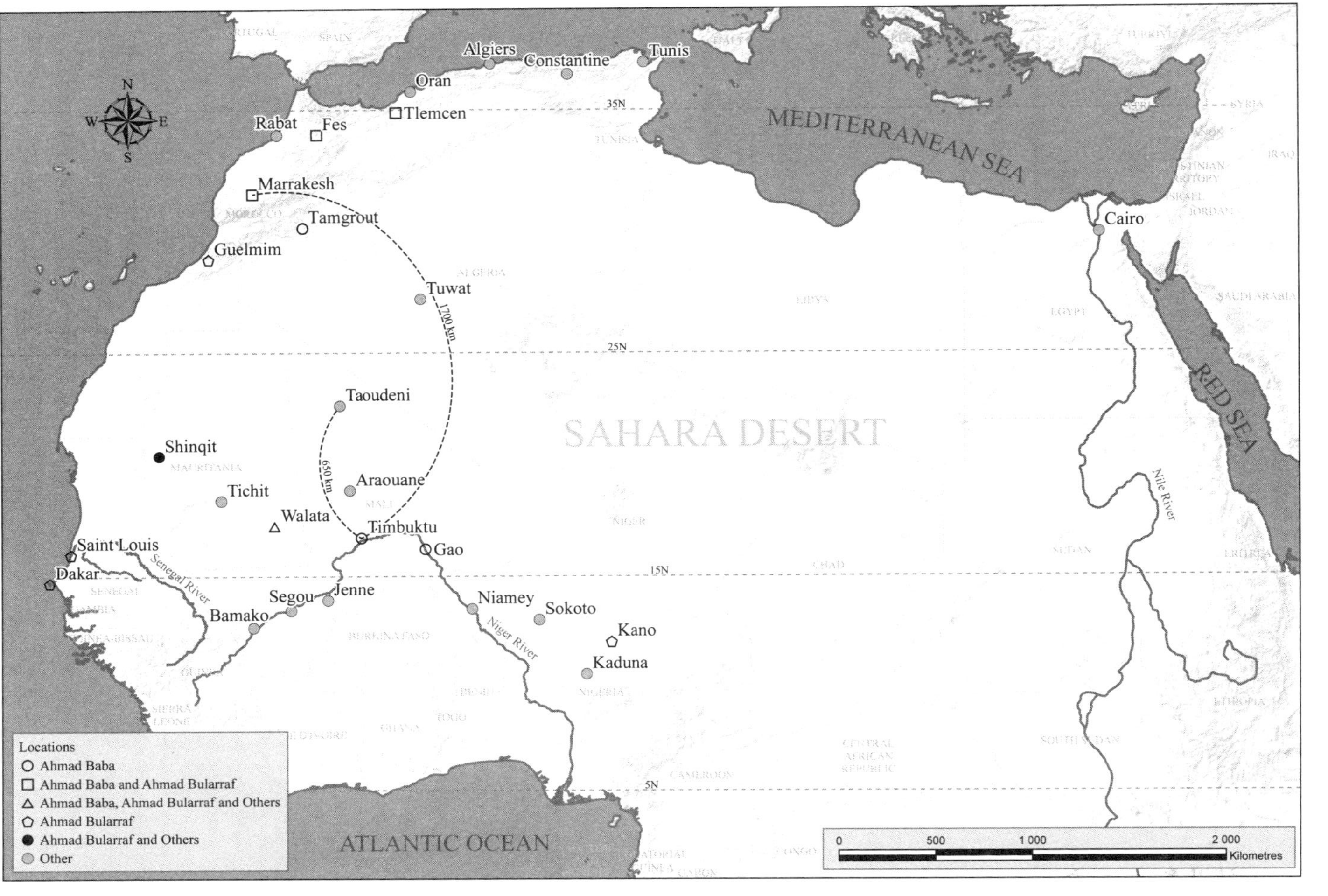

FIG. 1. Main places in which manuscript books and their writers circulated between the sixteenth and twentieth centuries.

FIG. 2A AND B. Two examples of the earliest extant writing in the region from Saney, close to Gao, Mali. Both are tombstones; the first, above, is for a Sulayman, son of a king (al-Malik), and is dated to 1115 CE (509 AH), with parts of Quranic verses 35:5 and 31:33. The stone is quartzite, measuring 82 × 34 cm, and the script is ornamental Kufic. The second is the tombstone of a woman, a queen (al-Malika) dated to between 1135 and 1155 CE with the Quranic verse 3:185. The stone is gray schist, measuring 47 × 34 cm, the script ornamental Kufic. These are two of the hundreds of epigraphic writings that reflect the levels of literacy in the region in the twelfth century.

Collecting, Papers, and Scripts

In early December of 2001, I traveled overland from Bamako with four South African archival and heritage specialists to make an initial assessment of the manuscript collections in Timbuktu. On subsequent trips, I visited other towns along the Niger River—Mopti, Jenne (Djenne), and Segou, and smaller towns—where there were smaller collections. However, except in Jenne, I was not taken to view these smaller collections, although I did get a sense of the landscape and the distances people and things moved. I traveled to countries in the wider region—Niger, Mauritania, Senegal, Nigeria, Ghana, Morocco—that have multiple manuscript collections, in various locations, with individual works or copies and commentaries on works originating in Timbuktu. These states did not exist when the history I recount in this book unfolded. But in this vast space—much of it desert or semiarid land with extremely low rainfalls, periodic

FIG. 2A AND B. (*continued*)

droughts, and often famines as a result—competing political elites exerted nominal control over parts of the region. This usually meant demanding some kind of tribute, which was collected on a regular basis. Timbuktu fell under what is commonly called the Mali and then Songhai states, often cast as empires, between the early fourteenth and end of the sixteenth centuries. There were towns, like Timbuktu and Jenne, with dynamic markets, and oasis settlements and nomadic camps that were connected to each other and the larger world through long-established trade routes that ran over vast distances reaching to the North African coastline. Paper was among the items of this commerce.

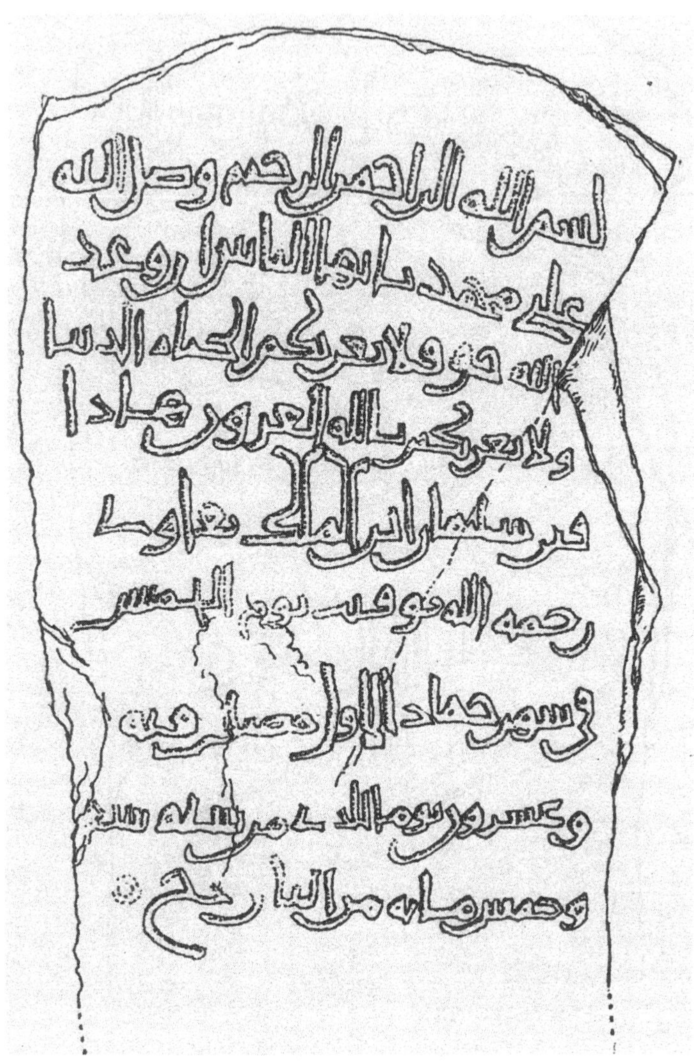

FIG. 2C AND D. Images of the inscriptions and line drawings reproduced by kind permission of P. F. de Moraes Farias and the British Academy, from P. F. de Moraes Farias, *Arabic Medieval Inscriptions of the Republic of Mali* (2003), 12, 20–21 (inscriptions 10 and 18, plates 4 and 8). The book is available online via https://www.fonteshistoriaeafricanae.co.uk/books-available-online/.

FIG. 2C AND D. (*continued*)

There was no paper production in northern Africa throughout the period covered in this book. Yet the manuscripts were all written on paper; there are very few examples of texts on parchment or vellum (prepared and treated animal skins). The importation of paper to coastal and interior settlements was of significance to the rate at which scholars could compose their work. International, long-distance trade involved multiple parties, from paper producers in southern

Europe to Africa-based merchants who distributed the paper among the other goods they exchanged. Gifting was another source of paper. Every sheet must have been highly valued and thus every thought carefully mulled over and prepared before the inked reed was applied to the blank surface. The inks and styluses were the least of the writers' problems because these could be made locally. The composition of a text, therefore, meant having well-formulated ideas in one's head and three things: paper, pen, and ink. And, of course, a smooth, hard surface to support the paper. A writer would sit on the ground when writing. Some of the manuscripts I was shown had suffered badly from insect infestation and other damage such as water stains, while others—most of them, in fact—were in good condition; they could be fifteenth- or sixteenth-century paper from a family's archive or late nineteenth-century paper made from wood pulp. Dating a text seems not to have been a common practice, and copying a text from an earlier period was not uncommon as a method of conservation. In the twentieth and twenty-first centuries, school notebooks from French manufacturers, identifiable by their gridlines, were used for making manuscripts.

The rulers of the early states that evolved in the region, such as the Mali and Songhai states, did not set down much, or anything, on paper. Rulers might have believed themselves above the need to write, although they had the power to instruct others in their court to write for them. While there was no pressure on them to write anything themselves, they did have at least one individual who dealt with correspondence with other rulers. How did they publicize their decrees, administer their realm? They certainly sent out their representatives to verbally give instructions and make demands of their subjects. Timbuktu and other towns were subject to higher political powers living in Gao, four hundred kilometers to its southeast, until 1591, when the Saʿdian dynasty of Marrakesh conquered the region; this is often simplified as the "Moroccan conquest of Timbuktu." During the periods covered by this book, there is, with extremely few exceptions, no written evidence of the laws the rulers issued, taxes they claimed, or other documentary administrative materials, until the coming of the French at the end of the nineteenth century. In the nineteenth century, up to the French advances and conquests—roughly from the early to mid-1800s—the frontiers of Islamic religiopolitical movements were shifting as they asserted territorial claims, and there was a proliferation of texts of a political nature revealing their arguments and claims. (See chapter 6, which focuses on the writers of the Sokoto state, named after the town where it was founded in present-day northern Nigeria.) However, these were not administrative materials. Much of what we know about the political history of the region comes from books written much later, not from administrative records or correspondence, between rulers and functionaries, or from diplomatic records. There are very few manuscripts from the earlier periods that directly deal with politics at the time. The movements of the nineteenth century, however, did generate a political literature filled with polemic and argumentation. But overall, the political communications or similar texts we have were mostly written decades after the events they describe. This is the case with the important chronicle, the *Tārīkh al-Sūdān* that we rely on for much of the political history of the region in which Timbuktu is located.

During my trips, there was no palace archive to consult the papers or official documentation of rulers or the elites close to them. I visited manuscript collections in family homes. On each trip, yet another family collection was revealed to me. Many of them were in poor condition, while others were well-maintained and curated collections. One collection was just piled up along the walls of a spare room; another was brought out into a courtyard in wooden boxes with books neatly and tightly pressed inside. These book collections were distributed in various homes in the narrow alleys of the town. Timbuktu's Ahmed Baba Centre had some facilities and expertise to conserve and work on the manuscripts, which the private collectors did not have. But in the years to come, the private collectors organized themselves and attracted foreign funding to establish such facilities.

Unlike European manuscript books, the codices of Timbuktu are all loose leaves, unbound sheets of paper. In other words, unlike this book, the pages were neither sewn nor glued together. They are written in the regional styles of the Arabic script. Some of my well-informed hosts would characterize the script of each manuscript—*Suqi, Sahrawi, Sudani, Maghribi, Hawsawi*—reflecting the area in which the manuscript was copied. To the untrained eye, West African Arabic calligraphy is all simply Maghribi because it looks like writing from Morocco, but there are, in fact, a variety of styles. These are not, for example, the Arabic calligraphy of Egypt or the calligraphy developed in Istanbul and used in the Ottoman Empire. A manuscript from outside the region is easily picked out by simply looking at the script style. The style developed by the Ottoman bureaucracy—*Riqʿa*—or the *Naskhi* were not cultivated by Timbuktu writers and copyists, and only in the later twentieth century would there be locals who could and might use such styles of calligraphy.

The manuscripts, when they had covers, were held together by their original, well-crafted, handmade leather covers. Some smaller texts had no covers, but modern paper files kept the pages together. In the beginning, I never saw manuscripts treated by their owners as precious museum objects; nobody wore gloves when handling them or treated them in the way I had experienced in rare-book libraries elsewhere in the world. But over the years, as more outside expertise appeared in the town, more of the custodians of family collections began to have what can be called a Western "conservation language." This came mostly from well-established professional and amateur conservators, and at times the owners strained to express the fragility and antiquity of their books. But the idea of conservation, before this sea change, was simply that one should store the objects securely and keep bugs far away. The manuscripts had survived for so long, and their owners used their own insights into what destroys paper. So why intervene? I could imagine these books in the past, passing from one home to another when there was a request for a text. I would later read about Ahmad Baba (d. 1627) writing about his teacher giving books out on loan with ease. And in the twentieth century, a scholar deep in the desert wrote to the collector Ahmad Bularraf (d. 1955), thanking him for the use of a book but complaining that a two-week loan was too short. The writing and collecting activities of these two figures stand at the beginning and end of this book.

In Timbuktu, among the learned elite, books were wholly seen as handwritten works even into recent decades. Therefore, in Timbuktu and the world around it, a focus on the uses of books means looking at a manuscript culture long after this kind of handwritten book culture had disappeared in most of the world. Even when Timbuktu scholars encountered print in the twentieth century, they continued to write out their works, which then circulated as hand-copied books. Into the twenty-first century, this is still a practice. When I met scholars there, they were still only writing out texts by hand; one in particular was especially prolific but never had anything printed until I offered to cover the costs of typing up a large biographical dictionary (*tarjama*) of scholars that he had compiled into a manuscript book. The persistence of the handwritten work meant that some curious developments had taken place. For instance, how many cases might there be of manuscripts that were once printed editions of texts, that somehow reached Timbuktu, especially in the colonial period? In other words, print became manuscript. Many years after my first visits, I discovered such a case, of an article from a Moroccan newspaper turned into a manuscript, and there are probably more. The scholars I write about in this book, and others who, at the time of my writing, are still active, wrote out huge tomes by hand. I have seen how researchers who wanted a copy of a work would have to wait until a copyist could be called to produce one. After a few days, a manuscript copy would be presented, looking like the original. However, the new copy would be made on lined paper. Copying a text by hand is much slower than contemporary so-called "print-on-demand" publishing. But until into the present it was possible to get a copy of a manuscript done by a local scribe; here then is a *manuscript-on-demand* culture. The absence of copyright and the capacity to make copies also opened the potential for making forgeries and fakes. This phenomenon is not unknown in Timbuktu.

I have visited, for research purposes and out of curiosity, many libraries and archives in various parts of the world and spent some time as a graduate student working in one. The archival materials and rare books were always hidden from the view of the regular user. A researcher never gets to see where the manuscripts are actually stored; they are brought out on request after the researcher has worked through often-arcane catalogs to identify items. The moment a manuscript materializes at your reading desk is often like a magical occurrence. So, coming to Timbuktu, I was somewhat disoriented by my almost-unmediated encounter with manuscripts. I had never seen so many books completely handmade and presented in such an unaffected, matter-of-fact way to a visitor or potential reader. One would expect to find such objects in the rare books section of archives and libraries or locked up in cabinets at antiquarian booksellers. This was the case, to an extent, with the state-run Ahmed Baba Centre. But on the whole, there was an informality and generosity around the materials. They were easily handled and passed around, with some of their owners giving running commentaries, if not on their often-rhyming titles then on their contents, or on how they were passed down in a family. Some of their owners had no idea what they were dealing with; they could not read the language in which the books were written. Arabic was and is a language of scholarship in the region and is not overall used as a lingua franca. A portion of the population speaks an Arabic dialect called Hasaniyya, but it does not have the same prestige as writing and speaking in what is considered classical Arabic. I was given handwritten lists of titles and authors by some owners who were hoping for collaborators to prepare proper catalogs. Extremely little about, not to mention in, the libraries were printed at that point. There were catalogs for the main archives, but they covered only a small percentage of the collections. As catalogs appeared in coming years, they mostly gave partial coverage to the holdings of a collection or did not give sufficient information about the actual books. To put it in specialist language, the codicology was undeveloped.

The collections aimed to conserve a tradition of book production and learning that privileged the hand and the handmade object. Aside from the writer, who literally wrote out his text, there was always a role for a person with a good writing hand, a scribe or copyist, who could make a beautiful final version or additional copies of texts. What I shall be describing is a world of writing that flourished but also fluctuated, roughly from around 1500 and into the contemporary period, in a severe, dry climate where populations had a precarious means of survival. Many of the writers themselves were pastoralists or connected to families who survived on pastoral activities. Conditions were always difficult but finding a hard surface to put down a sheet of paper and write was a part of that life, at least for the people like Ahmad Baba, Ahmad Bularraf, and others introduced in subsequent chapters.

When one encounters the term "manuscript" today, it mostly covers written material not meant for public circulation, such as private correspondence or drafts of all kinds, from administrative materials and formal declarations to drafts of novels. Nobody, other than archivists or historians, reads manuscripts or books that were handwritten and that were once meant to circulate in that form. There are always exceptions, of course, as we will see in some of the cases I deal with, in parts of West Africa and across the Sahara and Sahel to Ethiopia, for example, where handwritten texts remain highly valued and are still in use.

This is a book about books, *manuscript books*, which will sound strange if we have only known printed books and especially only books printed and bound by machines. The idea of having a print-on-demand book was unthinkable until a few years ago. To get a printed book was a long process; no longer. Then, of course, there is the digital book. These two types of books are even further away from the concept of a *manuscript book*, which was prevalent in medieval Europe until the emergence of printing in the last half of the fifteenth century. These are two ends of the spectrum: manuscript and digital book. Contemporary authors still speak of their manuscript when a work is in preparation, even as a typescript, before publication as a hard-copy or real book. The aim of authors and publishers is to see their books in print, and hopefully thousands of copies in both hardback and soft cover. A book only in the manuscript stage does not matter, not yet.

Writing was used for many purposes but what remains of the long writing culture in Timbuktu are the *books, the manuscripts*; far less, next to nothing, remains, especially for the earlier periods at least, of private correspondence, commercial records, or diplomatic records. Private correspondence is still kept by families but it is never given prominence or displayed like the manuscript books I saw and handled. Commercial records are to be found, and more could also still appear in collections because there were always contracts to write down, specifying weights and prices of goods. But I have much less faith that new documents from rulers, or the elites close to them, from the precolonial period will be found. Fortunately, whatever manuscript books or other items that I encountered over the years in Timbuktu were not burned by rebels. Timbuktu's return to the spotlight was reminiscent of the late nineteenth-century scramble to reach this city of untold riches.

Timbuktu and its three oldest mud-brick mosques were listed as UNESCO World Heritage Sites in 1988. The mausoleums that were attacked were therefore part of Timbuktu's local and world heritage. A number of individual manuscripts from Timbuktu have been included in the UNESCO Memory of the World Register. There are at least two dozen libraries in Timbuktu, with manuscript collections of varying sizes. A large share of these manuscripts was moved to the capital, Bamako. I have used the terms "libraries" and "collections," but there is not a single term agreed upon by locals to describe the Timbuktu materials. Some were consciously collected and preserved, while others appear to have been simply forgotten over decades, or longer, and hoarded until there was a flurry of attention to old books in the town in the 2000s. In Timbuktu, colleagues speak most frequently of *maktaba* (library) or *khizana* (store / storehouse) when referring to the collections. The most frequently used term in Arabic for "archive" is simply *arshif* (derived from French or English) although sometimes *mahfuthat* (lit. a place of protection) can be heard. But these latter terms are never used in Timbuktu.

Individual items within collections are most often described as *kitab* (book) or *risala* (letter/epistle), all collectively known as *makhtutat* (manuscripts). There are numerous books whose titles start out with the word "kitab." "Risala" also refers to a text but is used for shorter work or a piece of correspondence. The assumption is often that such a smaller text is a letter written to an addressee for either private or public reading; in this genre, it is not unusual to find a text running into a few dozen pages. There are, however, items that are strictly private correspondence.

What Kind of Book Tradition?

Writing Timbuktu uses "Timbuktu" to stand for a much larger area than the specific historical town of Timbuktu, although a good deal of attention is given to the place itself; many of the writers discussed lived there, passed through it, or had some other kind of connection to it. Timbuktu must be understood as a symbol of a much wider writing culture that stretched across and included the distant edges of the Saharan desert. Timbuktu the town, of course, also featured eminently in European visions of the continent, a mysterious location to reach, imagined as having untold quantities of gold. It became a place to conquer, lured by the "force of falsity" as Umberto Eco would have put it.[9] But as Leo Africanus observed after his visit in 1506, books, not gold, were the most valuable object in the town (see the next chapter). The scholarship on this fascinating traveler, writer, and captive of the Vatican is extensive but his observation on books in Timbuktu has never been commented on or used as a basis for investigating the place of books in that part of the world. By that time, there was already a tradition of writing, and manuscript books were circulating throughout the region. The book in West Africa in the early modern period was thus not an imported thing, a foreign object, but the product of local writers and copyists. The writers did not arrive on camel-back from Mediterranean Africa, from coastal northern African centers of learning to convert cultures of orality to literacy. Their ethnic and linguistic identities were diverse and claims to being from an "Arab" tribe hardly feature in genealogies from Timbuktu. Elsewhere, where and when this does happen it is, of course, always mythical. In fact, many, such as Ahmad Baba's ancestors, came from areas to the south of Timbuktu. The way of making a book—unbound sheets, always, and in Arabic scripts that were entirely regional—defined the book culture of this part of the continent for centuries. While classical Arabic was the language of scholarship—comparable to Latin at the same time in Europe—there are examples of texts in regional languages written in the Arabic script (this is referred to as *Ajami*). The Ajami writings were most often not prose works but poetry and used to add glosses to classical texts.

Ahmad Baba referred to his ancestors in the fifteenth century as being teachers writing books and having book collections. He himself would build up a large library. In terms of genre, they were works from within traditions of Islamic learning, but they were not merely copies of texts written in Fez or Cairo. When they did make copies of existing works, they added their own commentaries; they also used older texts as a basis for their own new works. They were educated within a well-established scholarly tradition, but also worked within their own contexts, responding to local issues. This was the only tradition of textual and book production in West Africa for centuries, and Timbuktu was central to it. The book culture was *both* Islamic and West African—to claim it was only one or the other would be to deprive the book culture of Timbuktu of its rich complexity.

When print arrived during the colonial administrations—Arabic printing was adopted in Morocco in the late nineteenth century—the manuscript tradition continued, with writers continuing their work and local copyists continuing to produce copies, usually on-demand. In various parts of West Africa, this book culture continued through the colonial period and the coming of print, persisted after independence in the 1960s, and survived into the first quarter of the twenty-first century. In Timbuktu now, even as I write these lines, a scholar is living who wrote out by hand a massive biographical dictionary of his contemporaries and predecessors. This is how he produced all his work. He is listed as having written twenty-four works in one catalog from 2003; since then, he has written more and made copies and commentaries. One of his works of great value to readers and researchers is a guide to the editing marks in Timbuktu manuscripts! He also produced a summary of the large text. Summaries are themselves part of this tradition of scholarship. A further step would be to release a versification of the work; this has not appeared yet. His main concern during the 2011 occupation of Timbuktu was to finish a manuscript he was commissioned to edit—he had to get a copy from Morocco to finish it. He makes his living as a teacher at a government school in the town, but his fingers never touched a typewriter or keyboard. Throughout the history of Timbuktu, there have been scholars like him, who wrote, edited, annotated, copied, summarized their larger works, and made a living by teaching or trading. There were also those who never wrote anything but were available to make copies, as we learn from colophons. On the other hand, we could speculate that there were those whose lectures were written up and compiled by their students and given as authors of a work. Even today, copyists are always available to copy a text from a library in the town. We can thus identify a West African precolonial book culture that persisted through all the invasions and crises that beset the town and region.

The book—as a material object, a tangible thing to hold, open, and read, and then store or pass along—thus has a striking continuity. Paper was imported but the habit of binding paper never came along with it. Travelers brought paper as gifts. Stitched pages, the bound book, almost never appear among the collections in the larger region. When they do, they are printed books brought in from outside, since the late nineteenth century. The reasons for this adherence to a way of bookmaking are not clear. It would be too simplistic to explain it away as simply "tradition." From among manuscript traditions that use Arabic or Arabic-derived scripts this way of bookmaking seems to be unique. Even in northern African Islamic scholarly centers—such as Fez and Qayrawan (Kairouan), or Marrakesh in the south, which had closer contact with Timbuktu—the book culture is different; books are bound, and a copying tradition died out long ago. Only a slightly modified version of the classical Maghribi Arabic script—done by a handful of experienced calligraphers—is used for book titles of the religious establishment, and in official missives of the king of Morocco, for instance.

For all this persistence of a style of book-craft with its unique Arabic calligraphic styles, the world in which this writing happened was filled with crises and instability: famines, droughts, invasions, rulers who hated scholars, and even periods without rulers. In the chapters that follow, many of these crises are identified, especially if they were captured in texts of the time. Books were obviously lost, damaged, and even destroyed during these moments. But the idea of the book did not disappear, despite the breaks and "the disappearance of learning," to use a phrase of Ahmad Baba.[10] When some calm returned and paper entered the markets again, a few learned men sat down and dipped their reed pens into locally made ink.

One of the challenges of working with the collections in Timbuktu has been the unevenness of available tools to find and identify materials. The manuscript catalogs have improved since the first ones that appeared in the 1990s, which were just lists of authors and titles. This was, however, a beginning. Even with the most recent, much-improved, catalogs there is still much to be done. A catalog of a collection—and usually of a set of collections in a subregion such as "western Sudanic Africa"—that gives usable codicological information on how to find an item should make research on West African manuscripts possible. However, we also have to contend with the real world of the collections, which are often held in precarious conditions. The siege of Timbuktu in 2011 and then the transport of whole collections out of the town, is one example of this precarity. Following these events and seeing the need for an account of the larger region's long encounter with manuscript books was one of the motivations behind this book. For our purposes, the range of issues, from the catalog to the collection to the manuscript copy—or in whichever order one wants to see these—constitutes Michel de Certeau's "historiographical operation," the practical procedures, labor, and experience of doing history.[11] An emerging field within philological studies—captured under the recently coined term "social philology"—attempts to bring the actual conditions of researching and cataloging collections into the foreground. The historical conditions described in this work present a good case for reading texts—manuscript books and other writings—not only as sources of information about the past but as part of the making of a past. At the risk of exaggeration, this is a case of manuscripts as actors. The cases of forgery, for example, are clear examples of belief in the force that words on paper could have; a significant case of forgery in the mid-nineteenth century is discussed in chapter 6.

Generalizations about the literary tradition of Timbuktu, and West Africa in the age of the manuscript book, must take the foregoing into account.

Interpretations of the history will shift and change as more manuscripts become accessible for study, existing ones are reread, and contexts—intimate and external to the text—become clearer. The standard history textbook account was that there were two Chronicles in Timbuktu and the anthropologist Jack Goody asserted from his fieldwork that literacy was limited to the writing out and reading of liturgical tracts and amulets.[12] Both accounts overlook a diverse and complex book culture that had specific regional characteristics and was the vehicle for sophisticated ideas and, importantly, debates. With all the cataloging and close-reading of manuscripts, we are now far beyond repeating rebuttals of these simplistic characterizations; there is ample evidence of a complex enterprise of writing (composition, copying, commenting) as a way-of-life, at least for a section of the population in West Africa. This book is therefore an account of material books and the ideas conveyed in them. It is a work necessarily concerned with the intersection of book and intellectual history, since sometimes there is more material that allows me to elaborate on ideas and thought, while at other times it makes more sense to discuss the book as an object, or the trade in books (more on this below). About the latter, chapter 7, on the life and times of Ahmad Bularraf, provides many examples.

This, then, is a short book about a large subject; it covers a vast territory and a long historical period. It is an introduction to writing in the Sahara-Sahel with Timbuktu as the focal point, a condensed history from epigraphy to typography with the bulk of the book focused on the impressive manuscript book tradition of northwest Africa. The subjects of each individual chapter deserve an entire, dedicated volume, and the endnotes could be extensive review essays in themselves. However, a coherent single volume on the written word and the handwritten book—the sign and its supports—has its place in a library today. The history of writing and books in this part of Africa is known far too little and is still seen as marginal to the big questions in African history. *Writing Timbuktu* draws on published research, but also contains new materials based on my own research, and it should provide fresh angles on old topics for specialist readers, whether Africanists, Islamicists, or book historians. The long history of writing and book production in Africa will hopefully get much more attention and inclusion in comparative discussions about topics ranging from epigraphy to philology to the materiality of the book. These, and related topics, have been covered, in various degrees of depth, in existing scholarship but in most cases this knowledge circulates in unpublished university theses and in specialist journals and monographs.

There are, of necessity, many gaps in this work for reasons of space and because of large gaps in the historical record, or sources are not (yet) available on numerous topics. My approach to this methodological challenge is to introduce writing as a practice and the manuscript book as an object but also give readers a sense of the range of the literature that was produced—that is, the contents of the books themselves. And so, at places, it was necessary to give more attention to the ideas than to the book as object, or vice versa. There was a temptation to give more attention to ideas—to do some sort of intellectual history—but this is not the central purpose of this work. Thus, some writers get more attention than others, and their works are introduced because they are available, although in many cases it is not possible to undertake close codicological descriptions of these works because all I had was a digital copy of a manuscript without accompanying data on its provenance or the circumstances of its copying.

In general, the tools for conducting research on manuscripts and manuscript books have only become available in the last two decades or so and are, thankfully, being continuously refined. For instance, the level of detail in catalogs has improved significantly since the first basic ones appeared in the 1990s for Timbuktu collections. While the advances in cataloging and counting the materials in the many collections are valuable tools, the challenge still remains of how to actually find the items. Any philological work necessitates copies of the texts, preferably hardcopies. Furthermore, there are few reliable editions, and still fewer translations, of even the most well-known works. The endnotes hopefully provide a guide around the materials for those interested in the state of the scholarship. There are manuscripts scattered in libraries all over northwest Africa that are hard to reach; only handlists or locally printed catalogs exist for them, and consequently they do not circulate widely—not to speak of seeing actual copies of the manuscripts. There are also a huge number of unpublished theses stored in university libraries all over the region, and elsewhere, that contain some fine scholarship and plenty of primary sources.

With all these caveats, this is a survey of the written word as a conveyance of ideas, and the manuscript book as a medium of communication, in northwest Africa. Many topics deserve separate treatment, such as how books were read, and the complex relationship between orality and literacy over time. A line had to be drawn to bring this volume to a close. But the writing continues.

1

Discovering Books in the Desert

THE INTERNATIONAL spotlight on the fate of Timbuktu's manuscripts led to curiosity about their authors and their past. Questions were asked about where they really came from, and about their contents. Interest in the town and region, by outsiders, has a long history. Over more than seven centuries, "Timbuktu"—or some version of the spelling, such as Timbuktoo, Timbuctoo, Tomboutou, and, much earlier, Tenbuch, Tombotto, and Tinbatu—was identified on maps, mentioned in correspondence, and graced book titles. The three short syllables of the word easily roll off the tongue in many languages.

The early nineteenth century marked one high point in the fascination with Timbuktu, as reaching the town became the ambition of numerous European explorers. These journeys went into the interior of Africa from different points on the northwestern coastline. Many communities on the African coasts had been in contact with European adventurers, merchants, and slave traders for centuries by this time. But in the early nineteenth century the slave trade was coming under increasing criticism in metropolitan centers, and European explorers were, on the whole, committed abolitionists. They were as appalled by the external slave trade as the internal slave trade on the continent. However, the explorers' own mobilization of local men to support their expeditions entailed great hardship and often death. For a few of the explorers, searching for Timbuktu was a long, demanding trek in the name of discovery and science. For others, the attraction of adventure and eventual fame, with the possibility of making a fortune, was a motivating part of the plan. By the end of the century, "Timbuktu was the magnet which drew Europe into the heart of West Africa," wrote the historian A. S. Kanya-Forstner in his study of the French conquest of West Africa.[1]

The Arabic writers since the eighth century used a range of names in their writing to refer to various parts of Africa.[2] *Zanj* for East Africa, *Habash* for Ethiopia and surrounds, *Nuba* for lands by the more southerly reaches of the Nile

River, and *Sudan* for all of what was known of Africa—often used in the expression "Bilad al-Sudan" ("Land of the Blacks"). In these Arabic works, *Takrur* and *Mali*, words of unknown or uncertain origin, became common terms for West Africa. They refer to a vast and rather unspecified terrain on the northern and western parts of the continent. Included in this space were broad organizational or political entities such as kingdoms and states and specific places ranging in size and significance classified as towns and villages. In the Arabic works, Timbuktu does not feature as often as might be expected from the later attention European travelers paid to it. However, Timbuktu is mentioned more than Gao (spelled *Kawkaw*), a political center, and Jenne and Walata, two centers of learning with which Timbuktu was long connected. The Andalusian writer who lived in Seville and Almeria, Abu 'Ubayd 'Abd Allah al-Bakri (d. 1094), completed a work of geography in 1068 that he titled *Kitāb al-masālik wal-mamālik* (Book of highways and kingdoms) that mentions numerous places in the region of the northeastern reaches of the Niger River. Al-Bakri's book is the earliest extant Arabic work that describes parts of the Sahara and West Africa. Among the places south of the Sahara that he mentions are actual historical locations such as Kanem, Takrur, Ghana, Tadmakka, and Gao. He writes with great confidence about the routes connecting the major locations in the region. He provides an image of the political and social organization of Ghana (not to be confused with the modern state by the same name) and mentions its gold mines, which are all under the control of the king, who was said to possess a gold nugget the size of a large rock. Nearly a hundred years later, in 1154, the Andalusian–North African Abu 'Abd Allah al-Idrisi (d. 1165) produced a map of the known world, commonly called the *Tabula Rogeriana*, made for King Roger II of Sicily. He also wrote a work of general geographical information, *Kitāb Nuzhat al-mushtāq fī ikhtirāq al-āfāq* (The book of pleasant journeys into faraway lands). His map was the most advanced of the time and positions Africa on top of the map and identifies several places across North Africa and the Sahara. East and West Africa are covered and the Nile River and the Niger River (although not named as such) are connected on the map. Timbuktu was not represented on the map. He further embellished the description of gold in Ghana, writing that the king had a huge block of gold weighing thirty pounds created by God. Such details are repeated in several other works, such as the anonymous *Kitāb al-istibṣār* (Book of observation) of around 1192.

The Damascene scholar Ibn Fadlallah al-'Umari (d. 1349) visited Cairo, then under Mamluk rule, after the Malian ruler Mansa Musa and his entourage passed through the Mamluk capital. The stories about the wealth of the mansa were recorded by Umari in *Masālik al-abṣār fī mamālik al-amṣār* (The itineraries regarding the kingdoms of the civilized countries). He gives the territorial divisions and organization of the historic kingdom of Mali, provides ethnographic details of its peoples and the king's quarters, and describes the flora and fauna. He writes particularly about Mansa Musa, his pilgrimage, and his sojourn in Cairo. He makes references to the generosity of the visiting ruler, who made numerous gifts of various weights of gold to members of the Cairene Mamluk aristocracy whom he met. These three geographical writers based their descriptions not on actual travel but on information gathered from informants and other travelers. Umari gives the names or ranks of the individuals he met in Cairo who had experienced the splendor of the Malian ruler's visit. The others do not give their sources.

Of the dozens of medieval Arabic writers who devoted some attention to describing Africa, most of them never lived or traveled in any part of the continent, beyond perhaps some visits to the more fertile parts of coastal North Africa. There are exceptions, such as Abu 'Abdullah ibn Battuta (d. 1368/69) who spent twenty-seven years of his life traveling the world, going as far as China. He passed through West Africa in 1352, spending nearly a year on this trip. In his written account, he gives details on the routes, the villages, and oases he passed through, and makes observations on Mali and the territory's rulers. He relates several brief anecdotes of his encounters with different kinds of people in towns and minor settlements but he does not recount visiting a gold mine and does not mention gold in the way the previous writers had. He saw gold only as a means of exchange. Thus, he notes the cost in gold of a certain amount of salt in Walata, where salt was itself a currency. He encountered preachers, teachers, and judges in various locations, but he rarely reports his conversations with them, nor their learning, and says nothing of their books or book collections. He mentions a single copy of a work by the Iraqi polymath Abu al-Faraj al-Jawzi (d. 1201), titled *Kitāb al-mudhish*—a large compendium on the sources of Islamic knowledge. In the entire area from Timbuktu to Gao, this is the only book he finds worth mentioning from his year-long journey.

Gold, real and imagined, as a means of exchange and an item of high value, appears in virtually all the writings, but books rarely appear, and paper never does, at least not as a separate object. Joseph Cuoq, the editor of a volume of extracts from seventy-two Arabic authors, was struck that a single book, the one mentioned by Ibn Battuta, was the only book title recorded in this vast region of West Africa. Concern with *tibr* (gold dust) appears far more often. There is no mention by any of these authors of book collections or authors in Timbuktu or Walata. Timbuktu was only coming into being as a trading settlement and entrepôt—probably more of a campsite than a town—when Bakri, Idrisi, and Umari were writing, so it is reasonable that they did not identify the place in their maps or writing. In the time of Ibn Battuta, while Timbuktu was already an established town, scholars writing and collecting books were not yet as visible or as much a part of the town's character as they would be a century later. Things changed from the fifteenth century onward. The first appearance in an Arabic dictionary of "Timbuktu" is in the *Tāj al-'arūs min jawāhir al-qāmūs* (The bride's crown from the pearls of Qamus) of Murtada al-Zabidi (d. 1790), the South Asian scholar and lexicographer. He specified how Timbuktu was to be spelled and identified it as a town in the far west, but nothing more.

Descriptions of Timbuktu, and even its inclusion in maps, appeared long after other places in the Sahara and beyond were identified. The European explorers arrived in the Sahara and at this illusive place many centuries later. Lured by the myth of immense wealth and pots of gold easy to take, arriving in Timbuktu became an ambition for adventurous young men with financial backing. The first European representation of Timbuktu, however, was not in a narrative description but on a medieval map.

Maps and Texts

Umari's and Ibn Battuta's pioneering geographical works could have been known in southern Europe. Umari's description of the Malian ruler Mansa Musa's generosity while in Cairo could have been the source for how the Catalan cartographer Abraham Cresques (d. 1387) represented Africa. Cresques produced a map in 1375 that holds the earliest mention of Timbuktu and neighboring towns in a European text (see a section that covers West Africa on a larger map, fig. 3).[3] He locates the towns he named "Tenbuch," "Geugeu," and "Melli" strikingly close to where we know Timbuktu, Gao, and the historic Mali can be found. The map depicts a ruler, probably Mansa Musa, on a throne with a golden crown, cup, and staff, sitting majestically atop this region. Whoever saw and heard of this map during the last quarter of the fourteenth century, at least in southern European royal courts, became aware of the riches of this part of Africa. Anyone who had the chance to see this map at the time would have concluded that there were societies like their own, where the king or ruler was rich and above everyone else, with towns located in a vast fertile space over which he ruled. The map does not depict emptiness, strange creatures, and dangerous predators but represents prosperity and a space not different to the representation of Europe on the same map.

FIG. 3. Section from *Catalan Atlas* of Abraham Cresques (d. 1387), showing part of West Africa. This is the first known representation of Timbuktu ("Tenbuch," on the map). It also shows a crowned figure with a staff in one hand, probably the ruler Mansa Musa. The cartographer Abraham Cresques made it on commission from King Peter IV of Aragon. *Image source*: https://en.wikipedia.org/wiki/File:1375_Atlas_Catalan_Abraham_Cresques.jpg.

Indeed, the depiction of Africa can be seen as rather more flattering compared with the lands on the other side of the Mediterranean. Whereas the African side has two impressive human figures and signs of wealth, this is not the case for Europe.

To the name "Tenbuch" (Timbuktu) fell the fortune, or misfortune, over the following centuries, of standing for a larger space with bottomless treasures, plenty of gold, and riches waiting to be traded for, or simply taken, if only it could be reached. The Cresques map is a unique representation of the northern regions of Africa. Unfortunately, the informants or texts on which Cresques drew to create his map have never been established. The map reveals a unique moment well before the growth of systematic prejudice about the peoples and cultures on the other side of the Mediterranean Sea. The lands across the Mediterranean had not yet become "the other" of subsequent centuries.

About 150 years later, in 1526, Leo Africanus (d. 1537), as he is commonly known in English, recalled his travels in the Sahara in a work that he completed as a manuscript but that only appeared in print around a quarter century later, in 1550, after his death.[4] Apart from Arabic—his mother tongue—he was literate in Latin and Italian. He also produced a trilingual dictionary and other smaller texts in which he relied on all his language competencies. The work in which he writes about his travels in the Sahara is based on his memories as a young man, when he only wrote in Arabic. By the time he produced his text describing this part of Africa, many years later, he could write in Italian, and that is how he wrote his text.

He was born after the fall of Muslim Granada in 1492, and his family fled with thousands of others across the Strait of Gibraltar. They settled in Fez. During this time, he was known as Hasan bin Muhammad al-Fasi (and sometimes also with the epithet al-Wazzan al-Gharnati), reflecting his origins and connections to Fez (al-Fasi) and Granada (al-Gharnati). The rulers of northern Morocco during this time, the Wattasid dynasty, had their capital at Fez.

He visited Timbuktu on two separate trips. Between 1506 and 1514, he traveled through the enormous territory beyond Fez and Marrakesh, and the places in the Sahara depicted on the Cresques map. The Wattasid sultan of Fez sent Leo's father—whom Leo accompanied—to pay homage to the ruler of Mali, Askiya Muhammad Turé (d. 1528). Leo did not meet the *askiya* (ruler) himself. In his writing, he described as "kingdom" a number of towns he visited, such as Jenne ("Regno dè Genia"), Mali ("Regno dè Melli"), Timbuktu ("Regno dè Tombutto"), and Gao ("Dè Ghago & suo Regno").[5] He might have seen the towns and their environs as having independent powers with no or little overarching authority.

Leo Africanus's *Descrittione dell'Affrica* (*Description of Africa*) was part of a larger work, *Cosmographia & Geographia dell'Affrica*, published first in Venice in 1550 by Giambatista Ramusio as part of a collection of travel writings. After the *Descrittione dell'Affrica* went from manuscript into print, it was published in more than thirty editions in eight languages. The text would be reprinted five times (the last one in 1613) and translated into various European languages in subsequent decades; a French edition appeared in 1556 and an English one in 1600. The work became a key text in Europe for information about Africa until well into the nineteenth century. The translations were used extensively by subsequent travelers on the continent, with a copy of "Leo" often taken along on the exploration. The French Orientalist Louis Massignon apparently even used it in the early twentieth century for empirical details when he was writing about Morocco.

Leo Africanus describes the Saharan environment, its human settlements, and the poor conditions for growing fruit-bearing trees or undertaking any agricultural activity in most places. He writes of the commercial activities in other places, items exchanged, and the origins of the traders. He also notes the levels of education. In what he calls "Melli" (Mali) he found no places of higher learning. This contrasts with what he found in Timbuktu, where he met many learned people, preachers, and judges, all supported by the ruler. He saw many books in Timbuktu, which were considered among the most valuable things in the town; he added that the books were all handwritten and originated in "Barbaria" (meaning coastal northern Africa). His remarks on Timbuktu are striking because he recognizes the book as a valuable object: more profit was made from trading in books than any other goods, he observed.[6] As an educated man, he probably spoke with people involved in education and book learning. Yet he does not identify the books as local but points to their distant origins. This was probably the case for some of the titles he saw but clearly not all the books, as will become evident in subsequent chapters.

While traveling on the North African coast, possibly heading to Istanbul, Leo was kidnapped, taken across the Mediterranean, and imprisoned in the Rome of Pope Leo X. He was held as a captive there from about 1516, and he was given the name Giovanni Leone Africanus (John Leo Africanus).

The Early Explorers

Human movement increased across the Mediterranean, and especially around the Western Mediterranean and the narrow Strait of Gibraltar, between the appearance of the *Catalan Atlas* of Abraham Cresques in 1327 and the publication of Leo Africanus's *Description of Africa* in 1550. There were centuries of mobility due to campaigns of conquest, religious struggles, and political and commercial maneuvering well before the fourteenth century. How much further beyond the coastlines of Africa the interaction went is another question. Cresques's *Catalan Atlas* depicts a solid, long, unmissable wall just beyond the coastline of North Africa. Could that have represented a view that penetrating into the interior, into the Sahara and beyond, was not possible, a physical and mental barrier hard to break through? The distances across the Mediterranean did not prevent mobility and movement and did not require more than a handful of men with basic seafaring vessels to cross back and forth. The Strait of Gibraltar is only about fourteen kilometers wide. The expulsion and forced migration of Jews and Muslims from the Iberian Peninsula was a long process throughout the fifteenth century, with 1492 being an emblematic date for the destruction of the Jewish and Muslim communities of Spain. The forced departures continued into the early decades of the 1500s. Jews and Muslims settled in places like Fez and Meknes but also further South, and even moved far beyond Marrakesh into Saharan oasis settlements like Tuwat, in modern southern Algeria, where the Jewish community would even build a synagogue.

Iberian naval competition saw Portuguese overseas expansion in this period. Ceuta, on the northern Moroccan coast, was taken by the Portuguese in 1415, a date that marks the start of their overseas empire. In subsequent decades, they made claims to territory along the Atlantic coast, gradually moving along what is now the Moroccan coast, down past Mauritania, and reaching the mouth of the Senegal River by the 1450s. They created sometimes heavily fortified enclaves from which some of their men attempted to penetrate the continent far beyond the shoreline, with variable seriousness and success.

The Portuguese—in many cases under the guidance of Italian-speakers from thriving commercial centers such as Genoa and Venice—came face-to-face with the inhabitants of Africa during their coastal expansion in the first half of the fifteenth century. In the 1430s and at the beginning of the 1440s, the explorers encountered the "Berbers," whom the Portuguese called *Maurus* (Moors) and *Azeneg* (Znaga), in the interior.[7] The term *Maurus* came to mean a distinct identity from Black Africans, but the term was at times used for dark-skinned people the explorers encountered. From the middle of the 1440s and 1450s, after navigating to the mouth of the Senegal River, the sailors reached lands inhabited by people they described as darker-skinned (*Negri*) people. Only a few adventurers went into the interior; they were mostly European fugitives assimilating into the African environment. The Portuguese noted the difference between the so-called Berbers inhabiting the Saharan coast and the peoples in the interior. The Venetian merchant Alvise Cadamosto (also Ca da Mosto) used the collective term "Negri" in writing about these peoples. Cadamosto made two trips to Africa, in 1455 and 1456, in the service of Prince Henry of Portugal, known commonly as "the Navigator." The work of Cadamosto was influential when it appeared because he was a keen observer and skillful in dealing with his African interlocutors and he was determined to collect all relevant information about the territories he visited.

During his 1456 expedition on the continent, Cadamosto met the Genoan merchant Antoniotto Usodimire. Nothing remains of the latter's writings except a short letter that he had sent to his creditors in 1455. Italians involved in the textile trade noted that there was possibly wealth in the interior of Africa, and one, Benedetto Dei, even noted Timbuktu's prosperity. Antonio Malfante wrote about a place he called "Thambet," probably Timbuktu, but he only reached the Saharan oasis town of Tuwat.

The explorers of this era often repeated stories they heard from others without visiting the places they wrote about; certain tropes recur in their writing as a result. Similarly, in many writings there were references to gold and treasures, and there began to appear references to monsters and other fantastical phenomena. There were also references to the caravans heading to *Tanbutu* and *Melli* and claims to have visited these places deep in the interior. The explorers' reports were compiled as manuscripts but eventually, with the arrival of the printing press in the Iberian Peninsula in the last quarter of the fifteenth century, the reports went to the burgeoning presses. There was a growing readership in Europe for books about the world beyond their own and probably as a result there arose the urge to embellish and invent things. The works circulated as single volumes, but also in compilations of travel reports, and they became standard references for details about the interior of Africa for generations afterward. For a long time—for some places even into the twentieth century—given the scarcity of documentation, travelers into the interior had to read even the fabricated narratives of the earlier adventurers.

European travelers believed there to be mines and minerals in the interior of the continent, and heard of places that sounded like Gao and Timbuktu. During the seventeenth century, coastal West Africa witnessed sporadic conflicts between European merchants-cum-explorers attempting to establish themselves in the region and launch their expeditions into the interior. Nobody ever made it deep into the interior; at most, they ventured there but did not return alive or live to tell their stories.

Timbuktu (as "Timbuktoo") appears in English as a playful, nonsense expression from the outset. It is a place in the Western imagination that was for generations associated with isolation and with being "the furthest place imaginable" as the Oxford English Dictionary still defines it. One reason for the perception of isolation is that numerous attempts by Western explorers in the eighteenth and nineteenth centuries to reach it failed and ended in tragedy.

The Association for Promoting the Discovery of the Interior Parts of Africa (called, in short, the Africa Association) was established in London in 1788 to explore the continent and to discover the course of the Niger River and reach Timbuktu.[8] Mungo Park, the Scottish traveler, and his armed entourage explored the upper Niger River in 1796, and in 1805 undertook a second mission into the interior, traveling on the Niger beyond the important towns of Segou, Jenne, and Timbuktu. After his return, his published journal of the trip became a bestseller. On his second mission, he sent letters back to the coast but never returned; he disappeared along the Niger, far beyond Timbuktu. The Mungo Park mission was met with hostility in the interior; he and his men would shoot recklessly and killed locals when they felt pressured. Park never entered Timbuktu—or if he approached it, he did not live to record his visit—but he kept alive the image of treasures to be found there.

James Grey Jackson, the English consul at the vibrant port town of Mogador (known today as Essaouira) in Morocco, added to the image of prosperity and of a high, learned culture in his book of 1811.[9] In his view, Timbuktu was the "Emporium of Central Africa," where trade was vibrant, the soils productive, climate comfortable, and gold mines in close proximity. He refers to a "state library, which is composed for the most part of manuscripts in the Arabic and contains a few in Hebrew" and what he calls "Chaldaic," adding that "it is probable there are many translations from Greek and Latin authors at present unknown to Europeans."

The popularity of Timbuktu in the nineteenth-century English-speaking world is perhaps best seen in the fact that the poet Alfred Lord Tennyson in 1829 chose to name his long, award-winning poem "Timbuctoo":

> Wide Afric, doth thy sun
> Lighten, thy hills enfold a city as fair
> As those which starr'd the night o' the elder world?
> Or is the rumour of thy Timbuctoo
> A dream as frail as those of ancient time?[10]

In 1825 the Paris Société de Géographie offered a prize of 10,000 francs and a gold medal to the first man to reach Timbuktu and produce a description of the town. By this time, British magazines had begun to parody the craze for Timbuktu. About twenty-odd exploration teams had set out to explore the interior of Africa from various points on the Atlantic coast by the 1820s.

Alexander Gordon Laing, who traveled in a north-south direction, was the first European to reach Timbuktu, in 1826, but he was killed after he left the town, probably by bandits who had trapped him in the desert. His journal was never recovered. By the time of his disappearance, the Frenchman René Caillié had left the French enclave at Saint Louis (in Senegal) on the Atlantic Coast and traveled eastward into the interior. He was an autodidact with previous travel experience in Africa and the Caribbean. While in Guadeloupe, he apparently read Mungo Park's account of his exploration. Caillié thought himself up to the task of exploring the interior of the continent. He took on an Arabic persona, including dress and name. He passed through Jenne, apparently the first European to visit this historic town with its large mud-brick mosque, and then went onward to Timbuktu, arriving in early 1828. He found the city wanting, sleepy, and rather dull; a disappointment compared with Jenne and especially given that the place evoked such fascination in Europe among potential explorers and investors. In both places, he stayed for only about two weeks. He was given protection by a notable from Jenne whom he named Sidi Abdullahi, with whom he engaged in long conversations. He recognized that there were men of learning, mentioned paper among the items for sale in the market, and noticed children learning to read, but books did not get a mention. He departed from Timbuktu in May 1828, stopping over at Arawan, about 220 kilometers north of Timbuktu, and then crossed the Sahara Desert back to the Mediterranean. In 1830 he published a three-volume account of his journey, and he won a prize from the Société de Géographie for his efforts. Publishing the results of an expedition was expected. Apart from elevating their authors in literary and scientific circles, the works were closely studied by others preparing their journeys into the unknown, such as German-speaking Heinrich Barth.

The Explorer as Philologist

Heinrich Barth went by the name Abd al-Kerim, introducing himself as a "Syrian notable," from the time his exploration of the African interior began in April 1850.[11] He was a devout Christian and he tells us that on only one occasion during his travels did he hide his religious identity. Unlike Caillié, he had a university education. He held a doctorate in classics from the University of Berlin, had studied Arabic by himself, and had a keen interest in learning languages, as is clear from the numerous word-lists and basic grammars that he compiled during his five years in Africa. Barth was recruited for a British exploration mission under the leadership of James Richardson and another German, the geologist and astronomer Adolf Overweg. They set out from Tripoli on a trans-Saharan route toward Lake Chad. Barth's luggage contained a small library that included a copy of the Quran he had bought in Egypt, a volume of Herodotus's *Histories*, and Mungo Park's *Travels*, among other books. Between the three Europeans in the expedition, they had books in classical Greek, Hebrew, and French, apart from books in English and German. Barth had also read the works of the early modern travelers on the continent; in his finished text, his citations go back as far as Cadamosto and Leo Africanus. He had a keen eye and ear for books. He was told that there was a big

"Christian book" when he was in the town of Katsina (now northern Nigeria) in early 1851. A few years later, among the Kel el-Suk people who were located further north of Timbuktu, he curiously found an English book, *The Life of Bruce*, which he bought from the locals. It was probably lost or taken from a previous English-speaking traveler, such as Gordon Laing, who was killed outside Timbuktu and whose luggage was thus left in the desert or taken by his killers.

In early 1852 in Bagirmi, southeast of Lake Chad, Barth met, in what he calls Bagirmi's capital, a blind scholar named Fáki Sámbo: "In this out-of-the-way place a man not only versed in all the branches of Arabic literature, but who had even read (nay possessed a manuscript of) those portions of Aristotle and Plato which had been translated into, or rather Mohammedanized into Arabic, and who possessed the most intimate knowledge of the countries which he had visited."[12] Barth visited this "very enlightened man" daily during his stay in the town.

In Wurno in 1853 Barth read a local work, *Tazyīn al-waraqāt* (Embellishment of the papers), by Abdullahi, the brother of the founder of the Sokoto state, and saw a work by the latter's son. Both works are of great value in understanding the thinking and events of the early nineteenth century in the region. (These figures and their works are discussed in chapter 6.) On Barth's arrival in Timbuktu in September 1853, the scholar Ahmad al-Bakkay al-Kunti, from the powerful Kunta family, offered him gifts of an ox, sheep, and other items he could live on. The opponents of Bakkay wanted him to expel Barth, which would have meant his death. Fearing that Barth could be poisoned, Bakkay therefore warned him to accept only food from his house and refuse it from anyone else. Bakkay was effectively Barth's protector at a tumultuous time in and around Timbuktu; and he showed Barth works from his collection of manuscripts. (For the literary heritage of the Kuntis and the situation in the area, see chapter 6.) The topics they discussed ranged from the size of the British Empire to the Arabic translation of the *Aphorisms* of Hippocrates, which was a gift from the Sokoto leader, Muhammad Bello, to Bakkay; Bello had gotten it from an earlier explorer, Hugh Clapperton, who made two voyages to West Africa.[13] On Clapperton's second trip to Sokoto in 1826, he brought for Muhammad Bello: Euclid's *Elements*, a work of Ibn Sina (Avicenna), a *History of the Tatars*, a copy of the Quran, the Old and New Testaments, and the Psalms.[14] Barth thought that gifts of books by Europeans would serve to break down barriers and increase European access to the learned elite of the region. Bakkay requested that Barth arrange for "her majesty's government to send him some good firearms and some Arabic books."

Barth wrote about a chronicle, which he called the *Diwan*, that recounted the history of the state of Bornu (around Lake Chad). In 1853, on the way to Timbuktu at Gwando, in Hausa-speaking territory, he was lent a collection of fragments of the *Tarikh al-Sudan* (Chronicle of the Land of the Blacks), "the most valuable historical work of Ahmad Baba, to which my friend, Abdel Kader, in Sokoto had first called my attention." Barth misidentified the author but was completely correct to identify the work as of great significance. He spent a few days making copies of parts of the text. His own commentary on the fragments shaped later scholarly perspectives on the chronology and history of the region. A German translation of these fragments was published after his return.

Barth left some books in Timbuktu while traveling further and was disappointed to find that they were destroyed in a fire. Earlier, in the market of Kano, a major commercial center, he found that paper—with the *tre lune* (three moons) watermark—was imported in great quantities, but he reckoned that it was sold as wrapping, not writing, paper. During the five years of his travels, most of the time without his travel companions, he kept a thorough record of his observations and encounters. He was particularly interested in the learned figures wherever he stayed. Barth and his two fellow travelers who started out together separated early on and planned to rendezvous at a later point. Richardson died in March 1851 in Kukuwa near Lake Chad and Overweg died in September 1852.

Barth's *Travels and discoveries in North and Central Africa* began to appear in 1857, with a print run of 2,250 copies, and a year later the last two volumes were published (1,000 copies); a total of 3,500 pages. The German edition—*Reisen und Entdeckungen in nord- und central-Afrika*—came out at the same time. He worked on each independently, so they are similar but not translations of each other. A French translation followed, and abridgements in English and German subsequently appeared. He published a *Collection of vocabularies of Central African languages* in 1862, which covers about seven languages used in the area he traveled through during his five-year sojourn in West Africa. He recognized that he was trained as a classicist and not in African linguistics and that sometimes his visit in a place was too short to appreciate the language fully. This was his experience with Hausa. In Timbuktu, he claims that life was hard, and the Songhay (Songhai) dialect spoken there was highly diluted. With Barth's substantial and scholarly reports, the fantasy of immense wealth and untold treasures in the middle of the desert, with Timbuktu at the center, began to dissipate (fig. 4 is based on Barth's impressions of Timbuktu). But the fascination with the name and reaching it did not disappear. Furthermore, the optimism about extensive trading possibilities remained on the horizon.

One indication revealing the place of Timbuktu among the community of explorers and geographers is found in a survey of the index of the *Bulletin de la*

FIG. 4. An image of Timbuktu made after the travels of one of the major European exploration missions of Heinrich Barth. Barth did not have artists in his traveling parties; this image is thus based on a mixture of the testimonies of Barth and the artist's imagination. *Image source*: https://www.posterazzi.com/africa-timbuktu-1853-ncaravan-approaching-the-city-of-timbuktu-in-the-saharah-7-september-1853-lithograph-from-heinrich-barths-travels-in-central-africa-munich-1857-poster-print-by-granger-collection-item-vargrc0114038/.

Société de Géographie. For the roughly forty years between 1822 and 1861, there are only two references to Jenne, one to Kano, none to Gao, and around sixty-four to Timbuktu. European explorers in the nineteenth century attempted to travel into the African interior in ever larger numbers to add to extant European geographical knowledge and for fame and fortune. The European press maintained a keen interest in their exploits. "Timbuktu" was the magical word to use in coverage of the subject of African exploration. The name had its effect at the time and in subsequent generations.

The War Correspondent as Manuscript Collector

Felix Du Bois was a correspondent in Berlin and Vienna for several French newspapers and magazines in the 1880s. In 1890 he accompanied an exploration mission in Guinea to the sources of the Niger River. Some years later, as French generals were leading their French and African troops deeper into the West African interior, *L'illustration*, the popular weekly famous for the drawings accompanying its stories, sent Du Bois as a war reporter to cover the course of the conquests. The concern with Timbuktu was no longer about its mythical gold and treasures but colonial conquest that would boost national pride. Du Bois arrived at the colonial port at Dakar in October 1894, after the leading military columns had already completed most of their conquests. No longer compelled to write about military matters and maneuvers, he was captivated by what Leo Africanus would have said were the true treasures of Timbuktu—its books. So, of all the European explorers who wrote about their travels and encounters in the major towns along the Niger River, Du Bois gave the most attention to education, manuscripts, and book collections among the locals.

Du Bois passed through several towns on the Niger River but Jenne captured his imagination—this "jewel of the valley of the Niger," as he put it.[15] He stayed in the town for several days, before heading toward Timbuktu. It was well after the town had been conquered in December of 1893 that his eyes fell on it for the first time. His role as a war reporter was over before it had begun. With no battle to write about, he went about exploring the town with his guides, who introduced him to scholars and people with book collections. This was never the intention of his trip. There is no indication that he could read or speak Arabic, or any other African language, or that he had training or experience that might have helped him deal with the materials he was shown in Jenne and Timbuktu. He had been to Palestine as a reporter just before this adventure but that did not qualify him to write about Arabic texts in West Africa.

By the 1880s, Orientalists in colonial Algiers had already begun to show sustained interest in the literature emerging from the Sahara. Jacques-Auguste Cherbonneau (d. 1882) and his successor to the chair at the *Collège arabe français d'Alger*, Octave Houdas (d. 1916), were the significant, pioneering figures who concerned themselves with this literature. In 1855, Cherbonneau produced a brief summary of the first biographical dictionary written by Ahmad Baba, and Houdas would edit and translate the two most important *Tarikhs* (Chronicles) from Timbuktu. Du Bois did not have the kind of education fostered for colonial officials in Algiers that could lead to a discussion about dictionaries and chronicles. Yet he wrote with great confidence about the books written in Timbuktu.

Shortly after Du Bois's return to Paris, in 1896, Édition du Figaro and Flammarion jointly published an account of his trip as *Tombouctou la mystérieuse*.[16] It went into a reprint in 1897 and, almost simultaneously, a translation—in places abridged and inexact—was published in Britain and the United States as *Timbuctoo: The*

Mysterious. The original French edition won the book prize of the prestigious Académie Française. The purpose of Du Bois's trip was to report on the conquest of the western Soudan, but that only covers about thirty pages in a volume of four hundred pages. The book does not convey much sense of mystery and the only suspense is his own anticipation of seeing the outlines of Timbuktu on the horizon.

Du Bois was genuinely charmed by Jenne, but Timbuktu disappoints him as "this wreck of a town" that had no mystery or inviting characteristics.[17] He makes repeated comparisons between the two towns. If there is a "main character" in the book, then it is the literary culture of the region, and in this Jenne is held in higher esteem than any of the other towns he writes about. He recalls previous visitors or writers such as Cadamosto and Leo Africanus from the earlier period, and Park, Caillié, and Barth from more recent times and evaluates the quality of their observations. He also notes the observations of the Arabic writers Bakri and Ibn Battuta. His purpose is to point to the limitations and weaknesses of his predecessors and the greater depth of his own engagement with the scholars and literary legacy of the region. The patriotic Frenchman Du Bois singles out for criticism the German Heinrich Barth. According to him, Barth was rather mediocre as a researcher since he spent most of his stay in Timbuktu hiding indoors, and "his utterances are mere amplifications of the facts acquired by his predecessor," meaning Caillié.[18] Du Bois does not inform his readers which version of Barth's work he read. He probably was referring to the French translation, which was based on an abridgement and had a number of peculiar translations. However, Du Bois was not disposed to praise Barth at all, irrespective of which version of his work he used. Du Bois's tone betrays the Franco-German rivalry of the time.

Du Bois mentions numerous works and scholars, including the famous chronicle *Tārīkh al-Sūdān*, by ʿAbd al-Rahman al-Saʿdi, of which he first found a complete copy in Jenne. He gives a long summary of it, devoting many pages to retelling the dynastic history of the Songhay people along the pattern of this chronicle. He mentions a number of works of Ahmad Baba, the famous Timbuktu scholar who was imprisoned and exiled to Marrakesh in the early 1590s (discussed in the next chapter). Two works of the Kunta family, who were prominent and influential in Timbuktu especially in the first half of the nineteenth century, are also briefly noted, as well as the figure of "Mahmoud Kati" and his *Chronicle* (Du Bois calls the chronicle *Fatassi*, a version of part of its title). Du Bois certainly had highly literate and literary informants in both Jenne and Timbuktu, who took him to manuscript owners and collections in multiple homes. He claims to have met the descendants of Ahmad Baba, one of whom was an excellent manuscript copyist. Du Bois was even allowed to borrow books, managed to buy a few, and had a complete copy of the *Tārīkh al-Sūdān* made in Jenne. He also says he had some manuscripts corrected in Timbuktu. His enthusiasm about the intellectual and educational past of Timbuktu leads him to coin the term, and title of a chapter, "University of Sankoré," for the important mosque of the town. In his view, while Timbuktu can be compared with places like Damascus, Cairo, and Fez, it was never really in their league because no great prose was ever produced there as in the great centers of Arabic learning. Timbuktu was "the younger sister" of those places but the greatest in the "land of the blacks" for "Her collection of manuscripts leaves us in no doubt upon the point, and permits us to reconstruct this side of her past in its smallest details."[19]

Du Bois notes the landscape, the habits of town-dwellers, and the goods bought and sold in the markets, but such observations are not his main concern. History and the books of the local scholars captured his imagination. In the last chapter, when he had to write about the French conquest, he writes that he will "show the taking of Timbuctoo in a new light, as it appeared to the inhabitants. They related it to me as the old Sudanese chronicles, whose art is unhappily lost, might have done."[20]

Du Bois's book was marketed for a popular readership. The book was advertised to both French and English readers as being richly illustrated, having "One hundred and fifty-three illustrations . . . and eleven maps and plans."[21] He wrote with the apparent learning of a highly trained Orientalist fluent in Arabic grammar and literature, trained at one of the French Orientalist institutes, whose aim was to write a general literary history of the region. In the French edition of his bestseller he had an appendix with the list of manuscripts he collected and brought back to Paris (fig. 5), adding to the impression that he was an Orientalist traveler who went on a mission to collect rare manuscripts.

However, Du Bois was a journalist and colonial war reporter, without the necessary linguistic or philological expertise. After this book on Timbuktu for a general readership, he would never return to the subject again. He had grand plans to return to the Sahara and become rich from the sale of the emerging transport technology, the automobile. Between his return to Paris and the publication of his book, he could have consulted a figure like the Orientalist Octave Houdas, who was then engaged in editing works emanating from the Sahara. We shall never know. Du Bois did produce a work filled with hyperbole but also with fascinating nuggets of information and insight. He was partly responsible, on the one hand, for the epithet "the mysterious" reemerging in descriptions of

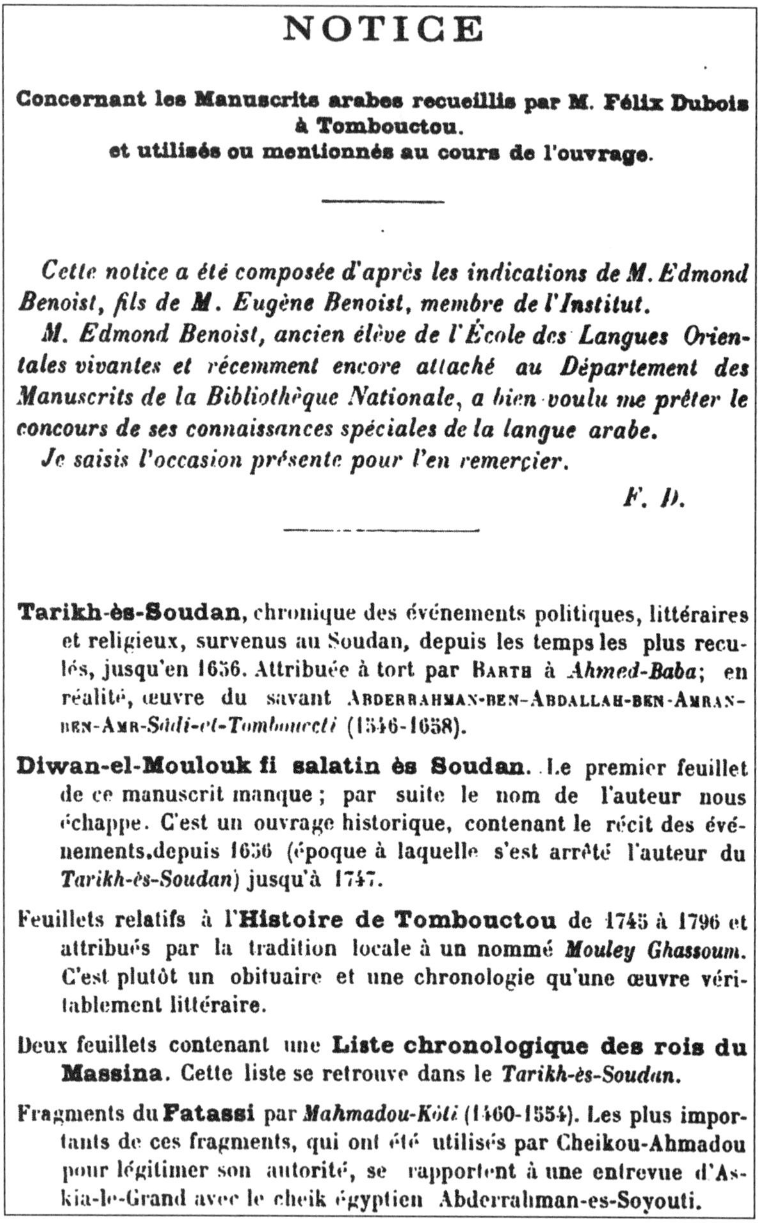

NOTICE

Concernant les Manuscrits arabes recueillis par M. Félix Dubois à Tombouctou. et utilisés ou mentionnés au cours de l'ouvrage.

Cette notice a été composée d'après les indications de M. Edmond Benoist, fils de M. Eugène Benoist, membre de l'Institut.

M. Edmond Benoist, ancien élève de l'École des Langues Orientales vivantes et récemment encore attaché au Département des Manuscrits de la Bibliothèque Nationale, a bien voulu me prêter le concours de ses connaissances spéciales de la langue arabe.

Je saisis l'occasion présente pour l'en remercier.

F. D.

Tarikh-ès-Soudan, chronique des événements politiques, littéraires et religieux, survenus au Soudan, depuis les temps les plus reculés, jusqu'en 1656. Attribuée à tort par Barth à *Ahmed-Baba*; en réalité, œuvre du savant Abderrahman-ben-Abdallah-ben-Amran-ben-Amr-*Sâdi-el-Tombouceti* (1546-1658).

Diwan-el-Moulouk fi salatin ès Soudan. Le premier feuillet de ce manuscrit manque; par suite le nom de l'auteur nous échappe. C'est un ouvrage historique, contenant le récit des événements.depuis 1656 (époque à laquelle s'est arrêté l'auteur du *Tarikh-ès-Soudan*) jusqu'à 1747.

Feuillets relatifs à l'**Histoire de Tombouctou** de 1745 à 1796 et attribués par la tradition locale à un nommé *Mouley Ghassoum*. C'est plutôt un obituaire et une chronologie qu'une œuvre véritablement littéraire.

Deux feuillets contenant une **Liste chronologique des rois du Massina**. Cette liste se retrouve dans le *Tarikh-ès-Soudan*.

Fragments du **Fatassi** par *Mahmadou-Kôti* (1460-1554). Les plus importants de ces fragments, qui ont été utilisés par Cheikou-Ahmadou pour légitimer son autorité, se rapportent à une entrevue d'Askia-le-Grand avec le cheik égyptien Abderrahman-es-Soyouti.

FIG. 5. In the French edition of *Tombouctou la mystérieuse* (1897), 419–20, Felix Du Bois, who went as a journalist to cover the conquest of Timbuktu, appends this list of manuscripts he collected and took with him to Paris. The English translation of the book does not have this Appendix. *Image source*: https://archive.org/details/tombouctoulamysoodubogoog/page/n457/mode/2up.

Consultation juridique et politique écrite par Mohi-ed-din-Abou-Abdallah Sidi Mohammed ben Abdel Kerim *El-Mogheili el Tilimsani* sur des questions posées par El-Hadj-Mohammed-Askia. Cet auteur arriva au Soudan vers l'an 1500.

Nil-el-Ibtihadj bitatriz-ed-dibadj. Supplément au dictionnaire biographique des savants malikites d'Ibn-Ferhoun, par *Ahmed-Baba* (1556-1627).

Miraz, ouvrage écrit par le *même auteur*, pendant sa captivité au Maroc, pour renseigner les Marocains sur les différentes populations noires du Soudan.

Eloge en vers d'un gouverneur marocain (17e siècle ?).

Lettre d'Abdoul-Kader, chef des colonnes de Cheikou-Ahmadou, rendant compte à celui-ci de sa campagne contre les Touaregs (19e siècle).

Lettre d'Ahmed-el-Backay-ben-Mohammed-ben-el-Mokhtar à El-Hadj-Omar (19e siècle).

Petit Taraïfa par *Sidi Mokhtar*, le jeune, ouvrage relatif aux populations du Sahara (19e siècle).

*
* *

Tohfet-el-Albab our Nokhet-el-Adjab. « Cadeau offert aux hommes intelligents et choix de merveilles. » Ouvrage d'imagination composé sous une forme sérieuse par Abou-*Abdallah-El gharnati* qui vivait à Mossoul vers le 12e siècle.

Dalaïl-el-Khairat, livre de piété très répandu dans l'Islam; œuvre du Berbère Abou-*Abdallah-al-Djozouli*, mort en 1465. Très beau spécimen de la calligraphie soudanaise ; titres et ornements en couleur.

Feuillets liturgiques, collection de carrés magiques, de talismans et de formules de prières.

FIG. 5. (*continued*)

Timbuktu since Caillé's first use of it in the 1820s, and on the other hand, for some parameters of the subsequent scholarly discourse about Timbuktu's learned culture and manuscripts.

When the next work dedicated to Timbuktu appeared, just over a half century later, the impression given was that the town did not have anybody who could read or write. Horace Mitchell Miner, an anthropologist trained at the University of Chicago, spent seven months in Timbuktu in the late 1930s, but his ethnography of the town, *The Primitive City of Timbuctoo*, only appeared in 1953. From "Timbuktu the mysterious" with its abundant scholars and libraries, it was a startling step backward when in the mid-twentieth century the town was cast as a "primitive city" with no literacy to speak of. Nor was there any mention of book collections among its population. When Miner was doing his fieldwork, the literary culture of Timbuktu that Du Bois strove to highlight—and embellish—was long gone. However, one man in the town known as Ahmad Bularraf (see chapter 7) was then deeply involved in writing, copying, and especially manuscript collecting. Miner and Bularraf's paths obviously did not cross in the narrow lanes or squares of the town.

What the European explorers set out to discover never materialized.[22] Gold was mined in West Africa, but the images of splendor and excess that had spread since the depictions of some of the Arabic writers remained elusive. The explorers made up for this by offering their sponsors, and the public, bulky books—often multivolume works—to satisfy their curiosity about a world still unknown to them. In various ways the explorers put themselves at the center of their narratives, but they were in fact heavily dependent travelers, uncertain of their surroundings. They were very often unwell, affected by the heat and hardship of such long journeys. While their reports placed their own concerns and observations at the center of their narratives, they were never, or seldom, alone. They all relied on local guides, intermediaries, interpreters, and traveling merchants they met along the way to achieve their objectives. Explorers' journeys also required large numbers of local young men to carry, pack, and offload the dozens of camels or horses they used as transportation. They took along tents, supplies of food and medication, equipment, and gifts for which the entourage servants had to care. Middlemen were crucial to the success of their visits and their names, or pseudonyms, were provided in some of the travel accounts. Explorers also had local protectors, prominent personalities who exerted influence in a town or region. Barth in Timbuktu, for instance, had the scholar and leader Ahmad al-Bakkay, grandson of the legendary Sufi scholar and merchant Sidi Mukhtar al-Kunti, who arrived in Timbuktu from Arawan. Barth could converse in Arabic and this facilitated his interactions with scholars but not with most of the ordinary people, because they would have used a Berber dialect, Bamana, Songhay, Hausa, or Fulfulde, depending on their origin. Barth does acknowledge the role of his local assistants in this work and mentions their names and where they assisted him. On his return to Europe, he took along two of them.

Felix Du Bois did not tell his readers much about his local assistants. He did not mention his abilities in Arabic, or any other local language, yet his work is filled with literary documentation that is remarkable, at least for a travel narrative of the time. He obviously used local interpreters but does not say so explicitly. Only a handful of European travelers reported witnessing any writing at all in West Africa; they recalled seeing inscriptions on rocks and tombstones, witnessing children with wooden writing boards, and finding Arabic manuscripts. The French agricultural engineer Georges de Gironcourt (d. 1960) was struck by inscriptions on tombstones and took drawings of them back to Paris.[23] He returned in 1911–12 on a mission sponsored by the Académie des Inscriptions et Belles-Lettres specifically to collect such epigraphic traces. Working with assistants and under extremely tough climatic conditions, his team managed to gather a large number of impressions of inscriptions at sites in Saney, Gao, Essuk, Junhan, and Bentiya. De Gironcourt did not find medieval inscriptions engraved in Timbuktu itself, but did find some that had been removed to the city from the Bentiya medieval epigraphic site. Figure 6 shows manuscript book copyists at work for De Gironcourt, who collected manuscripts and took impressions of inscriptions on his expeditions.

At the same time, De Gironcourt witnessed learning in progress. He commissioned copies of manuscripts and collected original ones—around 150 in all—at various locations along the middle Niger River. Colonial Orientalists did conduct surveys of the political landscape that included accounts of the scholarship in specific towns or regions. Tribal genealogies and chronicles were given prominence. Surveys, translations, and reproductions of manuscripts, such as in the many works of Paul Marty (d. 1938), were undertaken as an essential part of the emerging tools of colonial administration. These officials worked with the colonial military personnel on the ground, and they collected or copied texts sent to translators in the army in Algeria, such as Ismail Hamet (d. 1932), who undertook many translations of local materials.

Felix Du Bois was particularly critical of Heinrich Barth for his failure to correctly identify the author of the *Tārīkh al-Sūdān* (Chronicle of the Land of the Blacks). Du Bois's informants pointed out that Ahmad Baba was not the author of the chronicle, but that Baba was the most significant scholar of the town and

DÉCHIFFREMENT DE MANUSCRITS CHEZ LES PEULS DE SAY.
De gauche à droite : L'interprète, le marabout Isoufi Alilou, un marabout de Say apportant ses documents.

FIG. 6. Copies of texts being made for the French engineer Georges de Gironcourt (1878–1960), who made extensive agricultural surveys of parts of the French Soudan. While concerned with the potential of the land, he was also a collector of manuscripts, and commissioned a large number of works that were eventually deposited at the Institut de France in Paris. *Image source*: "Déchiffrement de manuscrits chez les puels de say," in G. de Gironcourt, *Missions de Gironcourt en Afrique occidentale, 1908–1909, 1911–1912* (1920), https://digitalcollections.nypl.org/items/510d47df-9d66-a3d9-e040-e00a18064a99.

wrote other important works. Du Bois was fortunate that he found such well-educated informants because Baba was indeed from the most prominent scholarly family that had arrived in the town in the late fifteenth century. Baba became a major scholar in his own right. Du Bois was also introduced to a man who claimed to be a descendant of Baba, whom Du Bois said was an excellent manuscript copyist. Du Bois's claim and that of his informant are both impossible to verify. However, the significant status of Baba in the intellectual history of Timbuktu was correctly identified. The remarkable career of Ahmad Baba deserves the spotlight, and to him we now turn.

2

The Education of Ahmad Baba, 1556–91

THE AQITS were a prominent family in Timbuktu, where they had been living since around the 1450s. They had moved to Timbuktu from Walata, a settlement four hundred kilometers to the west, but where they came from before that is not absolutely clear. They could have come up from Masina, a region that extends far to the south of Timbuktu where the dry semi-desert begins to become more savannah-like. Permanent settlements and towns like Walata and Timbuktu grew out of the needs of traders for stopovers near a watering source for themselves and their livestock. That might have been true until around 1100 CE, after which these meeting points started to become marketplaces and gradually grew into towns. Such permanent settlements were spread out in the desert. People were constantly on the move, much of the time in search of pasturage and water for their herds of sheep, goats, and camels. A nomadic lifestyle was common, and in some regions dominant, throughout the period that this book covers. Patterns of mobility and settlement were often reflected in names. After a long residence in one place families would add to their genealogies identifiers of place such *al-Tinbukti* or *al-Walati* ("from Timbuktu," "from Walata"). Recognizing and tracking individuals through personal names could be confusing. People seemed to draw on a small range of first names. However, with the help of a *nisba*—an identification of place or "tribe"—at the end of a long line of proper names, an individual could be more easily identified. So Ahmad Baba described himself or was identified by other writers as al-Sanhaji, al-Masini, Tinbukti, and al-Takruri. This indicates that his ethnolinguistic affiliation was to the Sanhaja, a Berber-speaking group, and his places of origin were Masina and Timbuktu; "Takrur" was a reference to the medieval Arabic term for West Africa.

"Aqit" also appeared in his genealogy, referring not to any place but rather to a familial line. 'Umar al-Aqit (d. 1468 or 1480) is the one descendant in the family line who emerges in the historical record as a resident of Timbuktu. His name is mentioned because he was a recognized man of learning who married the daughter, Sitta, of another prominent local scholar from the Anda Ag-Muhammad family. The offspring from the marriage of 'Umar and Sitta later provided the local judiciary with *qadis* (judges) and the *imams*, prayer leaders and preachers, of two major mosques until the end of the sixteenth century. Throughout the sixteenth century, the Aqit family name was associated with influential teachers, preachers, judges, and jurists in Timbuktu.

Ahmad Baba was born in Timbuktu into this distinguished Aqit family in October 1556.[1] Timbuktu is a compact town with mud-brick buildings lining narrow alleys. High walls enclose courtyards where families live, and Baba would have spent much time in such spaces playing and passing time with other children while visitors would come and go. The sturdy mud-brick mosques, with their minarets towering over the town, were built more than a century before the Aqits arrived in the town, and were the largest structures there. The town market is more a thing of time than of space; it happens in the open air or with makeshift covers as protection against the intense sun that at midday is around 40 degrees centigrade (104 Fahrenheit) year-round. Intense desert heat was possibly one reason why most men would veil their heads and faces with a turban as protection against the sun and ubiquitous fine desert sand when they were outside; over time this headgear became a dress style in the Sahara. Caravans from the salt mines at Taoudeni in the north brought salt slabs to the Timbuktu market and other traders brought their wares originating as far north as the Mediterranean basin and beyond. Among the items were glassware, textiles, leather goods, and—importantly, for a family like the Aqits—writing paper. This was the town that Baba grew up in. His birth into a scholarly lineage meant that from his early years, he absorbed the sounds of reading and recitation in the family quarters, with students and scholars coming to sit with his father and uncles.

This was a polyglot world. While the language of learning was Arabic, it was only one of a number of languages in use. Baba would have heard, and probably used daily, the dominant local tongue, Songhay, as well as Tamashek, a language widespread in the Sahara. He would have had some familiarity with, or even capacity in, a Mande language, or in Fulfulde and Hausa. The first lessons he learned would have come from his mother; by the time he was seven or perhaps ten, he would have been sent to a teacher outside the home. But with so many teachers close to him, he would probably simply have joined sessions his father or an uncle conducted. In his own recollections, he wrote of his father and his uncle as his first instructors.

Beyond the genealogy and devotion to learning, there is scant information about the family, and nothing about Baba's mother or siblings. His father—Ahmad bin Ahmad bin 'Umar bin Muhammad 'Umar bin 'Ali bin Yahya (d. 1583)—was by the time of his birth already a man who commanded respect in the town as a teacher, writer, and judge. Ahmad Senior would have had classes at home, received people with legal questions on issues such as marriage, divorce, or inheritance, or decide on cases about commercial disputes and contracts. There were no courthouses at the time, and a legal case could be pursued at the house of a judge, in a square, or a mosque, as long as the relevant parties were present or relevant documents, especially in commercial cases, were presented for inspection. A session at home would have been normal because a judge would have easy access to his law books and writing material. With time, the elder Ahmad built up a large collection of manuscript books at home numbering in the hundreds, according to his son, who wrote that his father was a "great collector of books with an extensive library which included many a rare treasure." Once he was old enough, Baba would have noticed that people visiting to consult his father also borrowed and returned books loaned from him. He would inherit these books. As we know from later evidence, library holdings were heritable property and split among children and sometimes siblings.

In 1549, seven years before Baba was born, his father went on the pilgrimage to Mecca and Medina, the holy cities of Islam in Arabia. To go overland on such a journey was a challenging and expensive undertaking that could last many months and even years; a pilgrim stood a good chance of never returning. For a man like Baba's father, a pilgrimage was also an opportunity to meet other learned men and either commission or personally make copies of works not yet in his library. Despite the challenges and costs of the trip, there was a long tradition of the educated, political elites and common people among West Africans who actually attempted such trips. The most famous was the mansa (or ruler), Musa, who in 1324 traveled with a large entourage and en route visited Cairo before reaching the holy cities. The journey was costly because the mansa had to pay for his large entourage's subsistence costs and take gifts for his counterparts along the way, especially in Cairo. He returned with much less wealth but enriched the town with the presence of a man of letters from Granada, Ibrahim Abu Ishaq al-Sahili (d. 1346), who played a major role in the design and construction of the main mosque of Timbuktu. But there were always humbler folk such as scholars and commoners who went on the pilgrimage as well. For some, there was spiritual benefit in the very idea of enduring hardship to reach the sacred destination. Ahmad Senior's journey had the dual benefit of being a pilgrimage and an opportunity for interaction with scholars who came from Central and South Asia and Egypt. This is possibly how texts by authors from such diverse regions came into the book collections in Timbuktu and throughout the West African libraries. Not only is the work of famous writers from western Asia, such as the eleventh-century philosopher Ibn Sina (Avicenna in the West), the twelfth-century theologian al-Ghazali, and the work of lexicographers Fayruzabadi and Zabidi, in the fifteenth and eighteenth centuries respectively, mentioned in local writing, but there are also copies—or copies of copies—in local collections. On the other hand, there were West Africans who traveled and settled in the holy cities and Cairo, and a handful rose to prominence as teachers (we shall learn something about them in chapter 5, on Shinqit).

Baba's father died in 1583, the very year that is given for most of Baba's writings in the first phase of his career. Baba would later write about his father: "He was a sensitive man of enormous prestige, greatly revered by both rulers and ruled. He used harsh words toward the rulers and those beneath them and they would act humbly toward him."[2] Out of respect and regard for Baba's father, rulers and their courtiers would visit him. The askiya Dawud visited Baba's father when the father was sick, "out of esteem for him." This askiya was a noted figure in a long line of the Songhay dynasty that had taken power in the 1430s and based themselves in Gao, some 350 kilometers (220 miles) south of Timbuktu. He and Askiya Muhammad (r. 1493–1529) paid some attention and even respect to the scholars based in Timbuktu. There were other rulers who persecuted the scholars, and in Baba's family there was a distinct awareness and memory of the fickleness of rulers, and more than this, their capacity for violence that did not spare scholars. The Songhay ruler who represented this tradition of violence was Sonni 'Ali (r. 1463–92), during whose reign Baba's grandfather and his entire family had to flee Timbuktu for the safety of Walata.

Coming from a family full of learned men, the path for Baba's entry into the same lifestyle was straightforward. We do not read of any traders, craftsmen, farmers, or praise-poets among the Aqits. It can be assumed that at least part of their income was covered by payments from students in a local currency, such as cowrie shells, or in kind, such as the provision of agricultural products from along the banks of the nearby Niger River, or the supply of labor for the family quarters and household needs. The Aqits did not split their time between trading and teaching. In Baba's writing, he exclusively focuses on the scholarly achievements of his ancestors, not how they made a living. He would elaborately describe those who made the most impact on him as a scholar.

Baba reserves most praise for his primary teacher after his father and uncle, Muhammad Baghayogho al-Wangari (d. 1593), who was from a diasporic trading group, the Juula, that spoke the Mande language. As the name "al-Wangari" indicates, he was from the people or region of Wangara, far to the south of Timbuktu, and had arrived with his parents when he was still young and completed his education in Timbuktu. Wangari was a student of Baba's father, with whom he read introductory works on logic and rhetoric. He had other teachers too in the town and, with the requisite training and certification (*ijaza*) to cover a range of subfields of Islamic law, he started offering classes. He became an outstanding and famed teacher, but only left behind five of his own works, of which only two manuscripts are extant.

After Ahmad Senior, it was Wangari who exerted the most influence on Baba. He would later write an extensive and loving portrait of this teacher, rich in detail about his habits as an educator and gushing praise for him as a scholar. The portrait Baba offers is one of a man of learning and scrupulous piety, including details of his rigorous daily routine of study, teaching, consultations, and prayer. Notably, Wangari treated everyone as equals. He possessed a large library and was generous in giving items out on loan, even to students whom he did not know, "and thus it was that he lost a large portion of his books,"[3] wrote Baba.

Wangari, the teacher Baba valued most highly, was present on the day when Baba and his family were arrested in 1593. The teacher remained in Timbuktu and died later in the same year. In an autobiographical note in the same work in which he writes about his father and his teacher Wangari, Baba lists twenty-five texts, ranging in size from two short didactic poems to large works, which had been the basis of his education. The titles cover the disciplines of Arabic grammar and rhetoric, law and legal theory, prophetic traditions, Quran exegesis, theology, philosophy, and astronomy. The classics of the Maliki law school are present in abundance including the *al-Muwaṭṭa'*, the *al-Mudawwana*, the *al-Mukhtaṣar* of Sidi Khalil, *al-Shifā'* of Qadi 'Iyad, and more works closer to Baba's own time such as the multivolume collection of legal responsa (*fatawa*) known as the *Al-Mi 'yar al-mu 'rib* of Ahmad al-Wansharisi (d. 1508), the chief justice (*mufti*) of Fez. Baba also had to study grammar and rhetoric. He does not mention poetry, a subject that was not systematically studied but was picked up along the way. He probably did not attend sessions where the classical Arabic poets were read and that might be the reason that he did not produce poetry in any significant amount or versify any prose works at any stage in his career. The use of verse to memorize the foundations of any discipline was a hallmark of the educational system in the broader region but became common only in the decades after Baba's time. Of the corpus he studied, law works were the most prominent.

This reading list could have been specific to Baba as a young man hailing from a scholarly family but at the same time it is indicative of the curriculum of his cohort in Timbuktu. The size of his peer group is not known but he was, by all accounts, an outstanding figure in his generation. The works he read point to what his family library would have held. Nothing in this list of books would have prepared him to write the book we discuss below.

Ahmad Baba's Advice to Scholars

In 1591, the world around Timbuktu started crumbling as the troops of the Sa'dian dynasty in Marrakesh invaded the region. This invasion and conquest of the capital, Gao, ended the independence of the Songhay rulers who held nominal authority over a large territory that included Timbuktu. The soldiers went about pillaging Gao for valuables and killing or forcing out the ruling elite. Timbuktu was bypassed in the first phase of conquest but, about eighteen months later, the town was attacked and the population terrorized. The scholars were not spared; indeed, many of them were either arrested, seriously injured, or killed. Some of the scholars spoke out against the excesses of the conquerors and even encouraged rebellion against the occupying troops, a good percentage of whom were of Iberian origin. It is unclear where Baba fit into this dangerous and chaotic situation. He was identified, possibly as a troublemaker or as a respectable figure with the potential to cause problems later, and instructions were given to arrest him and his family.

By the time Baba was captured and deported from Timbuktu in early 1593, he was around thirty-seven years old and had thirteen pieces of writing to his name. Key dates of his writing life run from 1583 (ten titles), 1588 (two titles), and one text begun many years earlier, only completed in 1592. Among this body of prose are abridgements, such as the one he made of the work by the Egyptian polymath Jalal al-Din al-Suyuṭi (d. 1505) on the advantages of marriage; glosses on passages from legal classics; longer commentaries on chapters of legal works such as the widely used *Mukhtaṣar* of Khalil bin Ishaq (d. 1365); and some writing on Arabic grammar. The final product of this first phase of his scholarship was a book on the nature and value, indeed superiority, of intention, when engaging in any action, a work that he had started ten years earlier. These writings have survived in parts. They are mostly, it appears, in poor condition and have not been collected, edited, or studied to see if they can tell us anything about the thinking of their author. There are copies of these texts spread across collections in the Sahara, so they were not private notes or rough drafts but were known and copied. One reason why these writings have received insufficient attention is that some might have judged these not to be among his best or "original" scholarship. They were possibly seen as the efforts of a scholar still writing in the shadow of senior figures in his own family because the works we have by him are abridgements and glosses. There is no trace of his own legal opinions on either theoretical or actual legal cases.

However, at least one work stands out from this period. For Baba, this intellectual effort is a departure from the other—what might appear to be unexceptional—subjects he had until then been writing about. Furthermore, for this period and the region, there is no evidence of anything of the kind written by any other scholar. Baba called it *Jalb al-niʿma wa dafʿ al-niqma* (Acquiring blessings and repelling affliction by avoiding unjust rulers) and completed it in 1588 (fig. 7).[4] This work of thirty-two pages has, until recently, not been edited, although it has always appeared in lists of his writings.

Baba does not give a reason for writing the *Jalb al-niʿma* except this: "To alert myself and my compatriots and peers against fraternizing with unjust governors." He is addressing the learned community about the nature of political power but this is not an advice-text to the rulers, although it draws on aspects of the "mirror for princes" genre (known as *nasihat al-muluk* in Arabic, *Fürstenspiegel* in German). He continues to describe his purpose, saying it was to cover: "The ruling on accepting gifts from these rulers in terms of its lawfulness or unlawfulness, in accordance with the Maliki school. I will not mention everything on these topics, but only some texts in each chapter, which will be an awakening for the intelligent through the grace of God."

In Baba's short introduction to the text, he lists the chapters of the book as follows: (1) Textual evidence from the Quran and hadith on distancing oneself from oppressive rulers. (2) Quotations from the generation closest to the Prophet Muhammad (*salaf al-salih*) and those after them on this topic. (3) Discussions from the words of the *hukama*—in other words, the wise and people with experience. (4) Vivid description of the calamities that afflicted some of those who kept company with unjust rulers. (5) Conclusion with a ruling against accepting gifts from rulers and interacting with them.

In *Jalb al-niʿma*, chapters two to four have individual titles indicating where the source materials originated, such as from "the pious predecessors, and those

FIG. 7. *Jalb al-niʿma* by Ahmad Baba is a work on scholars and rulers completed in Timbuktu before his exile. It advises scholars to avoid rulers using a wide range of examples from earlier periods. It makes no mention of the conditions in his own time. He wrote a summary of this work in Marrakesh. Length: 29 pages. Size of pages: 27 × 18 cm; text 18 × 12.5; thirty lines per page. Cedrab no. 775. *Image source*: From the archives of the Institut des Hautes Etudes et de Recherche Islamique Ahmed Baba (Iheri-Ab), formerly known as the Centre d'Etude, Documentation et Recherche Ahmed Baba (Cedrab) in Timbuktu. With thanks to its director, Dr. Mohamed Diagayete, for permission to use the images from Cedrab manuscripts shown here.

who came after them" (chapter 2); or from "the men of wisdom and experience" (chapter 3); and a few incidents of those "who accompanied the rulers," to which he adds the prayer "may God protect us from the calamities of this world and the next" (chapter 4). These chapters are the body of the work, where he displays all his proofs, and he does this by reproducing narratives from other books, some merely incidents captured in a single long sentence or paragraph, others long, intricate, layered narratives covering more than two pages. All of them carry a version of the same lesson: the wickedness of virtually all rulers, and how they have treated dissidents who refused to serve or indulge them. In many of these cases, he relates in some detail the cruel fate of the scholarly victims of such rulers.

The longest of these chapters, chapter 2, is filled with long extracts from a range of authors such as the famous Maliki scholar "Sahnun" bin Said (d. 854), author of the classical law corpus *Mudawwana*, widely used as a fundamental legal text in North and West Africa. Sahnun's advice could have been an inspiration to Baba and he cites Sahnun as saying: "Nothing is more detestable than a scholar who is absent from his own gathering and when someone asks about his whereabouts, they say that he is with the ruler or the minister or the judge." Sahnun, based in the North African town of Qayrawan, in modern Tunisia, was known to have a long and adversarial relationship with the Aghlabid rulers of his time. However, he would take up a judgeship close to the end of his life but only on the condition that, if necessary, he be allowed to prosecute those closest to the ruler. When he accepted the post, he is reported to have told his daughter: "Today your father has been slain without a knife."

We do not know if the books Baba used were the complete ones, compilations, or extracts collected in other volumes. There are titles that might seem surprising. There is his use of the work of al-Damiri' (d. 1405), *Ḥayāt al-ḥayawān* (*The Life of Animals*), which is not a text that immediately comes to mind for a discussion such as that which Baba was pursuing. This is a sprawling zoological lexicon that provides descriptions and folklore dealing with nearly a thousand creatures in alphabetical order. Beside the zoological materials, it has plenty of historical narrative strewn in between the discussions on the hawk, the cow, camels, birds, bugs, and so on, and by the end, the shrimp! He also includes an entry for the human (*Insan*). Baba cites a story from this work for its moral effect: do not befriend rulers and, if you were once friends with a man who became the sultan, then cut off ties with him. Baba attributes this compelling narrative to Damiri, but a comparison with the source text reveals only a faint resemblance between what is in the original and how Baba reproduces it.

The use of Damiri, even if it is hard to track and impossible to find precisely in the source text, is rather modest compared with Baba's use of the *Sīrāj al-mulūk* (*Lamp of Kings*), the work of political theory of the Andalusian Abu Bakr Muhammad Ṭurṭushi (d. 1126). Chapter 3 is taken completely from Ṭurṭushi's work and Baba tells his readers this. Indeed, this is Baba's style: he cites generously and gives his sources. He can be criticized for excessively long quotations but not for plagiarism. This chapter goes further than criticizing scholars who are close to unjust rulers; it advises scholars to avoid all rulers. Ṭurṭushi strings together a list of extracts from others who had written on the subject, such as the Persian Ibn al-Muqaffa' (d. 757), author of the famous animal fable *Kalīla wa-Dimna*, and other "wise men" among the Arabs, Persians, and Indians. Baba's extracts are taken from two chapters in the middle of the work, titled "Avoiding the Company of Rulers" and "On Keeping Company with Rulers." He gives a few statements that imply respect for rulers, but the weight of this extract is on total avoidance of rulers. It has some colorful descriptions and advice:

> Mu'awiya said to a man from Quraysh: "Beware of the Sultan, because he becomes angry like a young boy but attacks like a lion."
>
> Ibn al-Muqaffa' said: "Those most deserving of destruction are the ones who readily go to the Sultan."
>
> The wise said: "The most wretched of all people in relation to the ruler are those closest to him, just as the things closest to the fire will burn the quickest."

In Baba's use of Ṭurṭushi, he is far closer to the source text than in his use of Damiri. There are other narratives that Baba cites in large chunks that are relatively easy to compare with the sources. He relates a number of incidents, mainly from the history of the Abbasid Empire (750–1258 CE), such as a long story about the Caliph al-Mutawakkil (d. 861), the tenth Abbasid ruler, and how he treated those who appeared to be disloyal to him. Baba also touches on incidents from Andalusia taken from the courtier, historian, and poet Lisān ad-Dīn ibn al-Khaṭīb (d. 1374), and further stories taken from a work he calls *Al-tarikh al-kabir* (The great history) of Ibn Khaldun (d. 1406), the shortened title for the multivolume encyclopedic *Kitāb al-'ibar wa-dīwān al-mubtada' wal-khabar* (The book of lessons and record of beginnings and of information).

The conclusion of Baba's work, which does not wrap up the text but opens up new terrain, is titled "The Ruling on Accepting Gifts from Rulers, Interacting with Them, and Other Things Related to This, Presented in a Concise Manner."

It refines issues captured in this heading—"Gifts from Rulers"—with questions such as "What about accepting gifts out of fear?" Fear is not an excuse, says Baba. If you have any doubt, he advises the scholars, then examine how the sultan acquired his wealth. If acquired lawfully, then there is some possibility to accept the gift. What about judges and their payment? They are not the sultan's employees but are paid from the communal treasury. How should one treat the testimony of those who are close to the sultan? Reject it. Baba relies on Sahnun, the great Maliki jurist cited above, whose authority would have been difficult to contradict for any scholar in Baba's time. While referring to numerous titles of *nawazil* works (legal opinions based on actual events), Baba does admit at the end that there are differences of opinion on these topics within the Maliki school. The conclusion comes to an abrupt end, giving the impression of a writer rushing to finish his work, one who realized that there were still too many issues for which potential readers would want answers. Baba might have realized that he had spent too much space on stories from the past and ought to have taken the legal route earlier. So, in the conclusion, he addresses these questions in a nearly point-by-point fashion.

In short, *Jalb al-ni'ma* is an attack on corrupt, unjust, and oppressive rulers (*al-wulat al-ẓalama*). More than this, it advises against keeping company with rulers. What does "keeping company" (*suhbah*) mean? Baba is not really clear about what this constitutes, so that it could mean joining a large salon arranged by the ruler or a meeting of advisors. But the impression is clear: do everything to avoid rulers, and do not even pray for them.

Baba quotes extensively from the primary religious sources, offering minimal explanations, and stringing these quotations together to buttress his position. He mentions that he used two works by Suyuṭi (d. 1505), the Egyptian scholar highly revered in West Africa, whom one of his grandfathers had met on his pilgrimage travels to the East. Baba cites the exact sources that he used, namely the *Jam' al-jawāmi'* (a work on hadith) and the *al-Durr al-manthūr* (a work on Quranic exegesis). He quotes from numerous other sources; in all, around thirty books appear to have been available to him. He cites some texts, extracts a few quotes from others, and finally he simply reproduces a long extract as chapter 3.

Baba was well into his thirties at this time and had written other works, but they were mostly nothing exceptional and they probably did not give him any prominence. There is also the more general issue of how, in a manuscript book culture, a work circulated. How many copies of the texts that he wrote did he copy, or have copied, for wider circulation? Copies were routinely made, by students, of the lectures of their teachers but there is no indication that this was done with Baba's work. *Jalb al-niʿma* was not a text that he would have taught, in any case. We do not know who his peers were at this stage, what the young scholarly community of Timbuktu was like in the 1580s, or with whom he was in conversation through his writing. As we have seen, his previous writings were all standard contributions, the efforts of an apprentice. *Jalb al-niʿma*, however, of which multiple copies have survived, would have let him stand out. Perhaps it was even the cause of his later arrest.

Works offering advice to rulers have a long history and there are ample examples, from Persia to Andalusia, of which Baba would have known. He would even have read this type of advice literature. Indeed, one whole chapter in *Jalb al-niʿma* is taken from such a "mirror for princes" work. As indicated already, his chapter 3 is taken entirely from the twelfth-century Andalusian scholar Abu Bakr al-Ṭurṭushi's *Sīrāj al-mulūk*. Baba could have had such a work in mind but then realized its potential danger—who was he to address the ruler?—and instead directed it to scholars. It might still have gotten the attention of the governor of Timbuktu, or even the rulers in Gao, but he would have the excuse of writing for scholars and not their overlords.

The Aqits and the Rulers

About five years after the completion of *Jalb al-niʿma*, Baba would be arrested and deported to Marrakesh. It was referred to as the "red city," so named because of the reddish hue of the buildings. The city was then in the throes of an architectural and cultural revival under the Saʿdian dynasty (1510–1689). The Saʿdian rulers aimed to stress their sophistication and civilization, alongside their military prowess, in their claims to rule over the whole or a large chunk of northwest Africa. Here Baba would write his large biographical dictionaries, and several other works discussed in the next chapter. But his writing in Timbuktu seems already to have earned him, if not a reputation, then enough attention to be released from an awful imprisonment. Some influential scholars of Marrakesh, learning of his imprisonment, pleaded with the Sultan Ahmad al-Mansur (d. 1603) for his release. After about two years of imprisonment, Baba was released and allowed to teach in a mosque of the city; he even held special classes with selected students. In this way, he came to have students who went on to teach elsewhere in the region and who would later write about their teacher's influence. Marrakesh was once again beginning to flourish and, in this cultural and intellectual transition Baba made a small contribution to its flourishing. There were already highly regarded scholars in the city but that he was welcomed into this elite is a mark of their openness and the caliber of scholar Timbuktu could produce.

Did his reputation stem from his connections to the Aqit family, from his father and uncles having acquired an indisputable reputation? All this obviously helped Baba. Being recognized in the competitive scholarly environment of Marrakesh in the last quarter of the sixteenth century was no small matter. Baba's lineage and the right combination of name and scholarly competence allowed him to gain attention in Marrakesh. What we do not know is whether the scholars and students in Marrakesh knew about, or had read, his early writings, and how those scholars viewed the work. One of the extant copies of the *Jalb al-niʿma* is in the Royal Archives of Morocco, another in a private library in the remote southern Moroccan town of Tamgrout (Tamegroute).

Baba had to give a reason for writing such a work as *Jalb al-niʿma*. What he gave as his purpose does not, however, suggest the context or conditions that led him to compose the work. His experience of arrest and exile would be the logical reasons to write such a work. If this work had not been dated (1588) this would be an appropriate conclusion; indeed, about sixty years ago this was asserted in an article by the historian John Hunwick and it has been accepted until now. From the text itself, we learn nothing about whom he was writing against or for whom he was writing. He does not give any hint as to whether he was invited to write such a treatise or was responding to another writer or text. Some of the conventions of the time included stating the reason for writing a work, whether it was a request from someone or a response to another work. But there is nothing in the Timbuktu manuscript collections from this period that indicates a developing polemic around the question of how to deal with rulers. A possible longer-term factor was the experience of Baba's scholarly ancestors of abuse by rulers, and one ruler in particular.

The Songhay ruler Sonni Ali invaded Timbuktu in 1469 and he acted harshly against the scholars.[5] The reasons for his attacks are not exactly clear; perhaps he disliked the relative autonomy of the town, where scholars could largely teach without interference from authorities. He already had a reputation of intolerance against scholars and wanted to further curtail their social, and potentially political, role. Many fled, some to Walata, if they were lucky enough to be spared from death. The *Tārīkh al-Sūdān* (Chronicle of the Land of the Blacks) by ʿAbd al-Rahman al-Saʿdi (d. circa 1656) devotes plenty of space to the "great oppressor and notorious evildoer" Sonni Ali, to give only a few of the unflattering epithets he gives this ruler. Sonni Ali entered Timbuktu in January 1469 and, there and elsewhere, "tyrannized the scholars and holy men, killing them, insulting them, and humiliating them."[6] Sa'di describes in some detail what happened when Sonni Ali, the "evil oppressor," entered the town, and the consequences of his vicious actions against the scholars and the general population. We have only this source to rely on for this period of the region's history. There is circumstantial evidence to demonstrate that Sonni Ali was a vicious tyrant.

The ancestors of Ahmad Baba were among the scholars who had to flee Timbuktu. He had certainly heard from his elders about the oppression suffered by the scholars under Sonni Ali. These stories were probably circulating, or were in the background, when Ahmad Baba sat down to write *Jalb al-niʿma*. He did not make any reference to the events of the 1460s and, when he does give concrete examples of unjust rulers, he draws on distant examples. Indeed, he simply takes extracts from other works and other historical contexts.

After Sonni Ali's death, the new ruler was *al-Hajj* Muhammad, known as Askiya Muhammad, who was a devout man and treated the scholars with respect. They could teach and study again. For the scholars, life under the askiyas would never again be one of suffering, death, and expulsion. The askiyas were men of arms and went into battle with their soldiers; military campaigns were necessary for them to collect booty and maintain their prestige, among other things. While there were internecine conflicts and succession struggles among the descendants of the askiyas, scholars on the whole were not in their line of attack.

Ahmad Baba was born during the reign of Askiya Dawud. In late 1570, this askiya visited Timbuktu and made a contribution to the reconstruction of the Great Mosque, built under the patronage of Mansa Musa after he returned from his pilgrimage in the mid-1320s. Ahmad Baba was then about fourteen years old. He therefore did not himself have any personal experience of "oppressive rulers" either imposing their will over the general populace of the city or on the scholars in particular. He had heard stories of how scholars, including his ancestors, during the time of Sonni Ali, had suffered, been forced to flee, and had even been killed. He could also have witnessed the behavior of the rulers in his own time—Askiyas Dawud, Ishaq I, and Ishaq II—and their obsessions with worldly power, despite their acts of piety and charity. This is the broader context for *Jalb al-niʿma*. It was relevant to Baba's familial memory and his own life. A court historian in his narrative about the Saʿdian dynasty would later write that Baba had a single encounter with the sultan, for whom he had harsh words about his exile and his missing books.

In Ahmad Baba's worldview, there was only a limited place for sultans and askiyas. He seems to accept their historic existence and implicitly their necessity. He never asserts unambiguously the importance of central authority for social order. An explicit denunciation would have made him part of an "anarchistic" tradition of opposition to any centralized power in North Africa and the Sahara—embodied in the so-called *Kharijites* of early Islamic history, who had, centuries earlier, already been eliminated or put in their place. But, as a term of abuse, there was still a recourse to "Kharijite," so Baba is careful not to open himself up to this line of attack. Virtually all the rulers in his treatise have major flaws and he makes no excuses for them. He does not hold up one "good" ruler as a mirror to a "bad" or unjust one. He gives no counterexamples of good rulers, of rulers to emulate and in whose employ one should serve, or with whom one should cooperate. So, he does not hold up a cruel Sonni Ali against a virtuous Askiya Muhammad.

A cursory reading of *Jalb al-niʿma* reveals an author given to repetition, extending and repeating the same point: a scholar has no alternative but to avoid even mildly unjust rulers. However, the narratives Baba piles up are not merely pointless repetition because he was incapable of saying anything else. They are stories to educate (and possibly also to entertain, in a gruesome way). He wants to drive home the point, to create a vivid image of the excesses of men with arms and power. He does have a place for authority and order; it is only that the standards are so high that they make it impossible for any self-respecting scholar to even sit close to a ruler.

Jalb al-niʿma could have been written in any city of North Africa or western Asia. Baba does not use a single contemporary or historical example from his own region. There is nothing in its content that reflects its provenance. Was this a conscious decision by the author? Was it a kind of critique through analogy, an inversion of a "mirror for princes" work—here a "mirror for scholars"—the implications of which an attentive reader would have seen?

Was the manuscript, as it circulated, still a draft? From a contemporary reading of *Jalb al-niʿma*, this is a valid question. For instance, the conclusion is a continuation of questions and issues in scholar-ruler relations. There is no summary or concluding statement, which we find in Baba's other works. The conclusion has a rushed and unfinished feel to it. From his other writings, it is clear that he wrote with a good sense of order and organization; his texts follow a standard plot of beginning, middle, and conclusion. Here, he has a beginning and a middle but no conclusion, just more issues raised. In the work after this one, *Ghāyat al-amal*, which dealt with the issue of intention, he followed the standard pattern for prose works. He had started on the latter work much earlier and returned to it as the world around Timbuktu was falling to conquering forces.

Jalb al-niʿma contains insights into Baba's book world. As already mentioned, he cites at least thirty books, either mentioning them or taking quotations of varying length from them. These works must have been available to him in Timbuktu, as either part of his own library, his father's library, or other scholars' libraries. The books' circulation makes it clear that the town was not isolated from larger scholarly and book networks in Baba's time. Indeed, he was an heir to a longer tradition of book collecting. It certainly showed. Finally, how many copies of this book were made is unknown, but we are fortunate that at least three copies have survived. If Baba was uncertain of the fate of this work, then while in exile in Marrakesh he composed another, in 1598, that has the same theme and tone as *Jalb al-niʿma*. He called it *Mā rawāhu al-ruwāt* (What the narrators narrated). Indeed, it is possibly part summary, part supplement. It was audacious of him to take on this subject again while a captive in exile in Marrakesh. We shall turn now to his long trek through the desert and his nearly fourteen years of captivity and exile, teaching and writing in Marrakesh.

3

Exile in Marrakesh

IN OCTOBER 1590 soldiers and auxiliaries were gathering and preparing to leave Marrakesh on a major expedition across the Sahara. By the end of the month, several thousand cavalry and infantrymen, and thousands of camels carrying munitions and supplies for the expedition, finally marched. The men were armed with the latest matchlocks and harquebuses, but also with swords and lances, and with heavy artillery such as cannons. The soldiers came from all over the wider region, speaking various languages, and included Spanish-speaking so-called "Renegades" (*Renegados*, as the Spanish called the converts to Islam) and Moriscos (Muslims who were once forced to convert to Christianity). A Spanish observer, traveling in or close to Marrakesh at the time, wrote a short account of these preparations. He describes what he heard about the preparations and why and where the soldiers were going. The objective was to cross the Sahara into the Bilad al-Sudan (Land of the Blacks) beyond the treacherous Saharan Atlas Mountains and through the desolate, harsh desert. Sultan Ahmad al-Mansur had come to power in Marrakesh in 1578, and he was committed to enlarging his kingdom. His army was now on the march to conquer the last frontier.[1]

The Sultan's army passed through the Atlas and the Dra'a (Draa) valley and then entered the Sahara proper in December 1590. The troops were commanded by a "short, blue-eyed, eunuch," a soldier named Jawdar Pasha, who spoke Spanish like so many of his lieutenants.[2] After about two months on the move, the troops reached the banks of the Niger River. Then they prepared to go into battle. After another thirteen days of marching, they reached a place called Tondibi, around fifty kilometers (thirty-one miles) from Gao, seat of the rulers of the regional Songhay power. At Tondibi they encountered a large but underprepared and ill-equipped army of local fighters. It did not take long for the Battle of Tondibi to start and to finish. On a single day in early March 1591, the Songhay army was decisively defeated; the commanders were unable to quickly regroup and lead their men to offer further resistance to the invading army. The survivors fled from the battleground to come back another time. Ordinary folk, who were not armed, fled and many were killed in the mayhem. There was "loud weeping and lamentation, as people began, with much difficulty, to cross the river in tightly packed boats," as one chronicler put it many years later.[3] The askiya Ishaq ordered his subjects to leave and he sued for peace with the enemy. So ended around a century of rule by a dynasty—the Songhay askiyas—that was rooted in the region. As the capital was sacked, the conquerors searched for gold and other valuables to take with them.

Over the centuries, stories had reached Marrakesh and the southern Mediterranean lands, that in the vast unknown world beyond the Sahara, gold was plentiful, hoarded in large quantities, widely used and easily mined.[4] Medieval Arabic writers had coined the term "Bilad al-Sudan" but also "Bilad al-Tibr" for this region, referring to the gold dust (*tibr*) they believed was in plentiful supply there. Historically, in the larger region, especially to the south, gold had certainly been mined and goldmining was at the time of the conquest still undertaken, but the volume yielded was nothing compared to the exaggerated reports of earlier times. There was apparently none, or only negligible nuggets of gold, in the residences of the Songhay rulers and the royal elite at the capital, Gao, when the invading army searched them. However, the dethroned rulers promised to send 1,000 slaves and 100,000 *mithqal* (one *mithqal* is equivalent to between 4.5 and 5 grams; i.e, 500 kilograms of gold) in exchange for peace. This was sufficient for Jawdar Pasha, commander of the occupying army. Large numbers of his troops had fallen severely ill after the long march through the desert and having had to deal with the different, more humid, conditions by the Niger River. They may have defeated the Songhay army, but the weather and lack of supplies had defeated them. They could not tolerate the conditions and so Jawdar Pasha ordered the troops to leave with whatever slaves and gold they could take with them.[5]

Shifting alliances for political influence and trading opportunities as well as ruthless military agitation characterized this period; the rivalries were felt beyond the shores of the southwestern Mediterranean and the Atlantic coast of northwest Africa. There were the navies of the kingdoms of Portugal and of Spain, the English Barbary Company, established in 1585 to trade with the Moroccan powers, and Dutch-speaking merchants, all actively engaged in finding a foothold and trading partners in northwest Africa. Portugal established more forts at enclaves on the Moroccan coastline especially on the Atlantic coast, Spain had attempted rapprochements with the Sa'dians from mid-century, France made deals exchanging weapons to gain access to territory, and the Ottoman sultan in Istanbul asserted his power—from around Algiers, which was an Ottoman vassal state from 1515—because he believed he was the legitimate caliph to whom other Muslim powers ought to submit. The English were keen on an alliance with the Moroccans because of their concern about Spanish ascendancy. The Moroccans, in turn, were aware of the English naval capacities and the recent voyages of Francis Drake. Sultan Mansur was fascinated by reports of this voyage. Trade between England and Morocco expanded during the second half of the sixteenth century. England sold a variety of weapons to the Moroccans. This high-pressure geopolitical context forced the rulers in Marrakesh to act urgently to replenish their resources or make claims to more territory. The Saʿdian Sultan's expansion into the world around Timbuktu was in part a response to this broader political and military context. He would have more territory with which to bargain, and more space in which to maneuver, if necessary; there was the promise of wealth in the new lands, and he could continue to assert his claims of being the caliph, the supreme Muslim ruler, instead of having to subject himself to Istanbul. Sultan Ahmad al-Mansur, observing these developments from his Marrakesh palace, had no significant access to the coast, since important ports and enclaves were occupied by European forces or were claimed by his enemies from within the region. In the words of the historian, Mercedes García-Arenal, "Ahmad al-Mansur was compelled perpetually to counterbalance the influence of Spain and the Ottomans without becoming openly hostile to or making a clear alliance with either power."[6] He opted to expand across the desert.

Taking the Songhay capital at Gao was therefore of immense significance in the history of West Africa. Hardly two years later, taking Timbuktu was of no particular political or economic importance, yet defeating both Gao and Timbuktu was devasting to the political order. Timbuktu is about four hundred kilometers to the west of Gao and situated about fifteen kilometers from the Niger River. It had been bypassed on the march to take Gao but was now thought to be better, at least climatically, for the weary troops. Timbuktu would therefore become the base from which the new rulers attempted to administer their conquered territories. But Timbuktu did not have a reputation as a center of imperial or political power, so this was a new feature for a town that had always been in the shadow of the political center of Gao. As we saw in the previous chapter, the teachers and students of Timbuktu were among its most valuable assets; they attracted others to visit or live there and the rulers were well aware of the scholarly and spiritual reputation of the town.

From Timbuktu to Marrakesh

A new commander of the Sa'dian troops, Mahmud al-Zarqun, was sent from Marrakesh to replace Jawdar Pasha who had, among other things, proved too slow to pursue insurgents and capture their leaders who continued to resist the invaders. Zarqun chose to make his headquarters in Timbuktu. When the new commander arrived in August 1591, he proceeded to quell all expression of dissatisfaction with the occupation; any stirrings, uprisings, and resistance against his men were quashed. The members of the askiya royal family and their allies in Gao, who had survived and fled, continued to plot attacks on the occupiers, in a kind of ongoing guerrilla war that would last for many years. Timbuktu was a site for such resistance and the new commander had to deal with this. He did so brutally and systematically, as is recounted in the chronicle *Tārīkh al-Sūdān* (Chronicle of the Land of the Blacks). Its author, 'Abd al-Rahman al-Sa'di was too young to recall the chaotic years of the early 1590s, but would have heard stories about those days. Such stories were in circulation until the time that Sa'di was writing his work, around the 1640s or early 1650s. He was also an employee in the administration that had been established by the occupiers and knew from experience how they spoke about their conquests. He wrote, sometimes in detail, of the excesses of the commander and his troops who settled in Timbuktu. Despite being in the service of the occupying power, Sa'di did not diminish what they did, although at times he tried to explain the causes of their activities. Among the actions of Mahmud al-Zarqun were pillaging the town of all its wealth and imprisoning and killing dissidents. Zarqun "entered their houses and removed all the valuables, household goods, and furnishings. . . . His followers plundered whatever they could lay their hands on, and brought dishonour among the scholars, stripping their womenfolk and committing acts of indecency."[7] Others, he sent into exile. The collapse of political order meant that the judges and scholars were the ones to whom people turned for guidance on how to act in this situation. As Sa'di explained: "Some counselled that they should be repelled by force, if necessary, while others advised caution and restraint. Meanwhile, the harm they were causing continued to get worse."[8] The description of the continuous fighting, as the old political elites chose sides—with some leaving the area to regroup and attack later, while others were collaborating with the occupiers—provides a grim picture of Timbuktu in the 1590s. The attempts to subdue the region were ceaseless and, in Timbuktu, neither the ordinary residents nor the scholars were spared. For instance, in late 1593 the townspeople were told to assemble outside the Sankoré Mosque so that they could swear allegiance to the sultan in Marrakesh; a few days later scholars were rounded up and made to make the same pledge. In one incident, more than a dozen men from the learned community were killed by a soldier in response to a clumsy attack on him. Ahmad Baba and members of his family, as well as other scholars, were arrested in September 1593 and a month later they were sent on the long march to Marrakesh.

Between the two seats of the opposing political powers—Marrakesh and Gao—the terrain is mostly desert and desolate, demanding to traverse, with severe heat during the day and plummeting, icy temperatures at night. Around Marrakesh the winters can be severely cold, with mountainous and higher-lying terrain receiving snow in winter. Much of the territory is desert or semi-desert closer to Timbuktu and Gao. Water sources are limited, wells few and far between. However, between the time of the rise of both these places and the later sixteenth century, there was some significant development in the settlements around them. Some of the settlements had once been inhabited but would become deserted; others—such as Teghaza (Taghaza) and Taoudeni—were locations for mining the highly valued mineral salt. The learned towns of Jenne, Walata, and Timbuktu, for instance, attracted students and traders. Leo Africanus, when he visited some of these places in the early 1500s, wrote of each of them as separate "kingdoms," giving some impression of what they looked like to an outside visitor. Of course, these settlements and towns also drew the attention of the dominant political powers in the broader region. The Songhay elite incorporated the towns and expressed notional, but also sometimes aggressive, imperial control over them, especially when it came to extracting tax or tribute. The Sa'dian dynasty that emerged in the 1510s to the south of Marrakesh did the same closer to home. Ultimately, the Sa'dians, of course, overthrew the Songhay rulers. Beyond the rulers, their officials, and the army, there was a learned community that, for the most part, lived far from the halls of power and inhabited the very same geographical space that the rulers claimed. Political change and violence affected these scholars and students as much as anybody else.

The Scholar-in-Exile

News of the defeat of the askiya and his army in early 1591 traveled fast, and before long reached Timbuktu. Ahmad Baba and the learned elders of the town heard of these events but did not expect their town to be a focus of attention from the Moroccan army. Baba kept writing through the early months of the invasion, finishing in twenty-six pages a discussion on the importance of the concept of intention, *Ghāyat al-amal fī tafḍīl al-nīyya ʿalā lʿamal* (The object of hope in explaining the superiority of intention). In it, he discussed the meaning of the word *niyya* (intention) and defined it as an audible and mental pronouncement by the one who wants to do something. Intention is ultimately a product of the heart; in the conclusion, Baba returns to the subject of the purity of the heart. He cites the sayings of the Prophet Muhammad related to the importance of intention and discusses their authenticity. He cites a range of scholars who had addressed the subject before him, referring especially to the work of Abu Hamid al-Gazali (d. 1111). As soldiers were pouring into Timbuktu without resistance from the unarmed locals, Baba was finishing his text on the heart, the mind, and action.

Since there were no Songhay fighters in Timbuktu, there was a clear path for the Saʿdian soldiers to occupy the town.[9] The disruption of life in Timbuktu did, however, eventually stir the people to action. They reacted to the soldiers who demanded shelter and food. There were objections by the locals, followed by further provocations by the soldiers; but this led to more violence. The learned men of the town were then forced to play a mediating role and to begin to stand up for their people against the excesses of the soldiers. The *Tārīkh al-Sūdān* noted one moment when "the number of people wounded by the musketeers increased, the notables complained to the jurist Qadi Abu Hafs ʿUmar . . . who consulted the men of sound judgment about this. Some counselled that they [the soldiers] should be repelled by force, if necessary, while others advised caution and restraint."[10]

Baba was around thirty-six years old at the time of the invasion and would have been among the scholars consulted, since he was from a prominent, learned family and was senior enough to air his views among the conferring men. Noticing the prominent role of these learned men, Mulay Ahmad al-Zarqun ordered the arrest of a number of them, including Baba. Their houses were identified and they were led away by soldiers who took them to the outskirts of the town where some form of prison had been constructed near the encampment of the soldiers. After about a month languishing in the makeshift prison, the prisoners were sent into the desert with a north-bound caravan. They were forced to march, for at least three months, across the desert and mountains to banishment in Marrakesh. Long days in the desert under intense sun, and nights when temperatures plummeted steeply were punishing in themselves, especially to scholars who had lived by other, more serene, rhythms. The trek was demanding and Baba injured his leg along the way. Who of his family accompanied him is not clear. Later he would complain to the authorities in Marrakesh that his books were taken by the soldiers when he was arrested: "I had the smallest library of any of my kin, and they seized 1,600 volumes," Baba is reported to have remarked.[11]

Baba and his compatriots arrived in Marrakesh, the "red city," at the end of 1593 or in early 1594 (fig. 8). Caravans entering the town did not only raise dust but also created an atmosphere of festivity and piqued the curiosity of the locals. Led by soldiers, this caravan came with looted goods and men, women, and children from the elite of Timbuktu. The valuable loot seized in the latest round of attacks and in the occupation of Timbuktu was taken to the palace quarters as evidence of what the conquest had achieved. One report even included a young elephant among the things brought to Marrakesh!

The prisoners were led away to another experience of incarceration. They were kept in captivity until around May 1596, a period of between fifteen and twenty-four months in prison. The Sultan Ahmad al-Mansur was interested in seeing who was captured and held in his prisons. He had been educated in the traditional syllabus of the scholars of the time and maintained an interest in intellectual matters and books. He came to know about the Timbuktu scholars held in the capital and he ordered that Ahmad Baba be brought to him.

A historian of the Sa'dian period, Muhammad Saghir al-Ifrani, writing in the late seventeenth or early eighteenth century (his death date is given as circa 1743), wrote of Baba's meeting with the sultan. The sultan was then probably living in the newly completed Badi' Palace. Baba was taken to this impressive building for an audience with the sultan who sat behind a veil so as not to be seen by his subjects and by outsiders like Baba. Mansur believed himself to be a noble sharif, a descendant of the Prophet Muhammad, and therefore took the title *Mulay*, and made a claim to be the caliph of the Muslims.

One can only imagine Baba's condition after a long march and having languished in prison before the surprise order that he would have an audience with the sultan. He did not at first see the ruler because the powerful man was hidden from view behind a veil. But Baba was not intimidated by a voice, hidden behind a curtain, addressing him. He told the sultan that it was unbecoming of a human being to imitate the almighty by pretending to be unseen: "Now you are imitating the Lord of lords, so if you have anything to say, come down to us and remove the veil."[12] These were powerful words from a captured scholar to a ruler. Baba wanted to see the man who was speaking to him, and he wanted not only to hear and listen but to speak. Furthermore, Baba protested to the ruler about his capture, during which he endured an injury, the plunder of his goods and library, and then imprisonment and exile in a foreign land. Baba also denounced the illegitimacy of the invasion. Sultan Mansur listened but he did not respond

FIG. 8. When Ahmad Baba was exiled in Marrakesh, it was the center of impressive cultural and architectural developments. The engraver and painter Adriaen Matham (1590–1660) was with the Dutch Embassy when he produced this vista of the city. Although made more than thirty years after Baba's residence, it gives an impression of how the place was viewed in the time of the Sa'dian rulers. *Image source*: Adriaen Matham, "El Badi Palace" (1640), also known as "Vue de Marrakech." Found on https://gallica.bnf.fr/ark:/12148/btv1b530573367.

to or address Baba's accusations. Instead, he told Baba about his goal of bringing unity to the larger region, to which Baba also responded. Baba was fearless in his exchange with the sultan. This is perhaps not unexpected since he had nothing more to lose. Moreover, he was the author of a work that argues that rulers are to be avoided by scholars. Here Baba showed that, when one is forced into the company of rulers, then one should not hold back from criticizing them. The author of *Jalb al-niʿma* lived by his own advice to his peers. What he espoused in that work was not mere theory for him in this situation, nor did he forget what he had propounded there. He did not keep quiet in the hope of being released to return to his homeland. The sultan would certainly not have been impressed with Baba after this encounter. The sultan must have been shocked by such insolence. Baba was eventually released from prison, but not to go back home, and he remained in exile until the death of Mansur.

The names of the scholars in custody must have reached the learned men of Marrakesh because they petitioned the ruler to release Ahmad Baba. They pleaded, either directly or through advisors to the sultan, for Baba's release. The sultan had already promised Baba his release but these scholars requested that Baba also be allowed to teach in the town. Baba would have welcomed the opportunity to be free from his confinement and to teach, whether he was consulted or not. His role as a teacher at the Al-Shurafa' Mosque while restricted to the town allowed regular contact with local students and scholars. Was the request by the scholars an act of solidarity with one of their own?

Baba was not the only man of learning who was taken into exile, but there is no indication that any other of his cohort was released or given the same opportunity to teach. Furthermore, Marrakesh already had numerous scholars who came from all over the larger region, from institutions with high reputations in places such as Fez and Tlemcen in the north and the Sus (Sous) region to the south. Marrakesh was then already well into its revival, and from the 1570s onward they invested in numerous impressive buildings such as the Badi' Palace and mosques, schools, bathhouses, hotels, and saints' tombs with distinctive Sa'dian architectural features. Architects, craftsmen, senior scholars, and teachers were all in demand in the city. If Baba was part of a forced "brain drain" to help bolster the intellectual luster of Sa'dian Marrakesh, then the local scholars welcomed him as an equal. Furthermore, he found among them educated men, with status at the court and in the city, who wanted to study with him, such as al-Maqqari, al-Hashtuki, al-Marrakushi, al-Qassar, and al-Ghassani (more about them in chapter 4).

After Baba's release from prison to teach, we can assume that there was a relative improvement in his living conditions. However, the conditions for most people in Marrakesh, even the elites, were being tested, for in the 1590s the region was beset by drought, leading to severe agricultural shortages and recurring famines as well as plagues. The twin catastrophes of famine and plague returned and lingered throughout the entire period of Baba's life in Marrakesh. Additionally, there was the alienating experience of exile. He had the status of a scholar, was recognized by his peers, and could communicate in cultivated Arabic with them, even though some of them might have remarked on his accent and his apparent lisp. He could also still speak in Arabic and one or another language used in Timbuktu, such as Songhay or Hasaniyya, with his surviving countrymen who had been deported with him. There are reports of deaths among them—such as that of the judge Qadi 'Umar Hafs—but what happened to the rest of them we will never know. Most would never see their homeland again and would die in exile. We can imagine that for Baba and his countrymen, life in exile was overall unpleasant and hard but not completely unbearable. He and other scholars were at home among their Marrakesh peers who had similar academic concerns with language, law, and religion. Additionally, he was not isolated but had the company of students. According to Sa'di, Baba also had some family with him. But Sa'di does not specify what he means by family: wife and children, siblings, members of the larger Aqit family who were also scholars? So, we cannot say anything about Baba's family life in exile. All that we know is that he used his time, when not teaching, to write.

When the opportunity came to raise the issue of his return to Timbuktu, he took it up. This became possible when Mansur died in 1603 but Baba's departure only took place after a successor finally came to power in Marrakesh in early 1607.

Writing in Exile

Baba found a way to write when he was still in prison. "Despite the conditions of restriction and imprisonment that I am in, students have been frequently coming to me, and bringing books with them," he wrote at the end of a work he completed in prison. He finished *al-La'ālī al-sundusiyya fīl-faḍā'il al-sanūsiyya*, dated November 28,1595, which is devoted to asceticism and the way the noted ascetic of Tlemcen, Muhammad bin Yusuf al-Sanusi (d. 1490), defined and practiced it. Fortunate enough not to be isolated and forgotten in a prison, Baba was eventually released and given lodgings in the town. He was also allowed to leave to go to the Jami' al-Shurafa' Mosque where he gave his lectures. The mosque was in an alley close to one of the larger squares of the walled city. The main mosque complex, the Kutubiyya, with its imposing minaret that dates to the twelfth century, was on the outskirts of the town and would have been the preserve of scholars close to the court. Baba would not have been invited to teach there and one can only assume that neither would he have welcomed such an invitation.

In his role as lecturer, Baba would have had a variety of classes. He would have given classes to a general audience and then taken on individual students to read texts with him over an extended period. One of his students from this period, Abu l'Abbas Ahmad bin Yahya al-Tilmisani al-Maqqari, was born into a well-known, learned family in 1577 in Tlemcen, present-day Algeria. Maqqari referred to Baba as the "great writer and compiler" and listed the books written by Baba, books that Baba taught him and gave him the right to teach, in turn, a permission traditionally called an "ijaza." Another student was Abu 'Abdullah Muhammad bin Ya'qub al-Isi al-'Adib al-Marrakushi, born in Marrakesh in 1558, who received all his education among reputable scholars of the city. He studied with Baba over many years and grew close to him until Baba was freed to leave in 1607. From the Sus region came Abu l'Abbas Ahmad al-Hastuki al-Sanhaji (d. 1637) who also wrote about his teacher Baba. They would all become writers and all of them mentioned Ahmad Baba with great respect as one of their teachers. Abu l'Qasim al-Ghassani, who would rise to the position of Chief Judge of Fez, also studied with Baba and received his permission to teach several books. His students are discussed in the next chapter.

Baba certainly had a good amount of time for his own writing between his classes. Unlike in Timbuktu where he would have had to attend to legal queries and cases from locals, in Marrakesh he was free from this burden. His lectures did not demand extensive preparation and his more advanced students were few, so that he had ample time to read and write. There is no indication of what or whether he was paid by any of his students or if he lived off a stipend from the court, arranged by the scholars who had him appointed. He might have asked for paper from them or from his colleagues who had requested his appointment to the position. He had a tremendous need of writing paper during those years, more than he ever had in earlier years in Timbuktu or later when he returned. With plenty of free time and a steady supply of paper, pens, and ink, he could immerse himself in reading and writing prolifically. He turned his exile into an advantage. In his roughly thirteen years in exile, he would write twenty-seven works, among them two large volumes of data on hundreds of scholars of the Maliki school of law that was dominant in the region.

A Database of Scholars

In 1596, the same year that Baba was released to start teaching, he wrote the last lines of his first major work, which came to over five hundred pages as a manuscript (and in a published standard print format comes to nearly seven hundred pages). This was his *Nayl al-ibtihāj* (Achievement of joy), a work with descriptions, ranging from two lines to two pages, of the scholarly activities of 802 figures including his own family, the Aqits. Baba probably had plans for such a work before his arrest and had started making entries in prison. The final text was voluminous and entailed a large amount of research through existing works and the collecting of oral testimonies. In all probability, Baba prepared drafts and had peers and students look over the text. The full title indicates that the work is a supplement to an earlier work of biographies by another scholar. Thus, the first figure he writes about is the author of the original work, Ibrahim bin 'Ali bin Farhun (d. 1359), an Egyptian scholar who produced a major biographical dictionary of scholars from the Maliki school of law. In his introduction, Baba links himself to Ibn Farhun and the efforts of similar scholars to preserve knowledge of the great men of learning from this school of law. At the end of the work, he provides details of the two dozen books he consulted that were either part of his own collection that came with him from Timbuktu or borrowed from scholars in Marrakesh. He could have also relied on his memory of having read about specific scholars.

Two years later, in 1598, now no longer a prisoner but a teacher and scholar in the city, Baba completed a new version of *Jalb al-ni'ma*, the work on the relationship between scholars and rulers discussed in the last chapter. The new title was rather cryptic, *Mā rawāhu al-ruwāt* (What the narrators narrated). Given what he experienced and witnessed in Timbuktu and his own present condition as a victim of tyranny, it is not hard to see why he returned to the subject. He was reflecting on his own situation as a man unjustly arrested and deported and was therefore addressing the rulers in Marrakesh responsible for his condition. It could also be that, fearing loss of his writings, he began preparing new versions of them. Repetition, of works and themes, was not simply a result of a lack of imagination but had practical conservation reasons too.

At the same time, he continued with the biographical dictionary genre, and in 1603 produced another called *Kifāyat al-muḥtāj li ma'rifa man laysa fi al-dībāj* (The adequate supplement for those who want to know which scholars do not appear in the Dibaj [work of Ibn Farhun]) (fig. 9). The title indicates that it is an attempt to complete the earlier dictionary. On a quick reading, it seems that

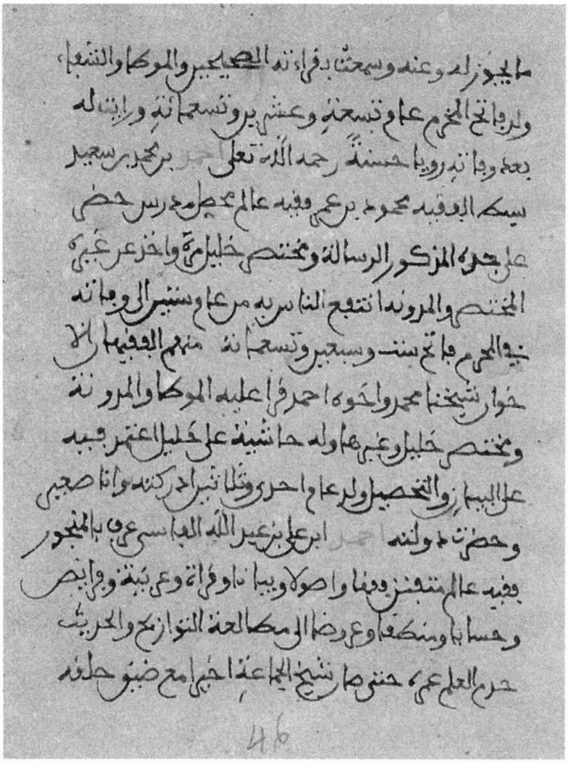

FIG. 9. Two leaves from a manuscript of Ahmad Baba's *Kifāyat al-muḥtāj*, a biographical dictionary that runs into more than six hundred pages, showing part of entries for letter Alif and Ya. It was arranged alphabetically. The names of the writers discussed (Ahmad and Yusuf) are in red. On other pages, there are marginal notes probably added later. Page size: 18.2 × 14.4 cm with text 12.2 × 10 cm. Cedrab 2460. *Image source*: From the archives of the Iheri-Ab (formerly Cedrab) in Timbuktu.

this is an abridgement of the previous biographical dictionary of 1596. This perception of the work as an abridgement is the most common view among scholars, based on the fact that Baba decided to exclude ninety-nine figures. He also decided to add an entry about himself. The introduction to *Kifāyat al-muḥtāj* is also rather similar to the one in the first collection of biographies. It was not uncommon for Baba to rework and rewrite a text, as he did with the work on scholars and rulers. There are other examples of this approach that make giving a count of his writings difficult. In a sense, many of his texts that were preserved for posterity were still works-in-progress. His reworking of the dictionary was

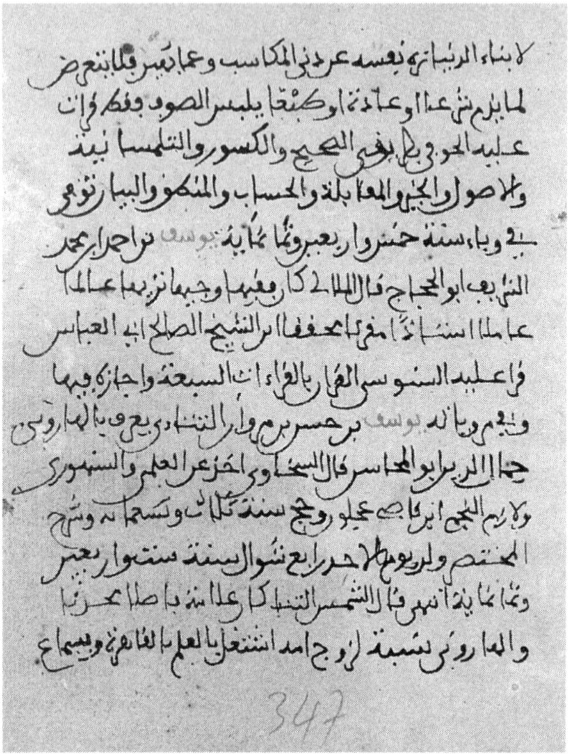

FIG. 9. (*continued*)

not simply an abridgement—in the sense of merely taking out some names—but also a rethinking of what he was doing. It is much more than a shorter version of the first dictionary he produced. This time he does not begin with Ibrahim b. ʾAli bin Farhun. Instead, he includes an entry on himself, which was largely in the words of one of his students.

Manuscript copies of both works are found in various libraries in Morocco and across North Africa, a measure of their popularity, and they have been widely used ever since. The *Nayl* was printed in Fez for the first time in 1909 and then Cairo in 1911.

Between the completion of the biographical dictionaries, Baba reworked his critique of scholars who mix with rulers. The dictionary genre and his advice to scholars were not unrelated. The latter is a work of prose advising men of his kind to behave ethically and stick to their calling. They are the people who deserve to be immortalized in a dictionary, not rulers. The chroniclers concerned themselves with rulers, but he ignores them.

Baba was conserving a tradition of learning through his compilation of scholarly biographies, and his view of that tradition was that scholars ought to avoid rulers. We know that he had in his library, either in Timbuktu or in Marrakesh, access to at least one biographical dictionary (Ibn Farhun's *Dībāj*). But there is a longer tradition of this genre that had various styles of organizing entries: by scholars of a discipline, scholars of a legal school, scholars of a specific place. There were those organized alphabetically with no regard to chronological order and those based on chronology. And there were mixed-genre works that combined a historical chronicle of events with a biographical dictionary.

Baba's biographical dictionaries focused, on the whole, on men who were writers and not mystics. He wrote a separate work on what he meant by "learning." *Tuḥfat al-fuḍalā bi baʿḍ fadāʾil al-ʿulamā* is the rhyming title of this work, typical of titles at the time of its composition, which when translated from the Arabic, might sound rather cryptic: "The gift of the persons of nobility about the virtues of the scholars" (fig. 10).[13] This is indeed the subject of this work: the merits, advantages, or superior qualities of those who live to learn and benefit society with their learning, as opposed to those who devote themselves solely to spiritual self-improvement, meditation, and an ascetic lifestyle. However, the superiority of people of knowledge rests on the condition that they act on what they know.

The work, as the title suggests, primarily deals with the virtues of seeking knowledge and striving to become a bearer of knowledge. For the author and his time, this meant preeminently to make the argument using the most prominent and earliest sources as evidence. There were two points of view that Baba had to entertain. "Seeking knowledge" has a great religious pedigree but so does seeking spiritual enlightenment, with only basic knowledge but plenty of devotion and meditation. Thus, an argument has to be made in favor of making a commitment to knowledge rather than an exclusive commitment to seclusion and prayer. Baba does this through marshaling an abundance of textual supports. He clearly demonstrates his command of the range of classical Islamic sources in advancing his argument. Perhaps the *Tuḥfat al-fuḍalā bi baʿḍ fadāʾil al-ʿulamā* was even conceived as a work precisely to do that: to show his erudition to his peers. Composed in Marrakesh after his detention, it could be that the work was meant as a marker of his capacity as a scholar, not only as the compiler of scholarly biographies in the *Nayl al-ibtihāj* and *Kifāyat al-muḥtāj*.

The *Tuḥfat al-fuḍalā bi baʿḍ fadāʾil al-ʿulamā* is relatively brief but it is dense; it is divided into three chapters and a conclusion. In the first chapter, Baba describes the rank of those endowed with sacred knowledge, quoting extensively from the Quran, using commentaries on citations, hadith, or sayings attributed

FIG. 10. The first and last pages with colophon of *Tuḥfat al-fuḍalā*, by Ahmad Baba, on the merits of studying law. He weighs the benefits of time spent studying against time in seclusion and contemplation. The date of the text is unknown, but this copy of the work was completed in 1702. It is thirty-six pages

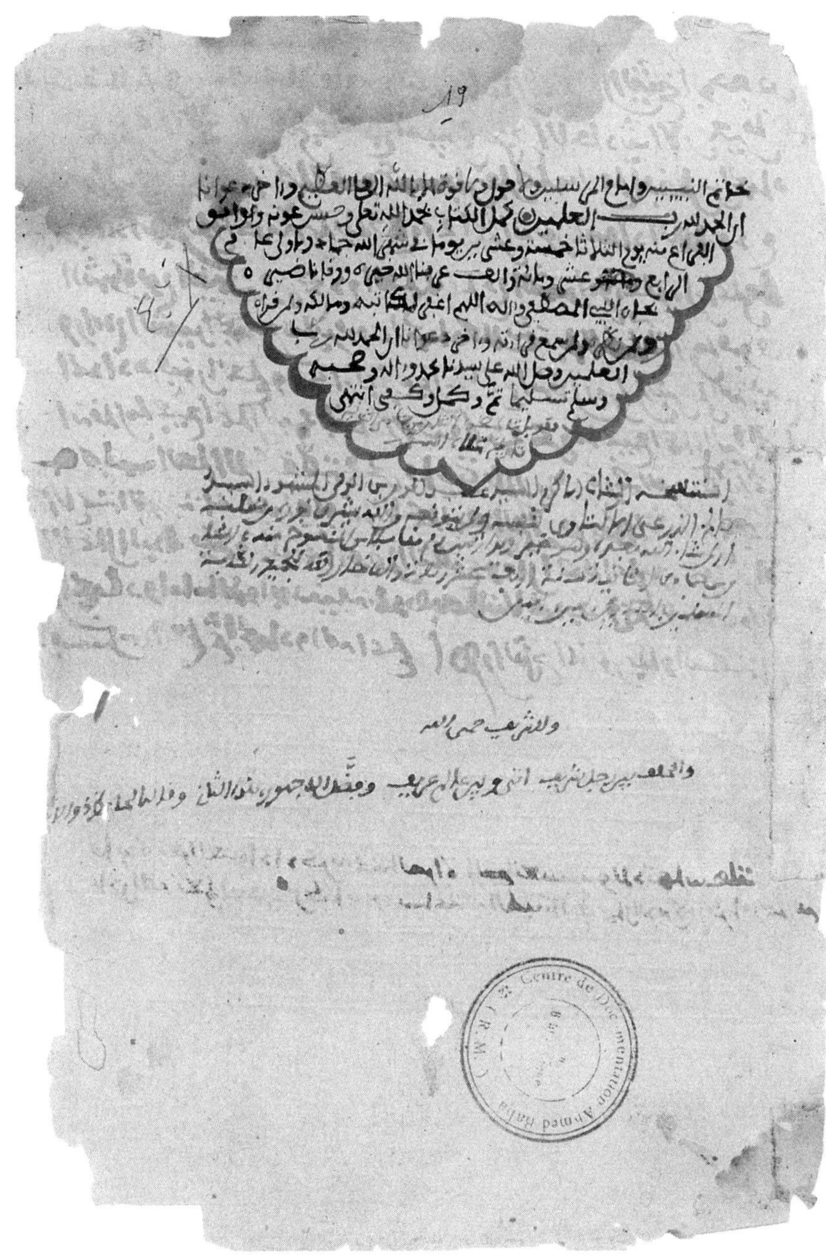

long, unbound, with paper size 24 × 15 cm, and twenty-nine lines of text per page. Cedrab no. 776. *Image source*: From the archives of the Iheri-Ab (formerly Cedrab), in Timbuktu.

to the Prophet Muhammed, and aphorisms of the earliest and most eminent scholars themselves. Besides citing these texts, the author also offers rational analyses of them. He steadily builds up an argument, in the course of this first chapter, that should make it clear that those with knowledge are superior to those without it.

In the second chapter, Baba establishes the superiority of seeking knowledge over all other forms of worship; indeed, seeking knowledge *is* a form of worship. Again, he relies greatly on the primary religious texts, this time the words attributed to the Prophet Muhammad, such where the Prophet advises: "One hour of a scholar reclining on his bed while looking at (some aspect) of knowledge is better than seventy years worship."[14] Baba continues to argue that all forms of good behavior are dependent on the search for knowledge.

In the third chapter, Baba makes a comparison between scholars who are occupied with the dissemination of knowledge and saints who display piety and righteousness. The main question is: Who is superior in the sight of God, the scholar or the saint? He presents two sides of the arguments, accompanied by evidence, and also points out the strengths and weaknesses of the arguments presented. One gets the impression that the society in which he lived had some kind of competition or perhaps rivalry between traditional scholars and the mystics or Sufis who displayed extraordinary spiritual powers.

Baba's personal inclination is that the scholar is superior, provided that he disseminates the knowledge sincerely and not as a means to accumulate worldly gain. Spreading beneficial knowledge helps society at large and not only the individual who possesses spiritual prowess. Willingness to act on that acquired knowledge is the ultimate argument for learning.

In Baba's conclusion, he mentions four different categories of scholars: (1) Those who have mastered various disciplines but do not act in accordance with the knowledge they pass on to others. They are undoubtedly doomed. (2) Those who have mastered the sciences but are only occupied with outward compliance, while they neglect purifying their hearts. They do not benefit fully from the knowledge with which they have been endowed. (3) Those who are fully aware of their faults but think themselves saved on account of the knowledge they have. They are in a state of illusion. (4) Those who have mastered all the outward sciences, and live their lives in compliance with them, but are also fully aware of their faults, and strive hard to combat these conditions.

Baba always believed that he would return to Timbuktu and longed for news from his homeland. He kept asking about his release and some of his new colleagues petitioned the ruler on his behalf.

Leaving Marrakesh

If Baba was already known in Marrakesh from soon after his arrival, then his prominence and eminence grew with the completion of his books. All his works found copyists that ensured their circulation beyond the single copy he worked on himself. The copyists could have come from among his students who were close to him or from the ones to whom he showed versions of his work-in-progress. The two biographical dictionaries probably brought him more attention than any of the other texts he wrote in exile. This was not a genre unfamiliar to his peers, but these works were meant to build on and contribute to a whole legal school, which was the foundation of the legal culture of Marrakesh and the entire Maghreb. The last attempt at completing such a work had been in the late fourteenth century.

Despite the scholarly community close to Baba, his relative security, and even some celebrity, he never stopped thinking about his return to Timbuktu. Though he was not known for writing verse, he composed a poem that expressed his longing for his hometown:

> O traveler to Gao, turn off to my city, murmur my name there and greet all my dear ones
> With scented *salams* from an exile who longs for his homeland and neighbors, companions and friends
> And condole there in my city beloved kinsmen for the masters who were buried there
> The young folk of my family have all departed to the Owner of all things in the days of my absence
> Woe to me and my sadness for them
> O Lord, grant them Thy widest mercy.

In Baba's first encounter with Sultan Ahmad al-Mansur in his court, while still a prisoner, Baba asked him when he would be released to return to Timbuktu. When he was released, it was not with permission to return to his homeland. He was let out of prison but not allowed outside Marrakesh. An attempt to escape would have led to torture or death. So, he suffered the life of an exile and tried to make the best of it by immersing himself in research and writing. When the opportunity arose, in the last days of the sultan, he raised the issue again. The son who became Sultan, Zaydan, promised Baba that he would be allowed to return to his homeland. There is no record of what happened to Baba's family, either those who had been imprisoned with him or those who remained behind in Timbuktu.

Baba was finally allowed to pass through the gates of Marrakesh in late 1607. His colleagues took him to the gates and said prayers for his safe passage home. The historian Ifrani reports that, despite the respect accorded to him by the scholars of Marrakesh, Baba told them as he departed: "May God not bring me back to this place, not return me to these lands." And so, he joined the caravan back home.

4

Ahmad Baba's Later Years in Timbuktu, 1608–27

FROM THE narrow alley in the heart of the walled city, he was led to the nearest city gates from which he would embark on his journey to freedom. There was, of course, not much fanfare, but several of his students and colleagues gathered to bid him farewell. Among them was a so-called Morisco—a Muslim forced to assume a Catholic identity after the conquest of Granada—who was then a translator in the Sa'dian court in Marrakesh. He was one of the thousands of this community who fled in the last expulsions from their homeland. Ahmad ibn Qasim al-Hajari had heard of Baba and had met this "outstanding faqih [jurist]" as he calls Baba.[1] He would later meet scholars in Cairo and Tunis who praised Baba's writing; he does not say how well he knew Baba but he certainly was acquainted with him and his writing. When Baba was leaving, he took the opportunity to join the group of scholars bidding him farewell. He was among the men who went with Baba part of the way beyond the city walls, as was their custom when an important visitor or traveler left the town's precincts. These men had been beneficiaries of Baba's teaching, writing, and company in Marrakesh, and were well aware of the conditions under which he had arrived there.[2] Baba's departing concern was with his library, which had been brought to Marrakesh; he had asked for the return of his hundreds of books. There is no record of them.[3]

Baba began his long trek back home in mid-1607. He was part of a larger camel caravan led by experts who knew the routes back to Timbuktu and had goods to sell beyond the desert. If soldiers were not sent along to ensure protection for the caravan, then there were some men with weapons to ward off bandits. They had supplies of water and basic sustenance and knew the oases or wells across the vast, harsh landscape. One settlement where Baba's caravan stopped, probably for longer than usual, was Tamgrout, about 350 kilometers southeast of Marrakesh.[4] Here he met the leading personalities of the town, who welcomed him. Over the previous half century, the isolated settlement attracted ascetics and scholars who, in turn, would go on to attract visitors, traders, and disciples. But in Baba's time, Tamgrout had not yet emerged as a center of the Nasiriyya Sufi brotherhood, which would in later decades attract its followers to the settlement. While in Tamgrout, Baba was asked if it was permissible for a Muslim to consume tobacco and was shown existing responses to the question from senior scholars in Fez and elsewhere. The question came from one Ibn Abu Mahalli, who had studied at the Qarawiyyin Mosque and college in Fez for five years and was a known Sufi who had written on Sufism. He also admitted to loving his tobacco. He wrote a work in its defense and was looking for more opinions on the subject—naturally, ones that argued in favor of the new leaf that was making its rounds even in distant Tamgrout. Mahalli had sent off questions to many centers of learning, including to Cairo. Mahalli had also noted its medicinal qualities, he claims. Baba was invited to give an opinion, and he duly composed a short response—*al-Lamʿ fīl'ishāra li-ḥukm al-tibgh* (The shimmering light regarding the ruling on tobacco)—that took into account all the existing arguments against tobacco. Baba concluded that tobacco is not a prohibited substance according to Islamic law. In his conclusion, he quotes from a text written by an expert on herbs that enumerates the medicinal properties of "this weed called tobacco." It is possible that Baba had already heard about tobacco, or seen smokers, in Marrakesh, which was a town full of people from all over the larger region and the coast carrying new things to sell. Tobacco was then the latest arrival from the Americas, brought by the Spanish and Portuguese back to Europe, with some of the plant brought from the Atlantic coast to Marrakesh and even into the interior settlements such as Tamgrout. In this way, the tobacco also reached Timbuktu and other parts of West Africa, if not by this time, then not long afterward. Tobacco would remain a contentious commodity into the nineteenth century (as we shall see in chapter 6).

This is the only text Baba wrote in Tamgrout but in later years, after his death, other works by him were found in collections in Tamgrout. For instance, there is a copy of his *Jalb al-niʿma*. After the Tamgrout stop, which offered a break from the rigors of the voyage, the caravan continued deeper into the Sahara. Other stops were probably at Taghaza and Taoudeni and then, closer to home, at Arawan. After some more days on the move, the caravan approached the outskirts of Timbuktu. When Baba was taken into exile, the journey lasted about three months, and the return could have taken as long if not longer.

When the caravan drew closer to Timbuktu and the outlines of the town in the distance could be seen, Baba was reassured that his return was finally a reality. Then just over fifty years old, he would have been exhausted and would have needed assistance to carry his few belongings and the books he had managed to bring back. Once he disembarked and walked into the town, he would have been shocked by the changes. Time passes slowly in the desert but, in the dozen years that had passed, the town looked like it had gone backward many decades. By the time Baba was deported from Timbuktu in late 1593, the town was already suffering under the Sa'dian conquerors. There were arrests, deportations, and migrations out of the town as people feared the ruthlessness of the occupiers and the general lawlessness of the occupying army. The population had witnessed the violence as the invaders searched for gold and other valuables to take away with them and then arrested or attacked anyone in their way.

The old order that Baba witnessed being destroyed at the time of his arrest and exile had not been replaced by a stable central authority. The leaders of the occupation had changed several times; many of them even fled while the regular soldiers stayed behind without the experience or motivation to establish a working government. Lawlessness and crimes against the locals were common for a long time. The region nominally fell under the Sa'dian empire but the ties were growing ever thinner and weaker. The Arma, as the new governors were called, would marry local women and set down local roots but had little experience or capacity to put in place the basic elements of political authority.[5]

With the chaos of the invasion, the exile of so many leaders and scholars—men with status and authority such as Baba—and the fear that had set in, the infrastructure of the town had been neglected and damaged in the subsequent years. As people fled and left their homes without occupants, their houses were either taken over by soldiers or simply left unoccupied. Trees were felled and the wood from the doors of houses was stolen to make boats. The inhabitants' household goods and furnishings were taken. There was ongoing movement into and out of the town as soldiers were ordered to leave to subdue rebellions in other towns such as Jenne, and their commanders were recalled to Marrakesh or sent elsewhere. The soldiers had to be housed and fed and the locals had to give them priority over their own needs. When Baba entered his hometown after more than a decade in exile, he must have been shocked by the sight and feel of the place. The occupying army had little interest in maintaining, not to speak of building, anything in the town. The farming lands close to the Niger River, which were cultivated by locals, were seen as sources of supplies for the army, not the population. The impressive mosques were still there and the layout of the town remained unchanged but the whole atmosphere was different. As the chronicler al-Sa'di wrote in the *Tārīkh al-Sūdān*: "Security turned to fear, luxury was changed into affliction and distress, and prosperity became woe and harshness. People began to attack one another throughout the length and breadth of the kingdom, raiding and preying upon property, (free) persons and slaves."[6]

Baba might have been aware of the situation, since, throughout his exile, there was somehow communication between the exiles and their families in Timbuktu. The exiles knew of deaths and burials back home and sent back information about their own situation. Those in Timbuktu heard about the comings and goings of the exiles. For instance, on their arrival in Marrakesh, the qadi (chief justice) of Timbuktu, Abu Hafs 'Umar, had written to inform people in Timbuktu of their safe arrival. And when he died in Marrakesh his people in Timbuktu received the news and knew that he was buried close to the revered scholar Qadi 'Iyad. Thus, Baba had some idea of happenings back home and he knew that he was not returning to the same city that he had left.

Baba had to find a place to live and start again as a writer. He soon found living quarters, which could have been the old family compound where he had lived all his life before his exile. When he arrived in Marrakesh, he was known by some scholars, and his name became even better known over the years because of his writings and students. There is no description of how he was received when he returned to Timbuktu. His former peers, still living in the town, probably had to be careful not to express themselves publicly or too loudly. It took time to settle down. Perhaps he had to move around until he could move into his old lodgings again. But his relatives from his Aqit family, and other scholars and students whom he had known and who had remained behind, had been killed or fled. His favorite teacher, Muhammad Baghayogho, for instance, died as Timbuktu was taken over by the Sa'dian soldiers. Finding a routine in this situation took time, but Baba eventually settled down to do what he knew how to do best—teach and write.

Baba's peers who had resisted suffered a similar fate as he had, and there were consequently few learned men who remained in Timbuktu. In a preamble to a text written after settling back in his town, Baba would write of the "need to say a funeral prayer for the disappearance of learning and its practitioners, the blotting out of its sun, the eclipse of its moon."[7] There had been an outflow of people who had lived most of their lives in the town. On the other hand, there was an inflow of foreign soldiers who were poorly fed and badly led, and thus quick to abuse and violate locals. Given their precarious existence, they were nearly as uncertain of their own futures as the long-standing inhabitants of the region.

Not long after the soldiers were established in Timbuktu the leadership decided to pack up and leave the town and return to Marrakesh. A new political order, under the Arma, as the soldiers were called, was being created, while the old administrative structure inherited from the late Songhay period remained nominally in place. Songhay political hierarchy and nomenclature remained in use combined with terminologies from Marrakesh and also the Ottomans. The Arma and their local collaborators were on the defensive and tried to fend off resistance more than to create a new order that would eventually ensure stability. The last of the leadership sent from Marrakesh were leaving the region when Baba arrived back in Timbuktu. The soldiers were left on their own to decide to return or to stay in place. Many soldiers made Timbuktu their home. They married local woman and, with time, would be seen as locals in the town. They had come with an invading army, but they did not have the capacity or interest to rule over the society. As a result, Timbuktu's inhabitants suffered; an old order had been destroyed but a new order failed to materialize. One factor behind Baba's release was probably the realization that the occupation of Timbuktu was coming to an end, and it was pointless to keep him in Marrakesh. He was far too independent and never reconciled with his jailers. They could not expect him to work for the occupation forces in Timbuktu.

In exile, he became the renowned Timbuktu writer. In contrast, Baba's return to Timbuktu saw him without the energy and probably without the conditions to pursue any major writing project. He was beyond his scholarly prime. He did eventually find his feet and in the following years he received students to teach, and questions and queries to address. Mainly, he received legal problems to answer and most of these were in the form of correspondence with other scholars. His writing took the form of opinions on issues of importance in the region at the time, such as the use of tobacco and the question of enslavement. Some of his works were rewritings of his earlier texts, such as his views on tobacco, written in Tamgrout. (Baba says in his text that he had already written on the topic in Marrakesh, but he could mean Tamgrout.) In total, what remains of his work in this period are about six small texts, certainly not as many or as substantial as what he produced in his Marrakesh period or pre-exile days. The prominence he achieved in Marrakesh did not lead him to any vanity or arrogance and his tone remained self-effacing, as when he wrote in 1615/16 in the preamble to a text we shall discuss below: "I am not, by God, a jurist, nor am I illustrious, neither do I deserve to be so described, either in reality or in metaphor. . . . I have a name, but there is no substance behind it, so if you are wise, do not be deceived by my name."[8]

Works in the Last Phase (1608–27)

The demanding journey back home probably wore him down; he was also much older and physically weaker. After he found lodgings, possibly in his old home if it was still accessible or habitable at all, he would have settled in and started to teach, read, and eventually write again. Those were still unsettling times in his birthplace, and it was some time before he could sit down to write again. His first dated work of this period is from 1610, two years after his return. Furthermore, it appears that he had already worked on the text in Marrakesh, as far back as 1603 and possibly earlier. It was titled *Minan al-Rabb al-Jalīl bi bayān muhimmāt Khalīl* and constituted a summary of the chapters on zakat (the obligatory tax on personal wealth) through to marriage from the legal compendium, the *Mukhtaṣar* (Summary) of Khalil, the famous work on Maliki law. These chapters were of practical value and could have been written to reinforce awareness of the rules regarding these matters in Timbuktu. In the same year, he completed *'Ayn al-iṣāba fī hukm al-ṭāba*, a legal opinion on the usage of tobacco, which is possibly a reworking of the text he had written during his stopover in Tamgrout on his way back home. Tobacco was then probably also in use in Timbuktu and the question of its permissibility, in terms of Islamic law, arose there as well.

A five- to six-year hiatus followed before new writing appeared. It could be that Baba's output during this period has been lost because the texts he did write were not copied, or not copied as extensively as some of his others. Then in 1615/16 a number of texts appeared. In 1616, he completed a short piece titled *Risāla fī taṣawwuf* (Letter on Sufism), which treats the question of the necessity of initiation into a Sufi order. His *al-Lum'a fī ajwibat al-as'ilat al-arba'a* addressed a number of questions including one about the concordance of the Gregorian calendar with the Islamic Hijri one, which is a rather curious issue for the time, both for Baba and for Timbuktu. It could mean that there were contacts between adherents of the two calendars in the region. Was the Gregorian calendar used by European Christians, or by the crypto-Muslims (the Moriscos), who arrived in large numbers from the end of the sixteenth century? This specific question could not have come from within Timbuktu and probably came from another place; it could have been an older question from his Marrakesh days. Another text, *Jawāb 'an thalātha as'ila*, is a response to three questions, about which nothing more is known.

Then there was a response to a set of questions concerned with a single but significant subject: Who could legitimately be taken as a slave? This text was titled *Mi'rāj al-su'ūd* (The ladder of ascent toward grasping the law concerning transported Blacks).[9] Though brief and a product of the end of his career, this response to questions about enslavement has attracted much attention; it is only the second work by Baba translated into English.

In terms of its form, the slim text was a fatwa (legal opinion), written in response to several questions posed by a scholar who is only known as Jirari. He wrote from one of the settlements in the oasis of Tuwat, a great distance to the north of Timbuktu, in what is today southern Algeria. Tuwat had been attacked by the Sa'dian forces in the 1580s, before they turned their attention to Gao and Timbuktu. Jirari must have felt certain that his correspondence would reach Timbuktu, given that the entire region at that time had some kind of Sa'dian dominance over it and caravans could pass in relative safety between these two distant points.

Tuwat had a number of reputable scholars and the fact that Jirari sought the opinion of Baba in Timbuktu shows the extent of Baba's fame beyond Timbuktu and Marrakesh. Jirari praises Baba as one of "the illustrious and revered jurists, lamps (of learning) of the region of the Sudan" which was, of course, reason enough to address the query to Baba. However, Baba's location was definitely a consideration, as the questioner writes: "Explain to us the realities of these lands, for you are better informed about them and are more knowledgeable about their state—may your reward from God be copious." The questioner means that Baba was located close to regions—he mentions Bornu, Kano, Gao, and Katsina—from which slaves were brought northward, and these enslaved peoples' "adherence to Islam is widely acknowledged among us."[10] Jirari wanted to know if the peoples in those regions were indeed Muslim or not, how and when they converted or accepted Islamic rule, and so on. These issues are all pertinent to whether they could be enslaved or not. Apart from a legal opinion, Baba was therefore requested to supply some historical or ethnographic details based on "continuous transmission and wide-spread (knowledge), or through a chronicle that can be relied on."[11]

Various forms of bondage and servitude were a feature of the labor system in the larger region. The slave laborer occupied a specific status in the hierarchies in many of the societies in the Sahara. One way of acquiring slaves was to engage in a war with another society and take captives who would be turned into slaves. The capture of those not killed in war was a common way of acquiring such labor. It was, however, prohibited by the Maliki school of Islamic law to take as slaves Muslims who were victims of such wars. Jirari raises an issue of concern that there was often doubt about whether a community was indeed Muslim and concomitant doubts about whether they could or could not be taken as slaves. To what extent should the background of such peoples (and slaves) be investigated?

In Baba's response, he restates Jirari's question: "What have you to say concerning slaves imported from lands whose people have been established to be Muslims . . . and others among whose [*sic*] adherence to Islam is widely acknowledged? Is it permitted to own them or not?"[12] Jirari had asserted that the "sole reason for being owned is unbelief . . ." but that many believers were being captured.[13] Baba revealed a geographical consciousness of the region and mentioned a range of places that he viewed as having largely Muslim populations, such as Bornu, Kano, Gao, Katsina, Kanem, and Songhay. Baba adds additional places to the discussion, those areas or ethnic groups with predominantly non-Muslim populations: Mossi, Gurma, Busa, Birgu, Dagomba, Kotokoli, and Yoruba. This gives some sense of the "Islamization" of the larger region because the questions deal with areas where the population or parts of the population had by then only recently converted to Islam. Some of the peoples were thought to be unbelievers and were taken as slaves when they were, in fact, Muslim. Baba engages in this discussion by referencing the history of conquests in the region. In addressing the reasons for enslavement, he also has to address Jirari's allusion to color as a factor behind enslavement. Baba responds by referring to the theories of color in Ibn Khaldun and other medieval Muslim scholars. But color was not a basis for enslavement, for he writes: "The cause of slavery is unbelief."[14] The starting principle for human beings is that freedom, rather than bondage, is to be assumed.

Baba concludes with two sayings of Prophet Muhammad: "Your brothers are your slaves," and "God caused you to own him, and had He wished He would have caused him to own you." Baba comments that there is thus an admonition to be kind and compassionate to "him among them who is owned, as well as others and to treat him kindly and compassionately, since the mere fact of being owned generally breaks one's heart, because of dominance and subordination associated with this condition, especially when one is far from home."[15]

There is no trace of any response to Baba's views, nor how and if his text reached Tuwat at all. The original letter was dated 1613 and Baba's replies were completed in 1615 because, as he wrote, he was distracted and forgot about dealing with the letter, for which he was rather apologetic. Baba was in a kind of argument or conversation in this text. He first presents himself modestly, stresses his weakness but then proceeds confidently to tackle the questions addressed to him, going beyond merely responding with affirmations or corrections. He adds detail and cites texts, as was expected. Apart from the subject matter and the details, the response is also interesting for the works that Baba cites. He mentions between six and eight books in his response, including: Jalaluddin al-Suyuti's *Raf' shā'n al-Ḥubshān*; Suyuti's *Azhār al-'urūsh* (which Baba mentions an abridgement of, *Nūr al-ghabash*); Ibn Khaldun's *Kitab al-'ibar*; Sahnun's *Mudawwana*; Abu 'l-Asagh 'Isa bin Sahl's *Nawāzil*; a fatwa of Makhluf al-Balbali; and finally, Idrissi's *Kitāb al-Rujār* and Bakri's *al-Masālik wal-mamālik*. Were these among the books that Baba had brought back from Marrakesh, part of his preexisting collection, or new additions to his library? What they do indicate is that, after his return to his hometown, he still had books and was always keen to cite from well-known works. His library, whatever its state after the trek from Marrakesh back to Timbuktu, remained in use. He used his books as a scholar to assert his claims and authority. It could be that he only remembered these works as having relevant information.

Hajari, who had bid Baba farewell in Marrakesh, remained in touch with him. Baba remained important to him and so, when he returned from his travels in Europe—visiting the Netherlands, France, and other countries—he wrote to Baba about his trip. He received a reply. Despite all the challenges and the possibility of caravans being attacked, the mail managed to reach the hands of its intended recipients. Baba thus wrote to Hajari and advised him to write as much and precisely as possible about the lands he was visiting. Baba's writing about tobacco, the calendar, and Hajari's trip to Europe, and Baba's interest in writing about it, are all indications of an engaged scholar open to the changes underway in the early modern world. Timbuktu might have then become infamous as a place at the very end of the world, but Ahmad Baba of Timbuktu was aware of a larger world beyond it.

Baba's Legacy: His Students

Ahmad Baba died in Timbuktu in April 1627 and he was buried in a cemetery in the town. There is no mausoleum marking his place of burial. He was not treated like a saint and his burial site never became a place of veneration. In recent times, a small house close to the Sankoré Mosque was said to have been his residence, which cannot be verified. It is not clear whether he had a wife or wives, children, or any other descendants, and if so, what happened to them. Similarly, we do not know the fate of any of the other Aqits of Timbuktu. There is one reference, from Baba's time in Marrakesh, to a son and grandson who died there, both named Muhammad. This could be possible but there are no details at all about these descendants. Felix Du Bois, the journalist discussed in chapter 1 who followed the French conquest, claimed that he met two great-grandsons of Baba during his stay in Timbuktu in 1894, but there is only his word for this claim.

Regarding the situation when Baba returned to Timbuktu, there are no references to members of his family who might have survived the conquest and subsequent disruptions. Could they have reunited after his return to Timbuktu? Did they care for the family property and did he live with them after his return? We are left with nothing certain, not a single detail relating to his personal or family life. Likewise, there were no descendants who became scholars and carried the Aqit name directly from Baba into the future. All these gaps mean that there was no information about his personal papers—drafts, completed texts, and correspondence—or documentation about what happened to his library, part of which he would have inherited locally. If there were descendants, his books could have been divided among them as part of a bequest or inheritance. But we do not know if this was the case. Copies of his works are scattered across the Sahel and North Africa, and many are later copies.

Some of Baba's students left behind impressions of their teacher.[16] A number of the men who read books with him in Marrakesh left a record of their interaction with him. However, of the students from his hometown, there is only one who mentions him, although he obviously had more students. The scholars who wrote about him were the most prominent of his students, but we must assume that there were others as well. There were also the auditors who attended his public lectures and who were, strictly speaking, not his students. Among those whom he taught specific texts, we only have information about a few: Maqqari, Marrakushi, Hashtuki, Sa'di, Fihri, Marrakushi, Ibn al-Qadi, Ghassani, and Tamanarti (to give only their shortened names).

A few of Baba's students in Marrakesh deserve some discussion. One of them was Abu 'Abdullah Muhammad bin Ya'qub al-Isi al-'Adib al-Marrakushi, born in Marrakesh in 1558, who received all his education among reputable scholars of the city. He studied with Baba over many years and grew close to him until he was freed to leave in 1607. He completed reading several works with Baba and received permission from him to teach them. His closeness to and high regard for his teacher is reflected in the entry on Baba that he wrote in his now-lost *Fahrasa* (catalog / bibliography), which speaks highly of his teacher, gives a number of titles of works he wrote, and names the works Marrakushi studied with him. Baba, in turn, used part of this description in his own biographical note on himself at the end of his second biographical dictionary, *Kifāyat al-muḥtāj*. It is worth noting that Marrakushi served as a secretary in the court of the Sultan Ahmad al-Mansur. According to Marrakushi's description of Baba, where he mentions the books Baba wrote, Marrakushi knew of the work on scholars and rulers (discussed in chapter 3) but this was not a deterrent to him serving at the court of the ruler. And Baba, in turn, did not mind having him as a student.

The other student was the widely traveled Abu l'Abbas Ahmad bin Yahya al-Tilmisani al-Maqqari, who was born into a well-known, learned family in Tlemcen, in present-day Algeria, in 1577. Maqqari was around twenty years old when Baba was released to start teaching, and was much younger than Marrakushi, who was then in his late thirties. By the time Baba arrived in Marrakesh, Maqqari was already living there and, despite his relative youth, he was known at the court. Maqqari was a scholar loyal to the ruling house. In the same work in which he gives generous space to Baba, he offers a dedication to Sultan Mansur who had, of course, ordered the invasion of Timbuktu that led to Baba's exile. Maqqari produced a biographical dictionary, *Rawdat al-ās*, and compiled a large, multivolume history of Muslim Andalusia, *Nafḥ al-tīb min guṣn al-Andalus al-raṭīb*. In Maqqari's biographical dictionary about the "scholars whom I met in the two metropolises of Marrakesh and Fez," he informs his readers about the works of Baba and displays immense respect for him.[17] Maqqari writes that he accompanied Baba on visits to local learned men when Baba was collecting information for his own works. Maqqari writes that his teacher from Timbuktu would allow him to use books from his own collection. Maqarri read Baba's works with keen interest and knew which of them were completed or still in progress. Baba granted him permission to teach numerous works that he had studied with him. Baba also shared a draft of his first biographical dictionary—*Nayl al-ibtihāj*—with him. A few years after the departure of his teacher, Maqqari became imam at the Qarawiyyin Mosque in Fez, one of the oldest and most significant institutions in the city. Maqqari died in Cairo in 1632.

There is one case in Baba's career of a student who learned from him entirely by correspondence. Abu Zayd bin Muhammad al-Jazuli al-Tamanarti knew about Baba and had heard about him from other students in Marrakesh, but did not meet him. Nevertheless, wanting to benefit from his learning, he wrote to Baba in Timbuktu asking for an ijaza to teach certain books. The exact arrangements of the teaching of the texts by correspondence is not explained anywhere. Tamanarti did get the desired permission, and wrote an entry on Baba in his biographical dictionary. He rose to the position of judge and mufti (chief judge) in Taroundant, a small town south of Marrakesh en route into the Sahara, where he died in 1662. Despite Tamanarti's exertion to have Baba in his intellectual pedigree, he did not consider Baba beyond criticism. He took another view on the question of tobacco to that of Baba, who argued that it was permissible to consume. Tamanarti disagreed, and said so.

Baba's Last Timbuktu Student

The nephew of Baba's own teacher from his earlier Timbuktu days, Muhammad Baghayogho, was also Baba's student, and so was ʿAbd al-Rahman al-Saʿdi. About the former there is no further information, but the latter is much better known because he emerged as the most important chronicler from Timbuktu. His writings were, for a long time, seen as among the handful of worthwhile written products from Timbuktu. There was even some confusion between Saʿdi and Baba for some nineteenth-century travelers, as we saw in chapter 1. Baba's own works were better known in the scholarly circles around Marrakesh during his time there but also after his return to Timbuktu and in the years immediately after his death. His student Saʿdi's *Tārīkh al-Sūdān* (Chronicle of the Land of the Blacks) became an important book in the latter half of the seventeenth century and thereafter, and was (and remains) probably much better known than any of Baba's works.

Only the bare outlines of the biography of Saʿdi are known; even his death date is unknown, but his *Tārīkh al-Sūdān* became an essential source for the history of the region. ʿAbd al-Rahman bin ʿAbd Allah bin ʿImran al-Saʿdi (d. after 1655/56) said that he studied with Baba but he does not say for how long or, more importantly, which books he had read with him. Saʿdi was about fourteen years old when Baba returned to Timbuktu and thirty-three years old when Baba died, so he studied with him at some point between his fifteenth year and his late twenties. Around the time of Baba's death in 1626/27, he was appointed the imam of the Sankoré Mosque of Jenne. He was then employed by the Arma rulers in the administration of Jenne and Masina and in 1646 he became the chief secretary of the Arma in Timbuktu.

ʿAbd al-Rahman al-Saʿdi probably wrote the chronicle after the death of Baba. In it, he discusses the rise of the major powers of the region until the Saʿdian invasion; the latter parts are based on his own experiences of the occupation. He wrote it to record "the stories and historical traditions that have been handed down about the kings of the Sudan, the Songhay folk [*ahl Sughay*], their conduct, and their military exploits, recounting the foundation of Timbuktu" and so on.[18] He includes in the chronicle a part of his teacher's biographical dictionary, the *Kifāyat al-muḥtāj*, when he writes of the scholars of the region. One of the ways in which the legacy of Baba was established or reestablished in subsequent centuries was through this extract in Saʿdi's chronicle. In chapter 1, we saw how Heinrich Barth attributed the chronicle to Baba, and later how Felix Du Bois corrected Barth. Barth made his assessment probably because he was given a part of the chronicle that was an extract from Baba's work. For many scholars in the twentieth century, it was Sa'di who had preeminence, because he provided the outlines of a political narrative for the region. His teacher had a larger and more complicated corpus ranging across of wide array of topics.

Sa'di, as author of the *Tārīkh al-Sūdān*, which he wrote as a government employee, was concerned with the past of the Songhay, Mali, the Tuareg, and the scholars of Timbuktu, and he did not spare criticism of the rulers then in power. There is little trace of the sources he used but he took an extract from Baba's *Kifāyat al-muḥtāj*, and also used his own observation, especially in his last chapter (chapter 30). He writes of Baba as the "jurist, the erudite scholar, unique in his time and alone in his age, who excelled in all branches of learning," recognized even in the Maghreb and the small settlements of the outlying areas.[19] He recognizes that his teacher did not accept the authority of the people for whom he himself was working. He adds a mystical touch to his teacher's body. He writes that the "name of Muhammad was written on his upper right arm as a birthmark in white letters."[20] About the latter, there is no other evidence. Sa'di earned an entry in a biographical dictionary prepared by a scholar from Walata named Bartili (d. 1805), who used Sa'di's chronicle extensively in his own work.

By the time of Baba's death in 1627, Timbuktu had for many years no longer been attracting students or scholars. The Sa'dian invasion and the chaos that followed in the 1590s left Timbuktu without its men of learning and without the qualities in which students from around the region would want to travel to study. The invasion had a long-term detrimental effect on living conditions in the town. Moreover, the learned community was dramatically reduced in size and importance. Baba's death was a symbol of the intellectual decline of Timbuktu that had started earlier. About thirty years after Baba's disappearance from the scene, the death of Sa'di in the late 1650s was another turning point in the history of writing and scholarship in Timbuktu. Sa'di was educated to be an influential scholar but chose an administrative career. To go from imam at the main mosque of Jenne to secretary was probably unheard of before this; it was a change in the career path in the region. It represents in stark terms the shift in attitudes and material conditions in Timbuktu. From the mid- to late seventeenth century onward, the locations where scholars and books were produced moved elsewhere in the larger region. The areas to the far west of Timbuktu began to emerge; there was a rapid expansion of learning centers and book-centered learning that took off in what was called the Bilad Shinqit, to which we turn in the next chapter.

5

The Rise of Shinqit

WHEN THE Sa'dian soldiers entered Timbuktu, education was dealt a severe blow. The death of the chronicler 'Abd al-Rahman al-Sa'di in the 1650s capped the decades-long dispersal of highly literate men. In better times, Timbuktu had welcomed scholars from elsewhere. Likewise, when Timbuktu was under attack, the elite had fled looking for refuge in towns and settlements where they had family or colleagues. Ahmad Baba felt the effects of the flight of the educated people after his return from exile. By the time of the death of possibly his last student, the chronicler Sa'di, the "disappearance of learning," as he would have termed it, was virtually complete. Sa'di's advanced literacy led to his recruitment as a scribe and secretary to the Arma rulers and he had to juggle this role with his calling as a scholar. Had he not been employed, he might have written more than his single, important work. Perhaps he did write more but there is no trace of his other works. However, despite the departure of so many educated residents, basic reading and writing skills did not disappear; they were far too deeply rooted in the society. There was always some teaching and learning in progress. Basic schooling in homes and among families did not come to an end during the occupation and there were always teachers who taught the essentials of religion and law. But there are no outstanding local writers to recall from the later seventeenth century.

The Arma rulers had seen to the production of at least two similar chronicles of governors, or *pashas*, as they termed themselves—effectively the rulers over Timbuktu—since their arrival on the scene. The *Dīwān al-mulūk fī salāṭīn al-Sūdān* and *Tadhkirat al-nisyān* are dated to the late 1730s and cover a 150-year period; the latter title is largely a summary of the former. By the time of their composition the Arma had set down roots and integrated with the native Songhay speakers and other groups. These works were meant to give them significance in a place where they were never completely accepted and at a time when their authority had, for some time already, been in serious question. From Timbuktu itself, there are few other works of scholarly prose that were written, copied, and passed down in the decades after these chronicles. The basic text of the chronicle, called the *Tārīkh al-fattāsh* (Chronicle of the investigator), was possibly produced in this period—the latter half of the seventeenth century—and was elaborated on and backdated a century later (about which more will be said in the next chapter). The arrival of the Kuntas in the early nineteenth century, headed by Sidi Mukhtar al-Kunti (see chapter 6), would eventually make the town attractive again for students in the quest for higher learning.

The impact of the conquest of Timbuktu was still felt for many generations, but the towns and settlements to its distant west, in a region called Bilad Shinqit, experienced a major expansion of literacy and indeed a literary revival. Whereas Timbuktu's writing elite almost disappeared in the wake of the occupation, in the lands to the west a series of battles that stretched over three decades had the opposite effect; they stimulated a small, highly literate elite to turn out a prodigious volume of texts. A series of battles of conquest destroyed a scholarly culture in the 1590s in one place, and in another part of the Sahara a war stimulated scholarship less than a century later, from around the 1640s to the 1670s, as if the fall of Timbuktu eventually enabled the rise of Shinqit.

Where Was Shinqit?

Shinqit, or Shinguitt, also transliterated as Chinguetti in Francophone scholarship, refers to a settlement in the western parts of the Sahara, the area called the Adrar.[1] Bilad Shinqit (Land of Shinqit) was a term used to describe the larger territory approximating to the central region of modern Mauritania. Bilad Shinqit was a colonial administrative entity created by the French in 1899. In some descriptions, it was much larger, reaching as far as Timbuktu. As a name for a specific place, it refers to a small town, or *qasr*, in local terms, that emerged around an oasis in the center of the country, the Adrar, famous for date palm cultivation and other agricultural activity in a series of oases. To the west Bilad Shinqit reached to the Atlantic coast, while its eastern boundaries included the settlements of Walata and Ni'ma. The latter settlements had close connections with Timbuktu so that, in practice, Timbuktu could be considered part of the Bilad Shinqit. Shinqit and Timbuktu, standing about 650 kilometers apart, both evolved into centers for trade, with effectively no great difference in the periods when they were said to have come into being or developed from watering and meeting points for long-distance traders traversing the desert. Significantly, like Timbuktu, Shinqit attracted writers, teachers, and poets. Both gained enormous reputations beyond their nominal borders. If Timbuktu's scholars often came from elsewhere, such as Jenne, and went beyond Timbuktu, then Shinqit was also connected with other settlements through migration; it was one of a number of places that came to have a reputation for their educated populations and scholars of great repute. In the late nineteenth and through the twentieth centuries (and into the present) in parts of the Arabian Peninsula, especially in the holy cities of Mecca and Medina, Shinqiti and Shanaqita ("Shinqitis") came to refer to men of learning who came from this part of West Africa.

In the vast, sparsely populated, mostly uncultivatable lands of Shinqit, two cultural processes were intricately connected: first, how the population, led by the elites, adopted the form of Islam that became dominant in the region; and second, how they began to use Arabic as a spoken and written language (and transformed the Arabic language). The two developments were intertwined. The Berber Sanhaja population of Shinqit converted to Islam gradually; in the mid-eleventh century, the Almoravid movement, based around Marrakesh, which they had founded, pressed southward and brought the Sanhaja population closer to their version of orthodoxy and proper religious practice. This meant ensuring the dominance of the Maliki school of law and a moderate Ash'arite theology. There is limited evidence from the twelfth century to the seventeenth century of the actual state of Islamic practice and learning in these lands. The Arabic writers relied on for this period, such as Bakri (d. 1094) and Ibn Battuta (d. 1368), discussed in chapter 1, all give us a sense that there were active, practicing Muslim communities with mosques, public rituals, and learning in progress in various small settlements and towns. Their reports describe mosques—or spaces dedicated to prayer—and encounters with teachers in some settlements such as Tichitt, Wadan (Ouadane), Walata, and, further from Shinqit, Timbuktu. In Ahmad Baba's work he described his ancestors as learned men who had active ties with Walata by the fifteenth century. When they were attacked by the ruler Sonni Ali, they took refuge in Walata.

Steady conversion to Islam, and the growth of Islamic institutions and public practices such as Friday prayers, did not, of course, mean that Muslims used Arabic outside of ritual and liturgical contexts. Widespread use of Arabic can only be dated, for the earliest, to the fourteenth century. The Arabic-speaking and self-declared Arab tribe called the Banu Maghfar (one of the tribes of the larger Banu Hassan confederation) moved increasingly into the region, leading to more linguistic change, that of Arabicization. In the process, in the fusion with the local Berber language, a new dialect was created that came to be called Hasaniyya (probably because it originated with the Banu Hasan). Writers would use classical Arabic but also this dialect for self-expression, using the Arabic script to write it. The native Berber language, Znaga, did not, of course, disappear. A similar process of Arabicization occurred across all of North Africa. The historian Charles Stewart has put it succinctly: "Berber populations adopted Islam, then absorbed Arab migrants, and finally emerged as quasi-Arabs themselves. At the same time, the Arab migrants absorbed local custom, their language took on loan words and, in a way, can be said to have become quasi-Berbers."[2] Literary output grew out of the contestation between those claiming descent from Berbers or Arab ancestors. But nobody among the still-small literate elite would have foreseen that a conflict that led to a series of armed engagements and that evolved into a war, would stimulate the distinctive poetry and prose of Shinqit.

The Shurr Bubba War of the 1640s to 1670s

In the late 1640s, conflict erupted in the southwestern areas of Shinqit, called the Gibla. With time, the sporadic local-level fighting spread over the larger Shinqit as more fatalities and injuries were reported. The skirmishes would drag on over many years and eventually grew into an all-out war. The battles took place between the fighters of the loosely allied confederations, the Zwaya, whose men were largely teachers and scholars, on the one side, and the Hassani Maghfar Arabs, on the other. The latter, properly called Banu or Awlad Hassan, claimed ancestry going back to eleventh-century immigrants from the southern Arabian Peninsula (contemporary Yemen). They were the so-called Arabs of Shinqit, who over the centuries had won the right to bear arms and levy protection taxes (called *gharama* or *hurma*) on groups they had conquered. Standing against these warriors were the mostly Berber Zwaya groups who were made up of literate and highly educated writers and poets who were schooled in theology and Islamic law. Bilad Shinqit was a highly stratified territory with the Hasan (warriors) and Zwaya (learned) occupying the upper echelons, and the warriors usually above the learned. Below them all were the Haratin, or slaves, and other servile groups. In theory there were definite, impermeable barriers that held back any movement up the hierarchies and between the various levels of the hierarchy. There was a discourse around origins and identity that drew on the past and found expression in poetry and song, expressing ethnic fixity and durability. But, in practice, these were the models of Shinqiti society that were challenged and transgressed, yet terms and categories like "tribe" with the connotation of fixed "tribal" identity, persisted.

The main cause of the war was a dispute over who had the right to specify which taxes were to be paid and who was to collect them. The scholars from among the Zwaya argued that the Hasan tribes had to pay the zakat tax—nominally a 2.5 percent tax stipulated by Islamic schools of law, including the Maliki school followed in the region—but they refused to obey the instructions of those they considered below them. The Zwaya saw it as an obligation on them to instruct others, including the Banu Hasan, in their religious duties, in this case paying the obligatory wealth tax. Members of the Zwaya could instruct the children of the Hasan but instructing the parents to pay a tax was going too far.

The protracted conflict that ensued—the so-called war of "Shurr Bubba," which was reportedly a war cry—was a turning point in the region's history. It seems that the actual armed conflict was of rather shorter duration than the longer and larger impact of the conflict. One figure emerged as the hero of the conflict: a leader known in the later narratives only as Nasir al-Din. He was behind a missionary project called the movement of repentance (*tawbah*) that was concerned with converting (and reforming those already Muslim) peoples in the south, on both sides of the Senegal River. When the conflict heated up, he is said to have assumed the leadership role among the Zwaya. He led the Zwaya against the Hasan but died before the end of the conflict, probably around 1674. The war ended in 1677 with the Hasani warriors ultimately the victors. In narratives of the war, Nasir al-Din of the losing Zwaya side was, however, ironically but ultimately the hero of the Shurr Bubba War.

The Hasani's victory gave them power of arms over others and also rights to collect taxes. The people of the Zwaya withdrew to concern themselves with studies. The groups that were considered Zwaya now had to find Hasani protectors; both of these sets had other clients, who were herders and cultivators. Among those at the bottom of the hierarchy along with the Haratin (freed slaves) were the praise singers, minstrels and singers, and metalsmiths. The Shurr Bubba War was a crucial occurrence and became a founding myth for later generations across Shinqit.

The defeat of the Zwaya did not, however, lead to their silence. Instead, as they turned to their duties there was a growth of education and scholarship in their ranks. This conflict was a milestone not only because it consolidated the power of the warrior groups and secured the hierarchies of Shinqit, but because the scholars responded with words, and with the written word in particular. The only problem with this narrative is that it could be a "myth" *not* in the sense that everything was made up and nothing happened in reality. The war does occupy a major place in the foundational narratives of Shinqiti society due to later descriptions by members of the scholarly elite. In this literature a template for the structure of Shinqiti society, as it then existed, was produced. The historian H. T. Norris has concluded that: "It is now apparent that the story of the war, and the martyrdom of its leaders, more especially of the Imam . . . Nasir al-Din al Daymani, is a record of several events which have been woven together into a hagiographical narrative, diversified into a series of Chronicles."[3]

Education: A Weapon of the Defeated

No matter how the Shurr Bubba narratives are read—as myth or hard fact—it is probably around this time that the Zwaya became even more committed to their role as educators. We do not know how or when this started but, throughout the territories covered in this book, the earliest travelers or writers on the region made references to some teaching and books. Bakri had already noted teaching at a mosque in the oasis settlement of Awdaghust in the eleventh century. This was probably not yet an example of the educational system in Shinqit, the *Mahadra*, as it is called in the Hasaniyya Arabic dialect. The Mahadra was the Zwaya educational innovation.[4]

The Mahadra was not for beginners, but for students with potential to become teachers themselves. However, there was an educational system in place that provided basic skills to all children. Among the Zwaya families, children were taught at home to memorize and read basic Quranic verses and the shorter chapters, and how to perform basic rituals such as ablutions and daily prayers. Memorizing the entire Quran (more than six thousand verses) by a young age was not an exceptional achievement at home or in the early stages of traditional schools. Mothers and other women teachers were important at this stage. All children got an education, but not of the same duration: this depended on gender and social rank. Of course, children from the learned Zwaya families were more thoroughly trained. Some basics were taught by mothers, such as the alphabet, stories from the life of the Prophet Muhammad, liturgies, and melodies, even before children went to school. After about the age of seven or eight, the talented boys would be sent to join an elementary school, usually one from within their "tribe." Each region had towns or qasrs with such schools, so they were widespread, and the genealogies of these schools, their founders and leading teachers, were easily recalled and known. The schools were sustained by nominal payments and gifts to the scholar; importantly, the pupils contributed their labor—for instance, herding cattle, working in the field at harvesting time, and so on. The schools were very often "on the move" in and under tents apart from regular sedentary locations.

All young pupils used a wooden tablet (*lawh*) to write out lessons; it would be wiped clean after verses were memorized. In some schools, the boards were sometimes cleaned with water, which was then drunk in the belief that such water had holy properties.

The Mahadra were places that entailed memorizing and studying texts, following tutorials or a one-to-one, scholar-teacher method. Over a number of years, the students would cover a series of texts, from basic grammar and theology through to law. They only needed a wooden board, reed pen, and homemade ink to join classes. This system evolved over many centuries and so did the curriculum. Poetry, for instance, was only studied from the early nineteenth century, according to the Mauritanian scholar Mokhtar Ould Bah.[5] Not all the students became scholars, but the years of learning among boys and young men studying the same or similar texts created solidarities and traditions that buttressed the values of Zwaya society and influenced the whole of the Bilad Shinqit.

There were also some regional differences in the schooling, so that in the east (a region called the Hodh), the children of the metalsmiths spent a longer time in school. In some regions, it was preferred to send children to the school of a stranger or anyone who was not a family member. The children of the teachers themselves left their homes to search for learning further from home. This traveling to learn is an old tradition and conforms to the *talab al-ʿilm* (going far in search of knowledge) concept, going back to an aphorism of the Prophet Muhammad in which he is reported to have advised going in search of knowledge "even as far as China."

The Mahadra was a higher level of schooling with several teachers, and is still an institution of significance in Mauritania. The Mahadra proper is introduced when a child is between twelve and fifteen years. The Mahadra was both a particular place and a nomadic institution; it started in towns and then moved with nomads. Al-Bartili, from Walata, (more on him below) described the study program. He mentioned the books studied. He noted the presence of women students and teachers, such as Khadija bint Muhammad al-ʿAqil al-Daymaniyya.[6] Apparently, among her students was the famous grammarian Mukhtar bin Buna al-Jakani.[7] She wrote a commentary on the famous *Umm al-barāhīn* (a work of theology) and composed works in the margins of the *Sullam al-Akhḍarī* and *Nazm al-ṭayyiba*, both on logic. She died in 1835/36.

The model of a curriculum, as described by Bartili and others, prepared students for going out to teach and eventually developing the competence to give legal opinions. For Quranic studies, students would become proficient in a style of recitation called *warsh*; some mastered seven variant readings of the holy book.

In *tafsir* (exegesis), the works of the great Persian scholar Tabari were the most studied, but other exegetes studied were Gharnati, Qurtubi, Ibn Kathir, and Suyuti, names familiar throughout the scholarly world of Islam. Few Shinqiti scholars wrote commentaries on the Quran; Muhammad Yadali wrote one and Sidi al-Mukhtar al-Kunti and a few others did brief commentaries on parts of the Quran. In hadith studies, the standard six books of hadith were read; the *Muwaṭṭa'* of Imam Malik was later added and *al-Shifā'* of Qadi 'Iyad read for the blessings. One commentary on the hadith work of Bukhari by a local scholar was also used. On the life of the Prophet (*sira*), students studied a poem by Miknasi and a work by Majlisi; for blessings, they read Busiri's *Burda* and *Hamziyya*. On theology, the works of the main theological school of Sunni Islam, the Ash'arites, were read. They also used the sections on theology from legal works. There were local works on the subject by A'mash and al-Jakani. Sufism was not part of the curriculum but the work of Ghazali (d. 1111) was read and Ibn Ata Allah (d. 1310) was known and became popular among the students. They did not confine themselves to North African Sufi writers but, from that region they read mostly the works of the Shadhili writers such as Ibn Ata'illah. Local authors included Yadali, and the Kuntis (see the following chapter), and then, in the later nineteenth century, Ma al-'Anayn (d. 1910). An informal part of the Mahadra culture was the making of talismans and amulets for healing and protection. Jurisprudence (*fiqh*) was heavily studied, not the Quran and hadith on their own. Fiqh was a practical subject that addressed the concerns of society, pastoral and sedentary.

The Mahadra spread from the towns, the qasrs, to the countryside (*badiyya*). Mobility was part of life and nearly everyone would move extensively in the course of his or her life. Only the very elderly stayed in one place. There are many cases of movement between schools; students sought expertise in a text and would follow whoever they thought was the best teacher. The lessons were oral: the teachers taught from memory. The scholar al-Mukhtar bin Buna al-Jakani (d. 1805) described his use of the back of camels as teaching lecterns. The historian Khalil al-Nahwi listed twenty-four well-known Mahadra; all had manuscript book libraries. Oral transmission of knowledge and memorization were valued, but so was the written word.

Scholars after the War

It is extremely difficult to pin down when and how the curriculum and teaching methods described above were adopted, or adapted, and spread in Shinqit, and indeed far beyond. The Mahadra is held up as the traditional system of schooling in Mauritania that has persisted through the centuries. Some aspects, such as memorization by the very young at home with the mother, could be centuries old; others were later innovations following the post-conflict flourishing of scholarship. Even after colonialism and the introduction of print, however, the use of printed books remained a rarity in these schools. Cultivating a good calligraphic hand and making texts into manuscript books were emphasized.

The Shurr Bubba War and its consequences were described by the writers who emerged in the aftermath of the war. Were these writers the products of this evolving system of education? We know only their names and works and, in a few instances, their main teachers, but get no sense of the system they went through to acquire their impressive skills of poetic and prose composition. They were not participants in the war and, to whatever extent the war was an actual historical event or series of events, the fact is that only *after* the date of its supposed termination are there scholars whose works and influence extended across Shinqit.

The following five writers are among the most important in Shinqit in the eighteenth century (and stretching a decade or two beyond, when the last of them passed on). There are many more whose names appear in biographical dictionaries, some whose works are still circulating, and others for whom there is no trace of a text, only a proper name and book titles. The following five were the most prolific and influential.

(1) ʿAbd Allah bin Muhammad bin Raziqa (d. 1731) is considered "the first poet" of Shinqit because of his poetic ingenuity.[8] He was known in short as "would Raziqa" (son of Raziqa), which was his mother's name. Such matrilineal significance in names was a feature of Shinqiti society. Numerous epithets were applied to his name, such as, "He brought the crown to poetry," as another scholar of this period Muhammad al-Yadali, put it.[9] He began his studies in Wadan then moved to southwestern Mauritania (the *Gibla*), and hardly knew a fixed residence, traveling for most of his life. Such mobility was not uncommon among students and scholars, although even by Shinqiti standards he was exceptionally mobile, always on the move. His incessant traveling included many trips outside the northern boundaries of Shinqit, even as far as to meetings with Mulay Ismail, the ʿAlawi ruler who conquered and ruled from Marrakesh between 1672 and 1727. At one stage, some members of his tribe considered him *amir* (here meaning the nominal governor) of the Traza region in the southwest, and this in addition to his status as a renowned scholar were the grounds for him to meet the ʿAlawite ruler. Wuld Raziqa befriended and grew close to Mulay Ismail's son, who was himself a man of learning, and the son reportedly gave him a large

library of books on one of his trips to Meknes. While Raziqa's name is known, his writings have not survived and remain, for the most part, missing, with only fragments surviving in private collections. Extracts of his poetry are found in the early twentieth century work *al-Wasīṭ*, discussed below.

(2) Muhammad bin al-Mukhtar al-Sa'id al-Yadali al-Daymani (d. 1753) was the author of numerous books including the praise poem (*madih*) to the Prophet Muhammad, known by its opening phrase *Ṣalātu Rabī* for which he was famous far beyond Shinqit.[10] It is still recited in Mauritania and elsewhere in North Africa and the Middle East. *Shiyam al-Zwaya* is a text attributed to him that seeks to describe Zwaya society. Works titled *Ghazawāt Shurr Bubba* (The Shurr Bubba wars) and *Amr al-wali Nāṣir al-Dīn* are attributed to him; given that they deal with the conflict, he is the most important chronicler of the Shurr Bubba War, although the events unfolded well before his birth. It is possible that he heard stories about the conflict from his parents because his father was apparently involved in the conflict. He followed what was then the educational program of the Zwaya children, memorizing a great deal of poetry, learning to read and write on wooden tablets, and gradually moving through the curriculum even as the family moved around. His story, much of it an account of his miracles, is told by Nabigha al-Ghallawi in a book he called *al-Najm al-thāqib*. Ghallawi was close to students of Yadali. In incidental fashion, we learn that Yadali's inkwell was one of his favorite objects, and that he kept a notebook with quotes from other books, probably for later use in his own writing. It was called a *shufrud*, which Ghallawi glosses as a *fihrist* (index). He wrote dozens of works in various genres. *Ṣalātu Rabī* was his most widely used text. Yadali once went to the Atlantic coast where he boarded a boat going to the small island of Arguin. The boat was rocked by strong winds but, because the *Salatu Rabi* was recited, the wind subsided. The sailors, who were Dutch, were so relieved and happy with him that at the end of the trip they presented him with "rare objects and a gift of laid paper."[11]

Yadali wrote on theology, grammar, legal works, exegesis, and poetry. His short work *Khātimat al-taṣawwuf* is a significant Shinqiti statement on the nature of Sufism and received its own commentaries in later years. He was not part of any Sufi order known in the region at the time and he was not writing as a member or leader of one, although there is a suggestion that he belonged to the Shadhili order. His commentary on the Quran had reached four volumes at the time of his death. It was said that "If he required the books, other than his own (for reference), he would read (the works) in two days, then return them speedily."[12] He wrote even when on the move, making sure that he found a shady place to write. He wrote when others slept and completed a stint of writing in the morning and again at night. He said that "had I not been a nomad I would have written as many works as al-Suyuti," referring to the great Egyptian polymath 'Abd al-Rahman al-Suyuti (d. 1505). Nabigha al-Ghallawi said that, when Yadali died, around a thousand works were found with him.[13]

(3) Walid al-Daymani, whose full name was Muhammad Walid wuld Mustafa wuld Khaluna (d. 1797) was an outstanding pupil of Yadali.[14] He is the author of a work on the saints of the Tashumsha branch of the Zwaya and, in particular, of his own tribe, the Banu Dayman. The historian H. T. Norris has shown how Daymani was pressed into writing the history despite not being able to verify any of the information contained in it. He wrote at least two long poems, of 280 and 180 verses respectively, in Hasaniyya meter and in the Znaga Berber language, filled with Arabic words. The poems include allusions to works highly regarded by the Zwaya.

(4) Nabigha al-Ghallawi (d. 1829) was from the Awlad Musa and is described as a man of knowledge and piety.[15] He left Walata sometime after 1794. He found a suitable teacher in the Trarza; he excelled in his studies, and was also a student of Muhammad al-Yadali. The works he produced on grammar and law are numerous.

(5) Lastly, al-Ṭalib Muhammad Abu Bakr al-Siddiq al-Bartili al-Walati (d. 1805) completed his biographical dictionary *Fatḥ al-Shakūr fī ma'rifat a'yān 'ulamā al-Takrūr* around 1800.[16] It contains just over two hundred entries. It is worth noting that Bartili uses the term "Takrur" and not "Shinqit" in his title.[17] In the medieval period, "Takrur" was one of the terms used by Arabic writers to describe West Africa. Bartili does not explain his choice, but his preferment of this term over "Shinqit" could be significant. Did he use "Takrur" to express a wider perspective than is conveyed by "Shinqit"? Bartili's work bridges the so-called Shinqit and Timbuktu divide. Later, the collector Ahmad Bularraf used "Takrur" and "Shinqit" together in the title of his biographical dictionary (see chapter 7). It could be that Bartili's location in Walata, right on the eastern edges of Bilad Shinqit, led him to embrace a larger perspective.[18] The earliest scholar in Bartili's work was from the 1460s, from Timbuktu, and was closely identified with it and the Sidi Yahya Mosque. He also included a long entry on Ahmad Baba, notably the first biographical notice on Baba since the mid-seventeenth-century remarks in the *Tārīkh al-Sūdān*, which had extracted heavily from Baba's own biographical dictionary.

Like all the other books from Bartili's time, *Fatḥ al-Shakūr* circulated as a manuscript book. Between three and seven copies circulated, not all made at the same time. The last extant one was made in 1818. It was edited and published by two prominent Moroccan manuscript scholars, Kattani and Hajji, in 1981, and edited again and translated into French by another Moroccan scholar, Chouki El Hamel, in 2002. Another edition published in Cairo appeared in 2010. c *Fatḥ al-Shakūr* ties together the preceding chapters of this book and the following chapters. Through the inclusion of Ahmad Baba, his ancestors the Aqits, his teacher Wangari, and Abdurrahman al-Sa'di and others from the Azawad region, Bartili indicated a path for us to understand a larger world of writing that places Timbuktu within the Bilad Shinqit and demonstrates the connections and links across a vast terrain over at least five centuries.

We have introduced five writers who were active from the mid-eighteenth to early nineteenth centuries. Many more could be mentioned. If we take only the writers mentioned by Ahmad bin al-Amin al-Shinqiti in *al-Wasīṭ* (The mediator), for instance, many more could have been mentioned. Based on names in the contents page of this work, at least seventy authors would have to be discussed. Around the time of its publication in 1911 there were more works by scholars who were collecting data for French colonial research projects in West Africa; they noted additional scholars. However, these five scholars cannot go unmentioned because of their enormous influence in their own time and beyond, as writers, poets, and leaders. The literary impact of Shinqit continued through the nineteenth century; we shall see how, through the Kunta family, Bilad Shinqit and the Azawad region around Timbuktu became much more deeply entangled.

From *al-Wasīṭ* to the Beginning of Colonial Collecting

In 1911, a scholar from Shinqit published a large tome of nearly six hundred pages, in which he introduced his homeland to the world beyond it, in a single volume. Ahmad bin al-Amin al-Shinqiti called his work *al-Wasīṭ fī tarājim ʻudabā Shinqīṭ* (The mediator on the writers of Shinqit).[19] *Al-Wasīṭ* became the standard reference on Shinqiti writers and any study of Mauritanian literary history has to start with it. As his name indicates, he identified as a man from Shinqit; an additional reason for this self-identification was that he lived far from his homeland, having taken up residence in Cairo over a decade earlier. This was the first work by a scholar from the region to attempt an account of the literary history of its people. It was also the first printed book about the Bilad Shinqit by one of its own writers.

Shinqiti's date of birth is unknown but estimated to be either around the 1860s or 1870s. We can see him going through the schooling system described above, from the lap of his mother to various teachers, learning to read and write and memorizing a copious amount of poetry and even whole books at a Mahadra. He left his homeland around 1892. The routes that he followed are unknown but he went to the east, and not only the Near East. He probably joined the annual pilgrimage caravan because he completed the hajj, visiting Mecca and Madina, where he met people from across the Muslim word. These encounters probably led him to travel further east. The editor's introduction to the second edition of *al-Wasīṭ* says that the author traveled to Central Asia, then under Russian imperial rule, and then back westward through Anatolia, where he visited famous mosques and libraries. He then went to Syria and finally arrived in Cairo in 1902. He struck up a relationship with Cairene scholars and especially with notable figures in the elite literary circles, such as the writers Muhammad Tawfiq al-Bakri, al-Manfaluti, and Ahmad Taymour. In Cairo, Shinqiti sat down to read and write, and to edit classical works. Apart from *al-Wasīṭ,* he published additional works, on Arabic grammar, pre-Islamic poetry, the etymology of the name 'Umar, and a polemical text on Sufism. Furthermore, he wrote commentaries on eight works. The Mauritanian writer Khalil al-Nahwi, who himself wrote a major work on the intellectual history of Mauritania, calls the author of *al-Wasīṭ* "The foremost Ambassador of Shinqit to the East."[20]

When Shinqiti arrived in Cairo, another writer from Shinqit—Muhammad Mahmud al-Talamidh al-Turkuzi—already had a reputation among the scholars of Al-Azhar University. It was common for students and scholars from the same region to gravitate to the living quarters of their countrymen in the neighborhoods close to the university. That is probably where the two Shinqitis met. They only had a brief two years at most to get to know each other. Turkuzi had by this time teaching duties at Al-Azhar and was working as an editor of scholarly editions of classical Arabic texts. He was a significant figure among the emerging publishers that were turning classic Arabic Islamic texts, until then only available as manuscript books, into printed ones. Cairo was then the center of Arabic book editing and printing. Turkuzi died in Cairo in 1904. It is possible that he introduced Shinqiti to this network of editors and publishers; Shinqiti also became involved in correcting and editing texts for publication in the burgeoning Arabic publishing world at the time. In this respect, Shinqiti's close relationship with the bibliophile and printer Amin al-Khanji was crucial. The Khanji library (*Maktab al-Khanji*) published *al-Wasīṭ* and his other books. Shinqiti died in Cairo in 1913.

How did Shinqiti collect the materials for *al-Wasīṭ*? Did others from Shinqit assist him? It is a tremendous feat of memory to reproduce all the poetry in the book, apart from all the other information. He might have traveled with manuscripts but even then, what his book introduces is far more than he could have carried on his travels, first to Mecca, then around imperial Russia, western Asia, and ultimately to Cairo. The work was produced far from informants and adequate written sources, and this shows in the unevenness of the coverage of the authors discussed in the book. He could have collected information from fellow countryman who had taken up residence in Cairo or were passing through, usually on the way to Mecca. But certainly, a large part of the text was produced from what he had memorized. Holding large amounts of material in one's head was part of the learning process at the time. Text-copying was accompanied by a great deal of memorization. In parts of Mauritania, this is still a practice.

Al-Wasīṭ covers a variety of topics: the name Shinqit, the geography, the conflicts and wars, the customs and music, the schooling system, and a host of other aspects of this *bilad* (country). Shinqiti tabulates numerous conflicts within and between regions and between various tribes. Importantly, he also covers the Hassan–Zwaya conflict, which, as we have seen, flared up only rarely as the latter were devoted to religion. He characterizes the Shurr Bubba War as a "religious war" given that it was caused by a contest over the religiously obligatory zakat tax. This description of Shinqiti history and culture is, however, not the main focus of the work. It was a supplement, of about 125 pages, to a book more than double that size focusing on important Shinqiti writers. They had all produced prodigious amounts of poetry and other kinds of writing such as the scholars discussed above (except for Bartili). Shinqiti discusses over 70 such figures, organized along the lines of their *qabila* or tribal affiliation. The complicated and shifting affiliations of so-called tribe, clan, and confederation, in theory structured along genealogical lines, were important forms of identification and social organization. Shinqiti belonged to the Idaw'Ali confederation and the poets and scholars from this group receive the largest share of the coverage. On the important early nineteenth-century figure Nabigha al-Ghallawi, Shinqiti includes an annex after the Idaw'Ali poets.

Shinqiti gives a number of biographical entries not arranged according to tribal affiliation, many of them on his contemporaries such as the Sufi leader Ma al-'Anayn (d. 1910), who had a following in the region west of Shinqit, in Saqia al-Hamra, and pursued a war against the French, eventually dying from wounds sustained in armed conflict. Shinqiti also included a short note on his colleague in Cairo, Muhammad M. Talamidh Turkuzi. The fact that he wrote on such contemporaries not only shows the breadth of his interests but also proves he was alert to news from the Maghreb and Shinqit, as is clear from his lengthy entry on Ma al-ʿAnayn, who was then negotiating with Moroccan rulers while battling the French.

Meanwhile, back in Shinqit, by 1913 the Sahara had been under French administration for just over a decade. The colonial administrators had been attempting to study this vast territory even before it was declared a French possession.[21] The death of Ma al-ʿAnayn in 1910 was a turning point. While he had called for an armed jihad against the French, his brother would become an iconic figure in the call against jihad and for cooperation with the French. Part of the French approach in colonizing the region was to use local knowledge and information. Ma al-ʿAnayn's brother, Saʿd Buh, was one such source of local knowledge. For this purpose, the colonial administrators collected oral narratives, testimonies about the structure of authority, and histories of conflicts and alliances among local notables. Written materials held a wealth of information on local conditions, about political conflicts among local groups, and about religious polemics. Such materials had to be collected from scholars and translated. Just two years before *al-Wasīṭ* appeared in Cairo as an Arabic printed book about Shinqit, in Paris a collection of Arabic texts about the same territory was published. The *Chroniques de la Mauritanie sénégalaise: Nacer eddine; Texte arabe, traduction et notice* appeared under the editorship of Ismaël Hamet in 1911. Hamet (d. 1932) was an Algerian translator for the French army. During his career, he would hold the position of *Officier interprète principal à l'État-major de l'armée* then *Professeur à l'École supérieure de langue arabe et de dialectes berbères de Rabat.* The *Chroniques de la Mauritanie sénégalaise* was collected and compiled by local scholars for the colonial official Théveniaut. Hamet provided a background historical essay to the collection, and other writers contributed essays on the history, geography, and other resources of the territory. The French translations of the texts are followed by printed Arabic texts, which had been presented as manuscripts, copied on commission by the French administrators. To what extent the Arabic texts reflect an "original" manuscript cannot be judged; but it is clear they were made on request or instruction, as each text says, "fait pour le commandant" (made for the commander). The French had found scholars prepared to work with them. The *Chroniques de la Mauritanie sénégalaise* included the narrative of "Amr el-oualy Nacer eddin," referring to the heroic figure Nasir al-Din, hero of the Shurr Bubba War.

In the following chapter we look at the Kunta family, who exemplified the Shinqit–Timbuktu connection. Then we look at Ahmad Bularraf, who enters this terrain from the Sus region of what is today Morocco. The Sus was never considered part of Shinqit or Takrur, but the Hasaniyya dialect was spoken there, just as in Shinqit, among some inhabitants. It is said that Bularraf visited Shinqit and spent some time there, probably reading texts with a scholar. His story is firmly placed in the colonial era, in the early years of the twentieth century. In the century before that, there were major conflicts and changes in the region, and Timbuktu was at the center of these historic events. The impact of the Kunta family in that era, as political leaders and merchants, as Sufis and writers, is a key part of the story of Timbuktu's significance in the nineteenth century. Their mobility and influence across the Sahara, across the Timbuktu–Shinqit and Takrur–Shinqit imaginary divides, deserves special attention.

6

The Kunta Writers

FROM TUWAT TO TIMBUKTU AND BEYOND

NO MATTER how generously one might want to stretch Bilad Shinqit on the map, it does not reach Tuwat, a name that is probably from a Berber dialect. Tuwat is a cluster of oasis settlements in southern Algeria, with a mixed population of mostly Arabs and Berbers. This thinly populated oasis is more than a thousand kilometers from Timbuktu and was only faintly on the radar of the medieval geographers, and the early modern and nineteenth-century explorers. However, it was not unknown: Ibn Battuta mentioned it in the 1350s, it appears on Abraham Cresques's *Catalan Atlas* of 1375, and the Genoan trader Antonio Malfante wrote about it after his visit in the 1440s. Malfante noted that in the tough desert setting, Tuwat had a relatively prosperous Jewish population. But about fifty years later, their situation changed from prosperity to precarity with the arrival in 1490 from Tlemcen, a Mediterranean coastal town, of the scholar ʿAbd al-Karim al-Maghili (d. 1505), who started a preaching campaign against the Jewish population. Despite stiff opposition to him from the local learned community, he succeeded in seeing them driven out.

One of the ways a desert settlement like Tuwat remained connected to other, larger towns was through the traders who would periodically show up. The traders often belonged to Sufi orders with members present in distant locations. At least two Sufi orders were established in Tuwat: the Qadiriyya, one of the oldest spiritual orders, going back to twelfth-century Baghdad, and the Shadhiliyya, whose founder hailed from the Maghreb but founded the order in Egypt in the thirteenth century. The Qadiriyya in the Sahara expanded rapidly when Shaykh Sidi Ahmad al-Bakkay, of the Kunta community in Tuwat, adopted the order in the early sixteenth century. According to Kunta tradition, his son Sidi Aʿmar al-Shaykh spread the order and the Qadiriyya spiritual center—Zawiyat

Kunta—was founded in Tuwat in the middle of the seventeenth century. Since the adoption of the Qadiriyya by a Kunti, the leadership of the order in the Sahara remained among them, from Tuwat to Timbuktu and beyond.[1]

Beyond the oases of Tuwat, further into the Sahara, a caravan would move across a harsh and sun-drenched landscape for many days, sometimes weeks, without encountering a settlement. Depending on the direction they took, the salt mines of Taoudeni could be reached. For centuries, mines were dug into the earth to chisel out slabs of salt. At the salt mines, large numbers of miners would be met by the traders and, after negotiations about the prices and quality of the salt, the camels were loaded with the salt slabs to leave for Timbuktu. Going there directly would take at least two weeks. Among the commercial interests of the Kunta was the vital supply of salt. The Kunta were heavily involved in, and came to dominate, the salt trade. Caravans with goods traversed the desert from Tuwat to Taoudeni, then Timbuktu; but between the latter two stops, there was a settlement called Arawan.

The Kunta were leaders of the Qadiriyya in a huge region and this, together with their political and commercial leadership, made them an impressive "enterprise" or "establishment," as they are known in recent scholarship. For around eighty years, the Kunta dominated the economy of the region. Between 1756 to 1826, under the leadership of Sidi al-Mukhtar and his successors, the Kunta were without peers as merchants and religious figures in the southern Sahara.

The Kunta had over time cultivated the valuable skills necessary to intervene and mediate in conflicts "in a particularly unstable universe that mostly escaped the power of any centralized authority," in the words of the historian Abdel Wedoud Ould Cheikh.[2] Political influence was enabled by commercial success. In addition to knowledge and spiritual exercises, economic independence was stressed among the Kunta. Sidi Mukhtar was himself a prosperous man and encouraged trading activities among his family and followers. As he wrote: "When the Kunta youth reached maturity their ultimate desire would be to travel in search of knowledge. After acquiring a substantial grounding in the religious and mystical sciences, they would concentrate on accumulating wealth. Then they would seek to marry into the noblest families. Each one of them would become distinguished for his knowledge, piety and wealth."[3] Sidi Mukhtar wanted only the most skillful herdsmen and access to the best possible pasturage for his animals. Camels were traded for other livestock and commodities, including grains, butter, honey, textiles, and gold. Sidi Mukhtar also kept horses. Commercial activities were viewed as necessary, provided that such activities did not detract from their devotional practices. The Kunta also accumulated wealth

FIG. 11. A historical image of Timbuktu from René Caillié, *Journal d'un voyage a Tombouctou et Jenne* (1830). Like Heinrich Barth's expedition (see Fig. 4), this image of Timbuktu was made after a major European exploration mission. Also like Barth, Caillié did not have artists in his traveling party, so the resulting image is based on a mixture of the testimonies of Caillié and the artist's imagination. *Image source*: https://www.meisterdrucke.us/fine-art-prints/Rene-Caillie/44264/View-of-part-of-the-town-of-Timbuktu-from-a-hill,-illustration-from-'Journal-d'un-Voyage-a-Tombouctou-et-a-Jenne',-1830.html.

through gifts from various groups, especially the so-called warrior tribes. On occasion they had to deal with goods that were of questionable provenance but did not refuse them in order to maintain good ties. The Kunta were a dominant force in the long-distance trade in the Sahara and anything tradable that entered the Sahara was traded by them.

In May 1828, René Caillié spent about ten days in Arawan, a village with only a few houses about 250 kilometers north of Timbuktu (which is pictured in fig. 11). He observed the significance of the salt trade and other goods that passed through the settlement, some of local origin, others originating in Europe.[4] He noted the diverse places from which the goods came. His host, he said, was a native of Tuwat.

This chapter introduces the Kunta scholars who were spread out over a vast territory and whose books and ideas reached as far as northern Nigeria.[5]

The Kunta figure to begin with is Sidi al-Mukhtar al-Kunti, who was born in Arawan in 1729. His mother died when he was not yet five years old and his father died about five years after that. The young Mukhtar was then raised by his older brother, his father's older brother, and his grandfather. Like the other children of the village, his early education took place at home and then with local teachers, but unlike the other boys in his cohort, he was an outstanding pupil and flourished as a student, with a reputation for his seriousness and devotion to his studies.

While still young, he traveled with caravans to other settlements in the Sahara to study with specialists such as the Tuareg scholars of the Kel Essuk. By the time he was fourteen years old in 1743, he had arrived in a nomadic settlement outside Timbuktu to study with Shaykh Sidi Ali ibn Najib. He visited Timbuktu during this time. He did not encounter much teaching and learning there, although he apparently encountered at least one merchant with a large book collection. His attention to politics and power came later. During this time he was initiated into the Qadiriyya Sufi order by his teacher. This was the same order his distant ancestors had adopted in Tuwat.

The young Mukhtar mastered works at various levels of the curriculum similar to those discussed in the last chapter: exegeses, prophetic traditions, the life of the Prophet, theology, jurisprudence, and rhetoric, among others. Later in life, he composed a poem in which he describes the merits of various disciplines:

> The best of knowledge if you desire to benefit
> Is the knowledge of the Book and of law, so do comply!
> Then syntax and morphology of structures and also
> The science of Principles without aberration and argument,
> Even if you are a linguist, competent and eloquent
> Then also Prophetic traditions—authenticating it, no foolishness!
> Whatever is besides these are futile and games
> And a type of sleep and a calling toward failure.[6]

These were the subjects he studied, and there was really no difference between the curriculum he describes and that used in the Mahadra in Shinqit. These lines capture the subjects well: Quran, Sharia, language, legal principles, and hadith. As Mukhtar completed the mastery of certain texts, he was then authorized to teach those books. In his scholarly and spiritual genealogy, he included the names of figures discussed in earlier chapters, Ahmad Baba and Baba's teacher Muhammad Baghayogho.

Afterward, Mukhtar returned to Arawan, his birthplace, but it was now too small and rather isolated for him and soon he relocated to Walata. This is where his ancestor from Tuwat, Sidi Ahmad al-Bakkay, died, was buried, and came to be recognized as a saint. Sidi al-Mukhtar was revered by the local population of Walata, just like his ancestor, whose tomb had by then become a site of pilgrimage. Mukhtar was still young and had the energy to move. From Walata he moved to Tagant, where he took the title of shaykh (the head) of the Qadiriyya around 1756. He was not yet thirty years old.

Sidi Mukhtar al-Kunti: Business and Books

Although no buildings were erected or endowed as schools or colleges in any of the towns in the larger region, there were teachers and students and the traditional method of certification or authorization (ijaza) was well-established. A spot with enough shade was sufficient for a teacher and his students to teach and study. There were also lectures, open to anybody, that would usually take place in mosques. Some writing was even directed at nonspecialists. Lectures might be in a local language such as Songhay or Tamashek, but scholarly books were written in Arabic. There are some examples of books written in Ajami (a local language written in Arabic script) but in most cases the writers of these works are not known. Shaykh Mukhtar wrote only in Arabic, whether he was writing for a general readership or for specialists. Among his materials are works counseling his followers and believers (ten titles), correspondence or epistles (twenty-eight titles), advice (four titles), and devotional writing (fifteen works) of which many texts were untitled. There are also certain invocations that served as a means of protection or as a cure for certain illnesses, such as the one, "Written for a student in a state of mental confusion."[7] Mukhtar also wrote innumerable short texts, on spiritual therapies and of a miscellaneous nature, probably directed at followers. These works were sometimes addressed to entire groups, such as the whole Kunta clan: *Nasiḥa al-baṭṭ li jamiʿ ahl al-Kunta* (Conclusive advice to all [the people of] Kunta) and *Risāla ilā abnāʾ ʿAli ibn Najīb* (Correspondence to the sons of Ali bin Najib [his teacher]). Sometimes works were directed at individuals.

His work in Islamic law is titled *Fatḥ al-Wahhāb ʿalā hidāyat al-ṭullāb* (The aid of the giver for the guidance of the seekers), a manuscript in four volumes, with each about seven hundred pages long. It is a commentary on an earlier work, *Hidāyat al-ṭullāb* (Guidance to students). Among his writings are collections of legal opinions and responses (*fatawa* and *ajwiba*) on everyday matters, filled with fine detail on almsgiving, trade, reciting the Quran loudly in the presence of another worshipper, family law, the confiscation of stolen goods from robbers and marauders, and whether a distinction should be made between these two groups of people.

Ahmad Baba was productive but he was not a Sufi master, political leader, or merchant. Baba had made use of his forced exile in Marrakesh in order to write. Shaykh Mukhtar combined multiple roles as well as writing, or at least he gave the lectures that were turned into books. He was, in his time, the most prolific writer, with a capacity to cover a wide range of topics. He did not specialize—as it might be said today—and his works also range in size from short commentaries of a few pages to large multivolume works of hundreds of pages. Even if it is true that he wrote most or all of his works in the last twenty years of his life, there is little detail regarding when exactly, in that two-decade period, he composed specific works. Similarly, the context for the composition of each text is exceptionally hard to specify. Dating a text was not of particular importance for him (or for the students who compiled his notes).

Sidi Mukhtar's Compendium for the People: *al-Minna fī iʿtiqād ahl al-sunna*

Despite Mukhtar's activities as a mediator, which entailed long deliberations with the parties in conflict and extensive travel, on the one hand, and his role as a Sufi master, which meant long, silent, and contemplative periods, on the other hand, he was a prolific writer. But it seems that he started writing rather late in life. The bulk of his writing was undertaken only in his last twenty years, according to his son Sidi Muhammad. Several works were attributed to Mukhtar by students (including his son) who compiled their lecture notes and turned them into books with his name as the author. To write, he had to read, and indeed, he did reveal something about his reading habits when he was young. He claimed that he needed only to read a third or a half of a book and could comprehend the rest without finishing it! He could also read multiple books at the same time and memorize them simultaneously. For writing exegesis of verses from the Quran, he said he had two angels with him, both giving him instructions.[8]

Shaykh Mukhtar was asked to produce a comprehensive guide for nonspecialists, "whether he be a free person or slave, woman or child," and *al-Minna fī iʿtiqād ahl al-sunna* (The divine gift in explaining the beliefs of the people of tradition) was the response.[9] He chose not to respond to specific questions, and instead wrote on topics he believed were relevant to ordinary believers. By the end of his writing, this work was just over five hundred pages: he included practical advice and discussed levels of faith and types of believers, categories of sins, the concept of predestination, eschatological matters, and a whole series of issues that can be classified as questions of classical theology. *Al-minna* is encyclopedic and has the character of a compilation written sporadically, rather than a coherent work that was planned and systematically articulated. Mukhtar also dealt with more historical topics such as the biographies of several companions of the Prophet Muhammad and controversies in the early period after the demise of the Prophet. Issues in the history of the Sahara, around where he and his followers were based, and the larger Bilad al-Sudan are given as titles to several sections. Section titles are also dedicated to the end of the askiyas, as well to the scholar al-Maghili[10] and a number of other figures from the history of the region. But in many cases, the section titles and the actual content are only thinly related. Thus, Mukhtar does not actually discuss Maghili and the askiyas, but only reproduces a prayer of the former relating to the latter. He also writes about his own travels in the region. As would be expected of a Sufi master, he devotes a good amount of attention to saints and their miracles, and to types of ascetics. He is insistent that sainthood had been integral to Islam since its earliest days. Similarly, miracles are not strange or outrageous phenomena, as proponents of certain schools of philosophy among the Muslims had held. At various places, he mixes historical narrative with unhistorical, miraculous interjections. For instance, he writes of a meeting between Maghili and his pupil A'mar al-Shaykh with the great Egyptian scholar 'Abd al-Rahman al-Suyuti (d. 1505) in Egypt, which is implausible. The purpose of this weaving together of history and myth is not immediately clear. As the work covers so many areas and is meant to educate the larger public, he was undoubtedly aware that some of the issues he was raising were highly esoteric. These were obviously debates circulating in the larger region in which he had followers—and antagonists.

Mukhtar had a broad, simple, and inclusive definition of a Muslim; whoever identified themselves as such, by saying the words of the creed, should be recognized as Muslim. However, there were others who sought more didactically to separate Muslims from nonbelievers and to delineate more clearly the boundaries of the Muslim community. There were scholars who asserted, for instance, that self-declared believers should be classified nonbelievers if they tolerated non-Muslims or their practices in their midst. Mukhtar was strongly opposed to the use of excommunication or *takfir*.

As *al-Minna* was meant to be for the common person and easy to use, Mukhtar also provided a list of prayers and invocations together with descriptions of their value and virtues. Among the surviving copies of the work is one that was made in 1840 using the calligraphic style, common in manuscripts from deep in the Sahara, that locals have named Sahrawi. It was made for Sidi Muhammad bin Ṭalib al-Ghadamisi by the copyist al-Khalif bin Muhammad al-Bukhari. Another copy was made in 1859, also in Sahrawi calligraphy, perhaps reflecting the uses of the text in the more remote desert regions where this style of writing prevailed.

While engaged in his writing, Shaykh Mukhtar was also active in promoting and growing his own branch of the Qadiriyya brotherhood, which was later called the Qadiriyya Bakkayiya and the Qadiriyya Mukhtariyyah (the former referring to his ancestor Shaykh Sidi Ahmad al-Bakkay, the latter to himself). He probably combined his travels as a merchant and mediator with his role as head of this Sufi order, inviting people and especially leaders to join the order. The first group to join was the Mashdhuf, a Berber group who claimed Arab descent, in a region between the towns of Walata and Tichit. However, the largest groups in this region, the Awlad Bella Arabs and their allies, who were the most powerful and populous residents of the region, did not join the Qadiriyya as quickly as others. It was only after considerable struggle and confrontation between the followers of Kunti and the Awlad Bella that he was successful as the spiritual head of the region.

In the Tagant, where Shaykh Mukhtar had many Kunta kinsmen, his interventions as mediator between rival factions were successful. This success resulted in the Awlad Bu Sayf recognizing him as the supreme shaykh of the Qadiriyya. This, in turn, led to other groups and holy men of the region, particularly from the Tajakant Zwaya families, resenting the shaykh. He was still young but already leader of the Qadiriyya and he was also attracting large numbers of followers. His detractors tried to mobilize against him and challenged him to a public debate. According to legend, he was given divine assistance through a vision that showed him the debate questions and how to respond. He sent the questions and his responses to his opponents in the form of a satirical poem before the debate took place. Thereafter, they accepted him and joined him. This was a turning point; after this, his position as leader of the brotherhood, with a strong political role, was accepted by tribes who were initially resentful and had resisted joining him.

One of Sidi Mukhtar's opponents was Ibn Buna al-Jakani (d. 1793/94 or 1805), who wrote on grammar, logic, and theology.[11] In particular, he wrote on the concept of Tawhid (the oneness of God). He wrote a commentary in poetic meter on the famous grammar of Ibn Malik, the *Alfiyyah*, which he called *al-Iḥmirār* because his poem was in red ink—the title referring to the color red—and Ibn Malik's in black ink. His *Wasīlat al-saʿādāt* (Path to happiness) addressed the subject of God's oneness. In this work, he makes a number of points that generated a strong reaction by Sidi Mukhtar, who wrote a work to refute him. In his rebuttal, Sidi Mukhtar defends the idea of sainthood as a reality, the miracles of the "friends of god" or saints, and the difference between their miracles and the unusual events that an ordinary person is capable of. He gives numerous examples of miracles of the prophets, companions of the Prophet, and the Sufis. He accuses Ibn Buna of word-games and indulging in speculative, Greek logic.

In 1811, Sidi Mukhtar al-Kunti died. He was eighty-four years old and was buried close to his ancestral Arawan. On his deathbed, he gave his string of prayer beads to his son Sidi Muhammad. We can assume that his collection of books and his own writings first went to this son. Sidi Mukhtar ensured that the continuation of his branch of the Qadiriyya order would remain within the family, in the Kunti line.

Son, Successor, Hagiographer: Sidi Muhammad al-Khalifa

Although Shaykh Mukhtar did not often explicitly speak about miracles his son and successor, Sidi Muhammad al-Khalifa (d. 1826), wrote a work that dealt extensively with this subject. He called it *al-Ṭarā'if wa'l-talā'id min karāmāt al-shaykhayn al-wālida wal-wālid* (The exquisite and rare narrations on the miracles of the mother and father) (fig. 12) and it ran to close to seven hundred pages even though it only reaches up to chapter 5 of a planned larger work of seven chapters plus a conclusion, according to the extant contents page. He mentions his mother, Lalla Aisha, at various points, and the conclusion was meant to be devoted to her life. She was respected as a saint.

The work is a hagiographical account of Sidi Muhammad's parents, which he had not completed by the time of his death in 1826. It is emphatically concerned with describing the miracles that appeared in the lives of his parents, while defending the miracles as real occurrences. He writes that sainthood, and the accompanying miraculous events that are possible for saints, are bestowed on a select few in history and that his parents achieved such a status. He writes of his father's virtues such as his forgiving nature, his perseverance, and his courage. The son-author describes how his father had studied and traveled extensively to find the best teachers in each subject he wanted to master. He also explains his father's teaching methods and names several of his students.

Sidi Muhammad never traveled to study and had only one teacher, his father. He would have read the same books, in the same fields, that his father had read with various teachers. The *al-Ṭarā'if wa'l-talā'id* is a monument to his father as his teacher, as a political leader, merchant, and spiritual master of the highest order, and to his mother. This was the work for which he would be best known, although he wrote several other works that address a range of topics. Another of his well-known works with numerous copies goes under the short title of *al-Risāla al-ghallāwiyya* (The ghallawi epistle) (figs. 13a and 13b) and is

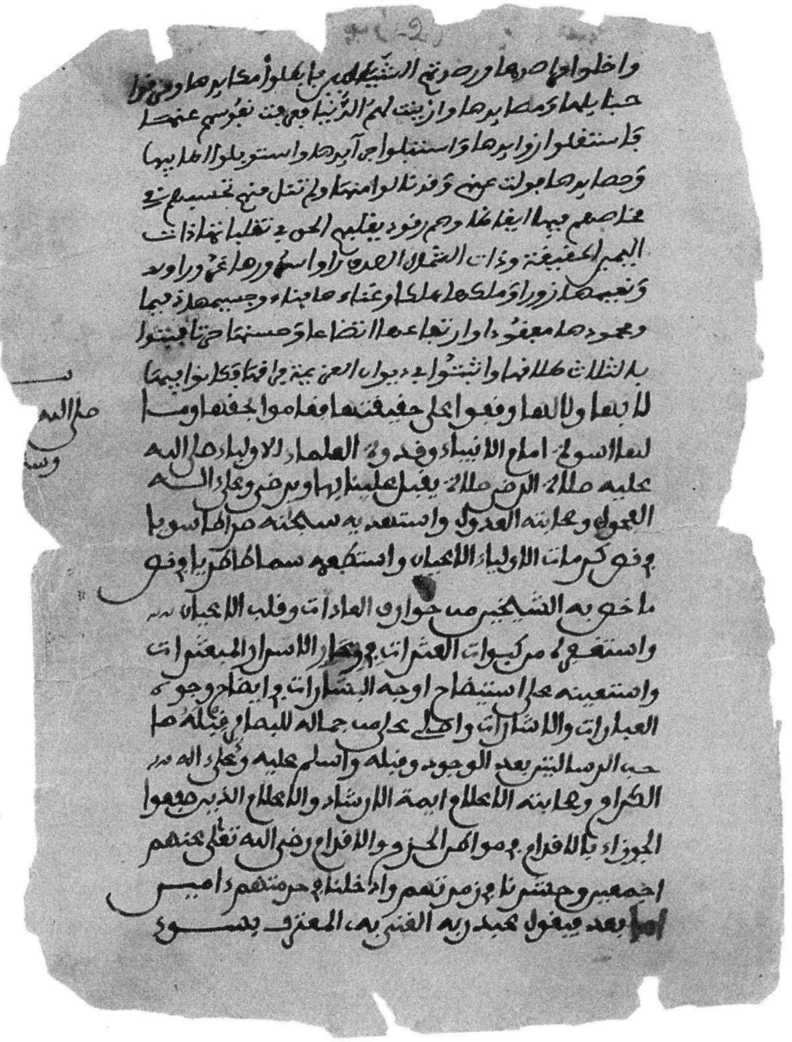

FIG. 12. *Al-Ṭarā'if wa'l-talā'id* was composed by Sidi Muhammad al-Kunti (1765–1826) to discuss, among other matters, the miracles of his mother and father (the "two shaykhs" of the full title). It is a large work of seven chapters with introduction and conclusion, reaching to 672 pages. This is from a copy with many pages damaged. Page size: 17.5 × 13.5 cm; twenty-three lines per page. Cedrab 2182. *Image source*: From the archives of the Iheri-Ab (formerly Cedrab), in Timbuktu.

FIG. 13A. *Al-Risāla al-ghallāwiyya* by Sidi Muhammad al-Kunti (1765–1826). This work covers a wide spectrum of topics, a brief history of the Kuntis, a defense of the Kunti family and their Sufi order against their detractors, and related topics. Ninety-six pages; twenty-six lines per page; text 18.5 × 13.5 cm. This is a twentieth-century copy on grid-lined paper. Cedrab 902. *Image source*: From the archives of the Iheri-Ab (formerly Cedrab), in Timbuktu.

FIG. 13B. *Al-Risāla al-ghallāwiyya* by Sidi Muhammad al-Kunti (1765–1826). Eighty-seven pages; twenty-six lines per page; page size 24.1 × 17.8; text 20.4 × 13.5 cm. Cedrab 329. *Images source*: From the archives of the Iheri-Ab (formerly Cedrab) in Timbuktu.

relatively short, at around ninety pages, compared with his *al-Ṭarā'if wa'l-talā'id*. The *Risāla* ranges over topics from the history of the Kunta and the region to matters of ethics and etiquette, law and spiritual practices, and disputes with and critiques of other tribes and Sufi orders.

Reading the Kunta Writers beyond Timbuktu

Further to the south, beyond the territories where the Kunta were recognized as scholars and successful merchants, in northern Nigeria, major political changes were in progress in the early 1800s. There, a movement emerged that challenged the reigning Hausa-speaking aristocracy. The scholar, Shehu Usman dan Fodio, had tried to convince the rulers to change their syncretic practices and conform to his way of understanding Islam. They persistently refused, and when he could no longer argue, he launched a jihad against them in 1804. His name reflects the multilingual context of the movement: *Shehu* is Arabic, related to "shaykh" (learned or elder), Usman is an Arabic proper name (Uthman), while *dan* is Hausa for "son," and *Fodio* is Fulfulde, "to be learned." Shehu Usman came from an erudite family and from a larger learned clan, the Torodbe, who had migrated from Futa Toro, located close to the Senegal River. Usman had studied with his father and other members of his family who were also highly literate. His closest associates when he launched his movement were his brother Abdullahi and his son Muhammad Bello. The three of them and large contingents of followers, seeing themselves as engaged in a jihad, swept through much of the Hausa-speaking lands and established a new order that they claimed was more closely aligned with the earliest, classical principles of Islamic government. The movement spread from Gobir in the east and eventually the settlement of Sokoto was transformed into their new capital in 1811. Since then, the name of the state became synonymous with Sokoto the town, and by the end of the twentieth century, "Sokoto Caliphate" was the common expression to describe this state, although the founders had never used it. Shehu Usman died in 1817 and his son, Muhammad Bello, assumed the leadership, while his brother Abdullahi remained the governor of the large western province of Gwandu.

Amid supervising military campaigns and with all the necessary attention to tax-collecting, security, and state-building, the three leaders of Sokoto exemplified a high regard for continuous reading and writing. Between them they produced hundreds of works of prose and poetry in Arabic, Hausa, and Fulfulde, with Shehu Usman dan Fodio writing at least a hundred prose texts, counting only his works in Arabic. The works were often polemics and arguments with opponents who held different interpretations of theology and law. Thus, the Shehu Usman's work of 1806, *Bayān wujūb al-hijra* (Discourse on the obligation to migrate), made the case for migration away from the territory of the established Hausa rulers. In response to his brother Abdullahi's book on governance, he wrote *Najm al-ikhwān* (Star of the brothers). In introducing the work, Shehu Usman writes that he had always tried to avoid controversy and disagreement but that it was necessary to write this rejoinder to Abdullahi.

Abdullahi (d. 1829) wrote a large commentary on the Quran, *Diyā' al-ṭawīl* (Light of interpretation), which he later abridged, and a series of works on governance such as *Diyā' al-ḥukkām* (Light of the rulers). A work on land tenure, *Ta'līm al-Raḍī*, deals with a wide spectrum of issues from waste lands to public pastures through to access to water and wells. In his *Tazyīn al-waraqāt* (Embellishment of the papers), he gives an account of the origins of the jihad movement and his involvement in it; he also includes his attempt to leave and instead go on pilgrimage to Mecca but tells how, on reaching the great trading town of Kano, he changed his mind. A copy of this work was later seen by Heinrich Barth during his travel through Hausa country, many years after the death of the author. He either owned or had access to a large collection of books, judging from the range of texts that he cited in his own work.

The youngest of the three leaders, Muhammad Bello (d. 1837), was said to have access to a library of thousands of works—20,000 in one report, which is probably an exaggeration. He wrote about 120 works himself. He was de facto ruler even before the death of his father in 1817. In 1812, he produced a large work—*Infāq al-maysūr fī tārīkh bilād al-Takrūr* (Easy expenditure in understanding the history of the lands of Takrur)—that covered the geography, ethnography, and contemporary history of the lands called Takrur; the work stretched from the eve of the jihad and up to his time. The work also describes the jihad movement, the territories under their control, and the larger region. The English explorer Hugh Clapperton saw a copy the *Infāq al-maysūr* when he met Bello in 1824 and had a copy of the work, or a part of it, made for himself. He carried the copy back to London and had it translated. It was added as an appendix to his *Narratives*. Bello wrote three works that convey a sense of the history of the lands of Takrur until the success of the jihad. Like his uncle Abdullahi, he wrote on governance in the form of "advice manuals" to leading figures serving under him, including one titled *Uṣūl al-Siyāsa* (Principles of politics), in which he lays out the principles of just rule and administration. In *Infāq al-maysūr*, Bello lists the names of important scholars from the region. For this list, he clearly had a copy of one of Ahmad Baba's biographical dictionaries (*Nayl al-ibtihāj*) at his disposal.

These writers from Sokoto reflect a knowledge of the longer and larger tradition of writing on law and politics by scholars across the larger world of Islamic scholarship. The legal school in which they were working was Maliki and thus their work reflects great familiarity with the corpus of Maliki works, of which there were probably multiple copies circulating. But they also cited non-Maliki scholars and were able to cite from the major collections of hadith and legal works from all the major schools of law. They used a wide range of Quranic commentaries in their work, and had a particular preference for the Persian polymath Ghazali across a range of fields. The Egyptian al-Suyuti, and Maghili, the scholar who had visited Tuwat, were quoted at length.

The Shehu and his son Muhammad Bello were spiritually linked to the Qadiriyya order. Abdullahi was in the Khalwatiyya brotherhood, and probably also in the Qadiriyya; as people would have been allowed to follow more than one. Bello wrote a work about the order that covered its practices, liturgies, and mode of initiation. Thus, among the three rulers, there are numerous works on Sufism.[12]

Sidi Muhammad Kunti's Advice to the Sokoto Leader

The predominance of the Qadiriyya order in Sokoto is one reason why the Timbuktu-based Qadiriyya leadership sought to advise them. Sidi Muhammad Kunti, sometime between 1811 and 1817, wrote a twenty-eight-page letter to Usman dan Fodio. It is an epistle in the manner of the classical Islamic tradition of the "mirror for princes," noted previously of Ahmad Baba's advice to scholars. Whereas Baba had adopted a strategy of advising scholars to criticize rulers, Sidi Muhammad wrote directly to the ruler. Like Baba's, his text is based on his thorough knowledge of a large corpus of classical texts such as those by Ghazali, Mawardi, and Ṭurṭushi. Having heard of the successes of the movement of Usman dan Fodio, he urges him to follow the respected predecessors among the Muslim rulers, practice moderation and justice, and stay within the bounds of the law in his exercise of power. The just sultan, according to Sidi Muhammad, is necessary to maintain order and balance in a realm, which is hierarchical and gives each rank its due. He writes: "No sultan without an army, no army without resources, no resources without taxes, no taxes without prosperity, no prosperity without justice, no justice without a sultan. Justice is the foundation of all foundations."[13]

The ruler also has to seek the advice of the scholars, when necessary, as Kunti writes: "The best of sovereigns are those who frequent scholars; the worst of scholars are those who frequent sovereigns."[14] This opens a contradictory relationship between the rulers and scholars and a potential contradiction in his advice: rulers go to scholars, but scholars avoid rulers. Of course, he knew that Usman dan Fodio was a scholar before he became a ruler. He gives an example of a worthy ruler—the Moroccan 'Alawite ruler, Mulay Sulayman (d. 1822), his contemporary who, not surprisingly, was also a supporter of certain Sufi orders. For the ruler to exercise just authority, he has to beware of his advisors and entourage, and avoid luxury and excess. Rulers should not hide in their private chambers, cut-off from their people.

Independent branches of the Qadiriyya were eventually founded in what is now Nigeria, Senegal, Mauritania, and southern Morocco. Despite internal divisions and controversies, the Qadiriyya was the dominant Sufi order in the Sahara and Sahel until the spread of the Tijaniyya order at the end of the eighteenth and early nineteenth centuries. Polemical writings questioning the claims of the founder of this order grew in number throughout the region, especially when former Qadiriyya followers joined the Tijaniyya. The latter did not allow dual membership; a Tijaniyya follower could not at the same time belong to the Qadiriyya (although the latter permitted such dual membership). The Tijaniyya was founded by Ahmad al-Tijani (d. 1815) in the early 1780s, in the region that today straddles Algeria and Morocco. It spread especially after his arrival in Fez from his native southwestern Algeria. The order spread through the Maghreb and into the Sahara and West Africa. By the 1790s, there were already followers among the Idaw'Ali (a group that produced important writers in Shinqit, mentioned in the previous chapter). From the outset, the Tijaniyya followers were seen to challenge the dominance of the Qadiriyya order that had a presence all over the Maghreb and Sahara. Criticism of the Tijaniyya focused on the founder's claims that he had seen the Prophet Muhammad while he was awake, not in a dream, and had received direct inspiration from him to found the order. In this way, he was also taught the litanies that he prescribed to his followers. As Ahmad Tijani earned followers, the writers among them wrote to propound the Tijaniyya views, which in turn generated an oppositional literature.

During Sidi Muhammad's twenty-five-year leadership, the Kunta were in an unchallenged position as a spiritual, political, and economic force. Timbuktu was the locus of this authority. Sidi Muhammad had two sons waiting to succeed him when he died. Mukhtar al-Saghir led the Kunta until 1847 and he was succeeded by Ahmad al-Bakkay. The latter gained valuable experience in leading a commercial and Sufi network while at his brother's side. By the time Ahmad al-Bakkay assumed control of the Kunta-Qadiriyya, their influence and commercial network had spread extensively.[15]

In the time of Ahmad al-Bakkay's predecessor, Mukhtar al-Saghir, in the early 1820s, opposition to the Kunta leadership of the Qadiriyya was already simmering in a community based to the southwest of Timbuktu, in Masina. A new settlement, called Hamdallahi, had been founded in 1817. There Ahmad Lobbo, also known as Seku Amadu, allied himself with the jihad leaders of Sokoto and refused to recognize the established Qadiriyya leadership among the Kunta of Timbuktu. This early Sokoto-Masina alliance would, however, not last. In the time of Bello's leadership (from 1817 to 1837), the relationship changed and the Masina leadership felt no obligation to follow Sokoto. In a letter asserting their right to have their own authority without allegiance to Sokoto, Ahmad Lobbo in fact cited from the book of Abdullahi mentioned above, *Diyā' al-Ḥukkām*; Bello in turn wrote a response to the letter. Such exchanges continued, leaving a trace of correspondence filled with scholarly citations indicating works then in circulation and held in libraries in the region.

When Bakkay assumed the role of leader in 1847, Ahmad Lobbo's son expected Bakkay to pledge allegiance to the fledgling Hamdallahi-Masina state. Lobbo's son was a scholar who seems to have written only one work. Among his group, there were teachers but only a handful of scholars with higher learning; they did not write as extensively as the Kunta scholars or those in Sokoto. Two names among them stand out, however: Yirkoy Talfi (also known as Sidi al-Mukhtar bin Wadiat Allah) and Alfa Nuh bin al-Tahir, who had both studied with the Kunta scholars of Timbuktu.

Lobbo and his allies—and then his successors—put increasing pressure on Timbuktu to align and follow them, but the Kunta and their followers in Timbuktu refused to do so. Furthermore, Bakkay was heir to a long, proud, and powerful family and economic network, who believed themselves to be the first propagators of the Qadiriyya Sufi order in the Sahara and Sahel. Among the issues that divided them was one that had long excited debate: the acceptance of the sale and use of tobacco by the Qadiriyya in Timbuktu. In Masina, the position was that it was not permissible for Muslims to consume the leaf. But the merchants of the Kunta were trading and transporting tobacco, so they had a lot to lose in accepting that view. As we saw in chapter 3, on the way from Marrakesh back to Timbuktu, Ahmad Baba wrote an opinion on the question of the permissibility of consuming tobacco. In his legal opinion, its consumption was licit. Thus, the Timbuktu merchants were not simply trading in a product about which there was ambiguity; in fact, there was a legal opinion in its favor, from no less a scholar than Ahmad Baba.

In September 1853, when Heinrich Barth arrived in the region, he was received by Ahmad al-Bakkay, who gave him protection until he left Timbuktu seven months later with a document of safe conduct that partly assured his safe arrival in Bornu.[16] Bakkay's protection of the European, Christian traveler further increased the enmity against Barth. The Hamdallahi leaders wanted him expelled and even killed.

Heinrich Barth went by the name Abd al-Kerim from the outset of his African exploration in 1850. In 1853, he spent around seven months in Timbuktu. He would probably not have stayed that long but the circumstances in the region left him no choice but to stay in or close to the town. He was fortunate to have the protection of Ahmad al-Bakkay. Without him, we might not have heard of Barth again. In Bakkay's Timbuktu compound, we can assume that there were a good number of books, which would have caught the attention of a curious traveler and visitor like Barth. But Barth never entered the home of his host and protector. He lived close to him and went with him to encampments on the outskirts of the town. Bakkay had inherited a rich collection of texts. Bakkay and his siblings would have inherited the books their parents and grandparents wrote, and their libraries would have been divided among them. Furthermore, Bakkay was himself a writer of poetry and prose. He was curious and valued books. Barth tells us that, while sitting with him in the camp outside Timbuktu, Bakkay, who had with him a collection of books, spoke about one book in particular: "Taking out of his small library the Arabic version of Hippocrates, which he valued extremely, he was very anxious for information as to the identity of the plants mentioned by the Arab authors. This volume of Hippocrates had been a present from Captain Clapperton to Sultan Bello of Sokoto, from whom my friend had received it, among other articles, as an acknowledgment of his learning."[17]

Even after Barth left Timbuktu, the opposition to Bakkay did not abate. The Qadiriyya based in Hamdallahi-Masina demanded that Bakkay and Timbuktu follow them. And the tensions between Timbuktu and Hamdallahi-Masina did not completely disappear when a new actor appeared on the scene who opposed both.

Al-Hajj 'Umar Tal (d. 1864) was a Fulbe-speaking leader.[18] He had met Bakkay when they were both visiting the leaders of Sokoto. While on pilgrimage to the holy cities of Mecca and Madina, where he spent about three years between 1827 and 1830, he was initiated into the Tijaniyya order by a senior figure of the order whom he met there. He was appointed the representative—*muqaddam* or *khalifa*—of the order for the central and western Sudan. On his return, he visited Hamdallahi, Sokoto, and Bornu. He proclaimed his objective to establish a state that would make it preeminent among the recently established "jihad states," but he found no supporters. At around the same time that Bakkay became head of the Kunta-Qadiriyya in 1847, Hajj 'Umar wrote his major work, titled *Rimāḥ ḥizb al-Raḥīm ʿalā nuḥūr ḥizb al-rajīm* (The spears of the merciful party on the throats of the accursed party), which has fifty-five chapters dealing with a large range of topics: Islamic law; the organization of his community or state; the status of Ahmad al-Tijani, the founder of the order; autobiographical notes by the author; and a range of mystical matters, from the relationship of the spiritual seeker and his master, to the nature of spiritual retreat. The bulk of the work consists of extracts and quotations from other works. Hajj 'Umar's work became a major text among the Tijanis and it was copied on the margins of the first major work in the Tijani corpus, the *Jawāhir al-maʿānī* (The jewels of all meanings) of Ali Harazim Barrada (d. 1856), the essential source on the life and teachings of the founder of the brotherhood.

The growing presence of the Tijanis threatened the social and commercial interests of the Qadiriyya led by Bakkay, who wrote to Moroccan leaders about the new order. In mid-1854, he wrote numerous letters, including one that ran to two hundred pages, to Qadiriyya leaders in Morocco. He also wrote a critique of the Tijaniyya order that he sent to Abu Abdullah Akansus (d. 1877), the Moroccan diplomat and scholar, who was a Tijani.

Meanwhile, in 1852, Hajj 'Umar had collected a large enough following of Tijanis to declare jihad and eventually establish an independent state. His ambition was that, through his charismatic leadership and committed followers, he would create a state that outshone Sokoto, at one stage an inspiration to him. But, in the words of the historian David Robinson, "he never came close to succeeding, because of the frenetic military pace of his campaigns and the absence of an intellectual cadre who could create a justificatory literature."[19] He spent nearly the whole of the next decade as a warrior, not a scholar and writer who wanted to win over opponents with clever arguments and copious citations. He did write during this period but his energies went into mobilizing men to fight. The fighting covered a vast terrain. In 1861 or 1862, Hajj 'Umar's forces secured Segu and parts of Masina, and if he had been successful beyond these parts he would have ruled over territory that might have resembled the extent of the Songhay polity of the sixteenth century. He captured Segu but his subsequent campaign against Hamdallahi and the Kunta—who set aside their differences in face of the threat of Hajj 'Umar—was a failure. His last major work, completed in 1861, was a polemic against the ruler of Hamdallahi—*Bayān mā waqaʿa baynanā wa bayna Amīr Māsīna* (The explanation of what happened between us and the ruler of Masina)—in which he recounts the recent history of the conflict between them. He forwarded an argument, supported by a range of texts, that those who are close to, or supporters of pagans, are in fact apostates. He was writing about the political dynamics in the region where his opponents saw the need to make alliances against him irrespective of their beliefs.

Bakkay, supported by the leaders of Jenne and Timbuktu, and, by this time the leaders in Masina whose previous leaders had opposed him, defeated Hajj 'Umar's forces at Hamdullahi in 1862/63. Hajj 'Umar died in 1864 during the fall-out from these events. Bakkay was then leader of what had been Hamdallahi, from 1863 until April 1866, when he was killed in battle.

During the tumultuous years when Bakkay oversaw Kunta affairs, he never stopped writing. Much of his writing was in the form of correspondence with his antagonists. Letters were sent to Ahmad Lobbo and his successor, replies came, and he answered in return, often sending detailed responses filled with poetry. He wrote to Hajj 'Umar in similar fashion. He also wrote to various scholars and leaders in Morocco, members of the Qadiriyya, to gain their support for his position in the Sahara-Sahel, and to former members of the order and other Tijanis, attempting to win them back or away from the newly arrived order.

The sons of Hajj 'Umar controlled a much-diminished version of their father's state until the arrival of the French in their territory in the 1890s. The French occupied the town of Segu and seized the remains of the library of Hajj 'Umar and his family. Colonel Archinard, who led the campaign that sacked Segu, saw to the transport of four large cases of books and letters. They were shipped to Paris and deposited in the Bibliothéque National de France's Arabic manuscript department under the name of Archinard. In the 1920s, items from this collection started appearing in the library's Arabic catalogs. But they received scant attention from the Orientalists in Paris, who saw little value in them. In a project led by Louis Brenner and David Robinson, beginning in 1979, a catalog of the collection finally appeared in 1985 as *Inventaire de bibliothèque 'Umarienne de Ségou.*

In the early 1840s, a chronicle began to circulate in the region called the *Tārīkh al-fattāsh* (Chronicle of the investigator), which was more than a narrative of past events. It contained a prediction or prophecy about the present, telling of a man who would revive the religion and lead the community as the only legitimate ruler. Not incidentally, the reformer of the age predicted in this text was none other than Ahmad Lobbo (d. 1840), the ruler of Hamdallahi-Masina. Few copies of the work, which was around a hundred pages in length, were made. At the time, there were rumors about this work, and about its prophecy in particular. The work was presented in the form of a genuine chronology of the history of the region, like the *Tārīkh al-Sūdān*, but with the addition of a prophecy. The author of the *Tārīkh al-Sūdān* recorded the mythical origins of the Songhay and gave a narrative of changing rulers (and scholars) and significant events, while the *Tārīkh al-fattāsh* was modeled as a typical chronicle but also had an eschatological element on the "end times" and prophesized that the reviver of the faith would come from Masina. The chronicle was backdated to the sixteenth century, with one version of the work passed down in the name of one Ibn Mukhtar, and the other in the name of Mahmud al-Ka'ti. It remains unclear if any of these are actual writers in the past or were invented figures, and it is still disputed how much of the text originated in the sixteenth century.

In the 1850s, Barth did not encounter this chronicle, although it had been in circulation for about a decade. Nearly fifty years later, Felix Du Bois was told about this *Tārīkh al-fattāsh* when he was in Timbuktu but never got to see a copy. He managed to take what he thought were fragments of the manuscripts with him back to Paris. Then word went around the French colonial administration about this chronicle and a concerted effort was made to procure copies. Octave Houdas and Maurice Delafosse, the editors and translators of the text, completed their work on the text in 1913. In their introduction to the work, they argued that there was a more-or-less coherent work that went back to the early sixteenth century, written by one Mahmud Ka'ti. They argued that there was a seventeenth-century version from the pen of the latter's grandson, Ibn Mukhtar, and that, in the nineteenth century, there was an attempt to interfere with the text. However, on the whole, according to them there was a stable core text, valid as a genuine historical source. *La chronique du chercheur*, the Houdas-Delafosse edition, was widely used by Nehemia Levtzion, with new speculation emerging about the composition nearly sixty years later. In 1971, Levtzion argued that this chronicle was a composite of works produced at two separate points in time. According to him, Ka'ti left some notes that were eventually collected into the chronicle. Houdas and Delafosse, and Levtzion, recognized interpolations in the text.

The *Tārīkh ibn Mukhtār* (Chronicle of Ibn Mukhtar) is an independent chronicle with an author—the Ibn Mukhtar of the title—about whom little or nothing is known. This chronicle probably goes back to the mid-seventeenth century. Then there was the nineteenth-century invention to support the claims of Ahmad Lobbo in Masina. It now appears that a scholar named Alfa Nuh bin Tahir (d. 1857/58), about whom there is little information but who was close to Lobbo, was the author of this *Tārīkh al-fattāsh*. Of course, he did not put his name to the work because it was purposely meant to be anonymous and seem like a product of an earlier epoch. His purpose was solely to assert the legitimacy of Ahmad Lobbo in Masina over the other leaders in the Sahara-Sahel such as the Fodios in Sokoto and the Kunta in Timbuktu. Nuh bin Tahir spent time in Arawan and had been a student of the great Sidi Mukhtar al-Kunti. He also worked under his son Sidi Muhammad but threw his weight and writing (and forgery) skills behind the opponents of the Kuntis in Hamdallahi.

The most recent and convincing analysis of the *Tārīkh al-fattāsh* places the work firmly as a product of the conflict for legitimacy and leadership in the events in Masina, Timbuktu, and Sokoto in the early to mid-nineteenth century. This argument was first offered in a detailed article by Mauro Nobili and Shahid Mathee, with an even more detailed and thorough argument in the subsequent monograph by Nobili.[20] Just over a century after the edition by Houdas and Delafosse, of a set of manuscripts that evidently had marks of forgery, the most significant question about the authenticity of the texts was raised. The events of the first half of the nineteenth century were complicated and fast-moving on multiple fronts, but critical history writing and text editing have been slow moving. However, the very idea of a fake chronicle, a forgery, points to the written word having tremendous value in these societies. A rumor based on a written source was potentially more persuasive than one without such support. The simple words "it was written" can have immense force. A narrative in book form—words fixed on paper—was believed by its proponents to have truth-value. In this case, the fake chronicle did not succeed; the man who was meant to be the reviver of the faith, and the ruler over all of West Africa, died two years after its circulation. There was a strong rebuttal from a Sokoto scholar and the marriage of eschatology and politics took a break for some years. The impact of the chronicle was and is now only an issue in the scholarly community, with periodic spasms of scholarship, some devoted to the authenticity of the text as a transparent source of raw historical data, others to a far more productive, critical philological reading of a forgery.

In 1920, Paul Marty (d. 1938), the leading French Orientalist on the Sahara and its southern edges, published a three-volume work on the Sahara. Most of the first volume was devoted to the Kunta. Marty published extensively on what he called *Islam noir* ("black Islam") before moving to work on Berber policy in the French administration in Morocco. For Marty and the colonial administration, having a clear and comprehensive overview of "the tribes" and the Sufi orders was essential to French policy. He saw the value of the orders to the colonial administration; he viewed them as unorthodox and local and a potential bulwark against an imagined pan-Islamic agitation emanating from places like Cairo, Damascus, and Istanbul. It is thus not surprising that he gave the Kunta so much attention because of their long and widespread presence in what was then French West Africa. Marty devotes close to forty pages to outlining the biography, works, and impact of Shaykh Sidi al-Mukhtar. Sidi al-Mukhtar clearly deserved such attention because he had initiated a major spiritual and intellectual movement in the Sahara and Sahel, with enduring and widespread political consequences. His own movements in the larger region, his writings, and large following point to an influential figure at many levels. Throughout the colonial territories, administrators were keen to find local written sources. As noted earlier in the chapter he genuinely founded a successful business and political "enterprise" that stretched across the Sahara. Chronicles and contracts, historical and geographical descriptions, and law and legal texts were collected or commissioned by colonial Orientalists. The French and the British were both engaged in such collecting. In the years after 1903, when Sokoto fell to the British, the works of the Sokoto scholars relevant to colonial administration were collected and translated.[21] For instance, Bello's *Infāq al-maysūr*, parts of which had arrived in London in the early 1820s with Clapperton, were read by the administrators. Now, occupying the country, they had access to a large variety of materials. Sir Frederick Lugard, who served as high commissioner (1900–1906) and then as governor-general of Nigeria (1914–1919), saw the value of these texts in crafting his policies of indirect rule.

7

The Collector of Timbuktu

AHMAD BULARRAF

AHMAD BULARRAF is the short form of the name of Ahmad bin Mbarak bin Barka bin Muhammad Bularraf al-Takni.[1] His birth date is uncertain but it could have been in 1884. He was born in the trading settlement of Guelmim in the arid Sus region of southwestern Morocco. From the early 1880s, droughts and the consequent food shortages impacted locals, and without opportunities to trade locally, many inhabitants packed up and left the region.[2] Like so many others during the next two decades, the Bularraf family went overland, going further southward until they crossed the imaginary boundaries that separated the Maghreb and what would become modern Morocco, from what was then beginning to be called by the French *Afrique-Occidentale Française* (French West Africa). They traveled through the Bilad-Shinqit. Bularraf never specified his exact itinerary from the time that he left Guelmim, whether he went first to the town of Shinqit itself and then to one of the early colonial administrative towns like St. Louis or Dakar. It is also possible that he visited one of the latter towns and then turned back, in a northeasterly direction, to the settlements in Shinqit. These were all then part, or fast becoming part, of the French-occupied territories of northwest Africa. The French colonial military had a long presence in these parts but colonial territorial demarcations and settled administration were still rudimentary. Nomadic groups and merchants, who had a long tradition of crossing the Sahara, hardly knew of the French encroachment and did not care for these divisions and names. They had their own ideas of space that gave significance to how far their camels could go before the next watering well, which routes to take to avoid potential bandits, and where they would meet their kinsmen. However, their trade had increasingly been steered into new directions, to focus more on the coastal routes and away from the interior. The traders increasingly headed toward the Atlantic coast and the settlements in colonial Senegal, such as St. Louis, which was the capital and commercial entrepôt close to the mouth of the Senegal River, as well as Dakar and Rufisque.

There is one reason why Bularraf may have gone to Shinqit or one of the settlements close to it: curiosity about the scholars living there.[3] Perhaps he had heard about some of the learned men of Shinqit, whose manuscript books had somehow found their way to Guelmim. It was helpful to him that there were already members of his Tikna clan in many parts of the Sahara and its borderlands, the Sahel, in the old, established towns and in the newer colonial towns. Locally connected family and friends in some ways eased his way through the larger region. But he was expected to trade, not study; the Tikna were known for their trading acumen, not for their learning or traveling in search of knowledge.

The Tikna had long-established commercial relations with the Sahara and the western Bilad al-Sudan (increasingly then being called the "French Soudan"). Throughout the nineteenth century, there was regular commercial traffic between Guelmim and St. Louis, which was the port for goods coming from Europe and for export out of the region. Tikna traders went with their camels and livestock over well-trodden desert tracks to make their living. Long before Bularraf left Guelmim, there was already a Tikna diaspora scattered from St. Louis to Timbuktu and as far south as Conakry in present-day Guinea. For instance, in the early 1880s, the Tikna merchant Muhammad Barka arrived in St. Louis, where his son Abdelkader was born in 1887. By 1894, the Barka family were in Timbuktu and they witnessed the French conquest close-up. The young boy was not kept in Timbuktu but sent to Arawan to get an education. Muhammad Barka traded in whatever goods the locals needed from outside, including livestock and salt. He was successful and prominent enough that the French colonial administration used him as an intermediary between themselves and the chiefs of the nomadic groups in the area. The elder Barka returned to Guelmim and died there in 1930, while his son remained in the French colony and died in Bamako a dozen years after Malian independence. The Tikna diaspora received some attention from the colonial officials and thus we know relatively more about their success than the other clans and families, such as the Tadjakant, who were also traders and worked through their own networks. The Barkas belonged to the people classified as "Moroccans" or "whites" by the French. By 1912, the so-called Moroccans comprised eighty-eight in a population of ten thousand in Timbuktu, nearly all merchants, with the Barkas the most prominent among them.

If Bularraf had gone to Shinqit because of its scholars, and spent even a few months there, then we can imagine that he asked to audit classes. This meant sitting with other students and moving from scholar to scholar reading a text or observing others reading a work. In such circles, he began to study law and its subfields. His time in Shinqit was never recorded either by himself or his contemporaries, so we can only imagine a young man, probably a bit older than the rest of any group he joined. There are no records or memories of him in Shinqit. However, some descendants of scholars in Shinqit recall the hospitality he extended to Shinqiti scholars visiting Timbuktu in the late 1920s, and his library is remembered as having a rich store of materials originating from Shinqiti scholars. The exalted status of the Bilad Shinqit in Bularraf's imaginary is confirmed in a compilation of the scholars of his time that he completed before his death.[4] The vast majority of scholars listed are from Shinqit.

The French *tricoleur* had already been flying over Timbuktu for about a decade when Bularraf arrived there in 1904. He could also have arrived later, in 1907, which is given as the date when he began his collection, but it seems likely that he first settled down and then, after some years, began to collect manuscripts and sell books. The French military expedition into the interior had finally defeated local armed resistance and the French were beginning to establish the basic elements of their administration. Timbuktu was a distant outpost of the expansive *Soudan Français*, but there were colonial policymakers and businessmen in Paris who entertained grand ideas that the fabled town could enjoy prominence again through large-scale economic projects, including trans-Saharan rail connections. In Timbuktu, Bularraf did not become a scholar-teacher, but continued in the Tikna fashion of making a living by trading. Like other Tikna traders, what he bought and sold in his early years in Timbuktu depended on what the local market required.

About ten years before Bularraf arrived in Timbuktu, Felix Du Bois had visited (see chapter 1). Du Bois found the remains of a once-great center of learning and enough literary remains to return to Paris with copies of a number of important manuscripts. Bularraf settled down in Timbuktu and probably met some of the same scholars—or their families and associates—as well as the same copyists and learned families who had interacted with Du Bois. If he had spent time in study circles in Shinqit, it was probably there that he cultivated a consciousness of the value of careful scholarly writing. He would have heard texts read aloud and cited approvingly or criticized. He would have seen scholars putting pen to paper and others reading silently with deep concentration. He would definitely have been affected by the high regard and significance given to books, all handwritten. Watching writing in progress, or seeing its end product as a manuscript book, as a deliberate practice to conserve ideas and not only to record transactions, was new to him. Arriving with a trader background in a town known for its commercial activities and for its legacy of scholarship, he soon took time off from his business concerns to read and then copy a manuscript, and then another one, and another. With time, and with enough surplus income, he got others to copy manuscripts for him, paying for the paper and the labor. Manuscripts were not among the things the Tikna traded or copied, and among them there were no known scholars who settled in Timbuktu or other settlements with a reputation for education. The Tikna knew well how to record prices, write contracts, get a basic letter off to a family member, but not how to copy the records of a legal case. They saw no value in collecting manuscripts. Bularraf would be the exception.

Some families in Timbuktu had manuscript libraries but Bularraf must have found them in a fragile or neglected condition. Evidently, these conditions moved him. Manuscripts could be copied and given a life, and so he applied himself to copying. He must have also encountered printed books, which were a new presence in the region. The increasing availability of Arabic printed books could fill a gap in Timbuktu. Before World War I, the Arabic printed book industry was still relatively young, but a new print market was in the making. Buying and selling printed books could have been seen as a commercial opportunity, and at the same time, a way to satisfy Bularraf's own religious and intellectual interests. A small set of his correspondence has survived and it has a consistent, nearly obsessive, concern with books. His earliest correspondence, 1911 and 1912, deals with books.[5] He wrote numerous times to a trader in St. Louis, Ahmed Ben Jelloun, possibly one of the Tikna traders based there. All the correspondence contains orders for books, and a few also include orders for other items, especially tea (*al-tayi*), but also sugar, cotton, copperware, and silk fabric. In one of the few letters without book requests, he ordered only fifty kilograms of tea leaves. In this period, he was looking for copies of something called *Kifāyat al-ṭālib* (Sufficient for the student)—a rather generic title—and *Jawāhir al-maʿānī*, a fundamental text of the Tijani order. One of the letters notes that Ben Jelloun had ordered books from Cairo that had been requested by Bularraf, but their arrival had been delayed.[6]

There is a break in the correspondence after this. The letters could be lost but World War I did disrupt communications and impose serious constraints on the flow of mail, imports, and exports. Colonial authorities directed everything to their war effort, including the recruitment of Africans to fight in the war. And so, getting mail or goods to Timbuktu was not a priority during those years. After the war, in the 1920s, Bularraf's correspondence was extensive, going to and coming from Kano in the south and Tangier and Cairo in the north. Books, publishers, and bookstores are mentioned in many letters. In 1922, Bularraf wrote to a merchant in Kano, the famous commercial town in the then British-ruled territories of northern Nigeria, seeking a number of titles. In 1923, he was in contact with a bookshop in Rufisque, one of the French communes on the Atlantic coast of Senegal. He wrote to Ahmed El-Harrouchi, offering to sell his books in Timbuktu. Harrouchi would supply Bularraf with titles in the following years. In 1924, Bularraf sent him 1,000 francs at the same time that Harrouchi mailed Bularraf three parcels of books, containing 11 titles in total, and including a list of titles available in his shop. The prices of books had increased: one had gone up from 80 francs to 106 francs. Through this relationship, Bularraf ordered gum arabic from Harrouchi's brother, also in Rufisque, while the brother inquired from his Timbuktu contact about the price of goatskins.

Kano had a number of specialist manuscripts copyists and booksellers. Bularraf made contact with a Moroccan in the book trade in Kano, presumably based in the old Kurmi market that had manuscript copyists and booksellers. Kano–Timbuktu trade and learned connections date back many centuries; the legendary Ahmad Baba's scholarship was known in and around this part of Nigeria. In 1922, Bularraf was corresponding with Muhammad Ben Mahjoub, who came from Marrakesh. In the case of correspondence with Kano, pound sterling was the means of exchange. In the colonial era, money had to cross new colonial borders and the French franc and English pound had to compete with each other. In April 1922, Mahjoub wrote to Bularraf to say that he could not send the books requested to Timbuktu because the sterling value of the items was too high at the moment. He suggested that now was the time for Bularraf to send merchandise, including livestock, to Nigeria. A few months later he wrote, noting the decline in the value of the sterling, and also asked Bularraf to send his greetings to a number of other Moroccans in the town, including the well-known merchant Muhammad Ben Barka.

In the 1920s, Bularraf's circle of book dealers expanded enormously. He ordered books from Al-Adabia, a bookshop in Tangier, whose owner offered him reduced prices. A Marrakesh bookseller wrote to him about the arrival of a consignment of books from Egypt. In further correspondence, the same bookseller noted other items that he had sent to Timbuktu, everything from carpets to cushions. The Casablanca bookseller Librairie Acharqia forwarded a list of sixty titles available for mailing to Timbuktu. From Rabat, the Librairie-Imprimerie Al-Ahlia offered Bularraf preferential prices on its current list and descriptions of its other, older books and publications, inviting him to act as its distributor in Timbuktu.

From 1924 until 1927, Bularraf was exchanging letters with the Zidane family in Cairo, who owned the Dar al-Hilal publishing house. One of the challenges Bularraf faced was getting books directly from Cairo to Timbuktu; he suggested that the Zidanes send the parcels via Paris, if they should have an agent there. Payment would be made via the Banque d'Afrique de l'Ouest in Dakar. He would face the same problem in his dealings with the Beirut bookseller La Libraire Sader, with whom he corresponded in the late 1920s. He wrote to a book dealer in Algeria, Muhammad al-Sayyid al-Zahiri al-Wahrani, thanking him for sending copies of *al-Wifāq* magazine and asking about specific titles. Another Algerian to whom he wrote in 1922 was the editor of the magazine *al-Shihāb*, with whom he sought to exchange books. Bularraf's dealings with booksellers, publishers, and general traders in Tunis and Algiers around this time did entail discussions about exchange rates, complicated money transfers, and mailing routes. The trader in Tunis who sold books, perfumes, jewelry, and clothing, among other things, did, however, advise him to deal with the Fez branch of the company.

In the roughly two decades of the 1920s and 1930s, Bularraf could order books from a wide range of publishers, printers, and booksellers, from Kano to Tunis, from St. Louis to Beirut. The larger French colonial infrastructure developing in these territories enabled his network, but French uncertainty about their rule over the population meant censorship and other controls and restrictions. For example, one published work in which Bularraf was interested was *Le présent du Monde Musulman* by Shakib Arslan, which Bularraf ordered in 1936, but it was apparently banned by the French authorities. This is quite plausible, for Arslan was a Druze notable and Lebanese intellectual who had been exiled by French mandate authorities because of his anti-imperialist political activism in the French-controlled Levant. A bookseller, in a letter to Bularraf, wrote that he would continue to try to obtain a copy of the book. The same bookseller also pleads with Bularraf to leave Timbuktu for a less isolated town where his "immense merits will be truly appreciated." The writer exaggerates his admiration for Bularraf by calling him the "philosophe du Grand Sahara."[7] That this book could not reach Bularraf because the French authorities had prohibited its circulation makes us wonder whether parcels of books sent to Bularraf—or to anybody else—were the subject of surveillance by the authorities. Were parcels opened? If the books were mostly, if not all, in Arabic, who judged what could pass through or what should be prohibited?

Colonial controls and censorship came alongside the possibility of moving correspondence and materials around with regularity and some predictability. The French had established a series of post offices in this vast terrain, and this facilitated Bularraf's correspondence and bibliophilic network. The colonial administration gradually expanded the colonial postal service, and later the telegraphic network, from the Senegalese coasts deep into the interior parts of its newly conquered territories. The postal service in West Africa and across North Africa connected cosmopolitan centers that had many booksellers and printers with outposts like Timbuktu without a single bookseller or printer. While French territories were separated for administrative purposes, the communication networks joined them.[8] The colonial postal service was crucial to the movement of official correspondence in the first place but, of course, private commercial enterprises run by Frenchmen were also meant to benefit from this system. Communication was the lifeblood of effective administration and growing business success in the colonies. Correspondence and goods could circulate in this way. Bularraf's correspondence and books could come and go. By the time Timbuktu was conquered, the French had fourteen *Bureaux des Postes* scattered across the vast space of its Soudan colony. But there were also what the French journalist Felix Du Bois called "secondhand" post offices in various places, by which he meant a petty officer who ensured the departure and delivery of letters in every town with a French presence. Du Bois observed that the French mail was meant to arrive and depart once a fortnight. It apparently traveled at a rate of thirty-five miles per day.

Transport of correspondence and books by writers from the colonial territories would still have been conducted through the trans-Saharan camel caravans on which many generations of predecessors in the region had relied. However, Bularraf came to use the colonial postal service, "al-bustah" as he called it, extensively, for his correspondence and for sending and receiving manuscript works and printed books.[9] By the end of the nineteenth century, the postal service was developing steadily in the areas around Dakar and St. Louis. By the start of World War II, these services had reached the larger settlements of the interior of Mali. By this time, telegraphic lines spanned many thousands of kilometers. Various forms of transport were used to move mail internally between the different parts of the colonial territories, including motor vehicle, rail, river, and air transportation, when these forms of transport arrived in the colony and where they were possible. After World War I telegraphic and telephonic lines were in various stages of planning and implementation for the entire French Sudan colony. There was always the possibility of attacks by bandits in the desert—a concern expressed in letters from the period—and the colonial military presence ensured the relative safety of the movement of mail. As a merchant, Bularraf had many reasons to be concerned about the safety of the region, because his goods—such as tea, sugar, leather goods, and perhaps paper—had to come and go.

Bularraf would have continued using the older means of transporting books, but he was also concerned with the effectiveness of the postal service. In one of his letters, he wrote about postal rates and the length of time it took for items to move between two points by post.[10] The postal service, in theory, had an elaborate collection and delivery schedule for a number of locations in the colonial territories, and Timbuktu was among them. Schedules indicate the routes of certain cycles of collections and delivery. By 1929, Timbuktu was one point in a collection–delivery circuit that ended in Ansongo, passing through Kabara and Gao. For instance, collection was at Timbuktu on Tuesday at 7 a.m., with delivery in Gao on Friday at 11 p.m. and at Ansongo the following evening at 8 p.m. Mail would have to join other circuits to get to its intended point of arrival, and it seems this was rather slow-moving. On the other hand, it was regular, predictable, and secure, and Bularraf saw its usefulness.

There are archival materials and oral testimonies about other traders in Timbuktu. None has such a legacy of manuscript and book buying and collecting. For instance, there was Muhammad Ben Adbelwahab, also from Guelmim, who was an important merchant in Timbuktu and head of the Moroccan diasporic community in the town. All the letters to and from him in the 1920s and 1930s are about products other than books for resale, such as rice, couscous, salt, tea, jewelry, gold, and so on. His commercial contacts were not as extensive as Bularraf's and were largely confined to the Malian towns of the French Sudan.

Copying, Editing

While writing to booksellers, Bularraf was also working on gathering local manuscripts from within Timbuktu as well as from other towns in the region. In a number of cases, his copying and editing of manuscripts led him to write to contacts or strangers in distant cities to complete his copying and editing work. For instance, in a letter to Sayyid Muhammad, a descendant of Mukhtar al-Kunti, dated September 1945, he requests a copy of a work by another descendant, Ahmad al-Bakkay (recall the Kuntis from chapter 6). He believes that his correspondent had a copy of the work because it was cited in a text by the latter's deceased father. The owner of the work is located somewhere in a desert settlement called Taku. In this work, Bakkay responds to another scholar's promulgation of the views of the Tijaniyya Sufi order. Bularraf was keen to have this work. Bularraf says that there used to be copies of this work in the Timbuktu area, but they were all consciously destroyed. In his inquiry, he asks about the possibility of having the book copied and sent to him. He enquires about the cost of copying. He is prepared to pay for the copying and for the paper to be used. It turns out that Bularraf had a hundred pages of the work, but he could not fathom where they fit, since the pages were random. A good part of the letter is his citations of the beginnings and endings of the various sections he owns. Right at the end of the letter, he mentions the title: *Fatḥ al-Quddūs fī jawāb ibn ʿAbdillah Muḥammad Akansūs.*[11] An intermediary is mentioned, a tailor, who would assist with transferring the completed copy to Bularraf. We do not know whether Bularraf was successful in this request and added this work to his collection. This is, however, an example of Bularraf's work: he writes to the owner of a work in another location, requests a copy, offers to pay for copying and paper, identifies intermediaries to transfer the item or make sure it enters the rudimentary postal system then operating in the region, and finally receives the copy that goes into his collection.

Making copies of texts overlapped for Bularraf with writing his own works. In many instances, Bularraf's own writing begins as a copy of an existing work, which he ends up commenting on. This conforms in some ways to the classical Islamic *sharh* or commentary tradition; he even includes this term in some works. In earlier styles of this tradition, commentaries were interlinear, but his commentaries were added at the end of a text. He was not merely a copyist concerned with conserving a work under threat of disappearing or becoming difficult to read. He had an active interest in each work. There is also a possible pattern in the works that he chose to "save" through his copying and commentary. These works reflect the learned polemics and legal controversies of the time. The entanglement of copies with his own ending commentary leads to difficulties in how to attribute works: to him or the author whose work was copied? However, there are works that reflect his own thinking without reliance on another, "original" text.

Bularraf's Legal Writing

Many of Bularraf's writings were what we could call legal case reports and verdicts, or opinions on cases, a genre called *nawazil*—a term used in a number of works. A similar genre is the fatwa—a term also found in his work. In many instances, he includes his own view or "legal opinion," which would have been mostly an exercise in legal thinking without any practical impact on a case.[12] The French colonial authorities wanted him to take on the role as the head judge of Timbuktu, and there were people who regarded him as a judge (mufti) with the right to issue legal opinions (*fatawa*). There was perhaps recognition, in some quarters, for the volume of writing on legal subjects that he was collecting. One can only imagine him discussing cases with local scholars and friends and, over time, receiving greater recognition. There are examples of cases, from his own time and from much earlier periods, that he copied for posterity. Through these copies of legal cases and opinions, he preserved not only manuscripts, but a large and fascinating part of the history of Timbuktu and the region, because the cases deal with ordinary people and the issues that affected them and led them to seek mediation or legal redress. These cases contain details about marriage and divorce, commercial transactions, crimes, and all kinds of disputes. For example, one fatwa that shows how he combined his roles as copyist, commentator, and pretender judge is a case that involved a marriage proposal, a dowry, and a death. A man—no names are given—paid a dowry to his prospective wife, well ahead of the formal marriage ceremony. Thereafter, the bride and her family arranged their future living quarters in preparation for the ceremony and celebration. Unfortunately, before the wedding the man was attacked and killed by a lion! In Bularraf's rendition of the case, he adds that the woman's family also requested a share in the inheritance from his estate. In Bularraf's commentary—his "judgment"—he wrote that local practice on what constitutes a recognized marriage contract had to be taken into account, and ruled that there was, in effect, no marriage. The woman was not owed anything, since there was no formal, recognized marriage contract. This view went against two legal opinions supporting the woman's case.

In 1945, Bularraf wrote an opinion on the case of a woman who, within a space of about six months, took two husbands. Two scholars had already produced judgments. The case, he reports, is as follows: one Abd al-Qadir married a woman named Dhat al-Jamal and soon after their marriage, he went on a trip out of town. She objected to his travel plans but he said that he would not be gone for long. He apparently told her that, if he was gone for more than fifteen days, then she could divorce herself. There were no witnesses to the exchange. After fifteen days, with no husband back at home, she declared herself divorced from him. After the stipulated "waiting period" (three months) for women after a divorce, a man called 'Abd al-Mun'im asked for her hand in marriage. The two were quickly married and the marriage was consummated. After a few months, her first husband returned only to find her married; the new husband refused to let her go. Moreover, she was now pregnant with 'Abd al-Mun'im's child. Bularraf commented that the woman made up the fifteen-day rule, which had no grounds in the laws of marriage and divorce of Islam. The legal scholars of Timbuktu were asked by the first husband to express an opinion on the matter. In this way, Bularraf added his view, and wrote out the case like a story, and supplied the names of the main characters! In so many of the legal cases that he copied or on which he commented, there are elements that lead one to think of him as a kind of storyteller who enjoyed relating the real-life stories of Timbuktu. He wrote or copied and then commented on around thirty texts that have been classified as fiqh, under which these legal opinions, nawazil and fatawa, fall.[13]

In 1944, Bularraf was asked for by a scholar who had already given his views in a complicated paternity and inheritance case. This was not a fatwa, although Bularraf gave an opinion; his contribution was more like detective work, conducting an investigation that a judge would deal with. Bularraf first worked to establish all the relevant facts. He included the letter of the plaintiff in the case and added two texts of his own, based on his painstaking investigation of the issue. Was the person who is claimed to be the father really the father? Bularraf actually went to speak to people involved in the case; many of the witnesses were called on for their views, and he recorded the conversations.

His legal writing was often rich with detail, at times shocking, and could even evoke humor. The scholars were clearly argumentative. There were legal principles and rules in the region and he had to work with them in order to produce a plausible opinion. The opinions must have taken time for him to prepare, and he had to read other opinions on the same case, perhaps consulting other scholars and referring to his collection of books, as well as writing a convincing text of his own.

Another set of his manuscripts—as discursive texts and correspondence—concerned spiritual life, good behavior, and character. In his collecting, there was also some concern with Sufism and the controversies involving the major Sufi orders in the area. The Kunti family played a major role in Timbuktu (as has been shown in the previous chapter) and they assured the presence and powerful position of the Qadiriyya Sufi order in the town. But this Sufi order's hegemony was, as we saw, challenged with the rise and spread of the Tijaniyya. By the time Bularraf arrived in Timbuktu, the contestations and polemics might have subsided, but tensions were still shimmering under the surface. He appears to have been interested in following and putting together a position on the arguments of the respective actors in the region. It is still unclear if he belonged to any one of the two orders, or left the one to join the other. However, by the end of his life, it appears that he was not a member of any *tariqa* or rather, there is little evidence of his participation in the practices of any one in particular.

Doubting Bularraf

Bularraf was at the opposite end of a legal dispute with another scholar recognized to issue fatwas, Muhammad bin Ibrahim al-Kunti. They exchanged acerbic and sarcastic letters, dismissing each other's status and qualifications to give judgments. Bularraf mocked Bin Ibrahim, opening his text in the traditional fashion with praises and flattery, only to say that those words of praise are what he, Ibrahim, says about himself! In fact, he says, Ibrahim is a simple liar, arrogant and ignorant. Despite his claims to learning, he is incapable of dealing with elementary aspects of the law. In his response, Ibrahim denounces Bularraf for his lack of proper scholarly credentials, for being an imposter; he should stick to making money and not dabble in law or give legal opinions, for which he has no education! Bularraf's critic then hits where he believes it will hurt most. He points out that Bularraf makes many exaggerated and false claims about the book trade, the cost of books, and other items of trade, and in general is not a trustworthy man. He points to his copy of a particular work—*al-juz' al-Nafrāwī*—as flawed and inferior, contrary to Bularraf's claims. This happened in the mid-1940s, when Bularraf was late in his career as bookman, copyist, and legal opinion writer. Informally, he was probably regarded as a kind of lawyer and therefore his views were solicited. During his time, there were a number of qualified scholars who were respected by their peers and the general populace. The French were fostering a new legal system and were trying to get some of these scholars to work within the system, with uneven and limited success. Litigants decided which cases they wanted to take to the colonial courts and which to the scholars who lived among them.

Bularraf was a kind of transitional figure at the further reaches of the colony. He was a modern figure and, by all accounts, a pioneer when it came to the town's history because of his work to both revitalize and conserve the manuscript book arts of the town. His labors, of course, coincided interestingly with the growth of printed books reaching the Sahel. This increased circulation of printed books ran parallel to nearly the entirety of the French colonial period, with its postal system and other innovations. The great emphasis on handwritten books and other materials today easily leads one to forget that printing has been around in the region for more than a century. There was no aversion to print; no fatwa against its use has been found. Bularraf's manuscript-copying project was not a reaction against technological innovation and modernity. Bularraf's library held printed books; among them was *Kitāb Sībawayhi*, a work in two volumes, published in Paris in 1885. This was a classic work of Arabic grammar. He also arranged for the printing of local works, and he went way beyond the confines of Timbuktu in this pursuit. One claim is that at least ten such works were printed under the patronage of his library. Tunis is the only place of publication given. The apparent local preference for the manuscript over the printed form, until very recently—and even today—deserves further reflection.

Late Works

When Bularraf was seventy-six years old, he completed a work he called *Izālat al-rayb wal-shakk wal-tafrīṭ* (The removal of doubt) (fig. 14).[14] It was a biographical dictionary of his time. This type of work is standard in the history and world of Islamic scholarship, as we have seen; biographical dictionaries with various amounts of detail have appeared, and some chronicle not only the names and lives of Islamic scholars.[15] There are biographical dictionaries for other professions and fields of endeavor. Bularraf's dictionary is considered his major work of original scholarship, and he makes a place for himself in it. Listed under "Ahmad bin Bul'araf al-Musu Ali al-Takni," he is described as the compiler of twelve works at the time of the dictionary's composition in 1359 Hijri (1940 CE). He writes of himself as a compiler, not an author. It seems highly unlikely that the rest of his writing came after this—whether we number his works as few as 30 or as many as 150. But when describing his own scholarly efforts in his biographical dictionary, or *tarjamah*, he limits his scholarly contribution to work he did as a *compiler*. He lists his ten compilations of fatwas of local scholars. He had gathered the legal opinions (fatawa, nawazil, ajwiba) on numerous matters from a host of scholars. He also mentions two commentaries by himself, one on abrogated hadith by Ibn Jawzi, and another on a work by Ibn Hajar. He confidently includes himself among the greats of his era and region, but merely as a compiler. The entry on himself is of average length (fourteen lines of printed text), not the shortest but neither is it long. A number of entries are merely one line, noting, for instance, that someone was a writer of poetry or of legal opinions. There are around thirty entries that are extensive; one covers twelve pages. The twelve-page entry, which is the longest, is devoted to Muhammad Yahya Salim al-Wallati al-Yunusi.[16] He knew Bularraf but died much earlier, in 1936. We are not told much about Wallati's life, only given a long list of his works and poems. Most of Wallati's writings dealt with the details of law; he made a number of abridgments of classic Maliki law books. Several of his poems were attempts to summarize legal works in poetic meter.

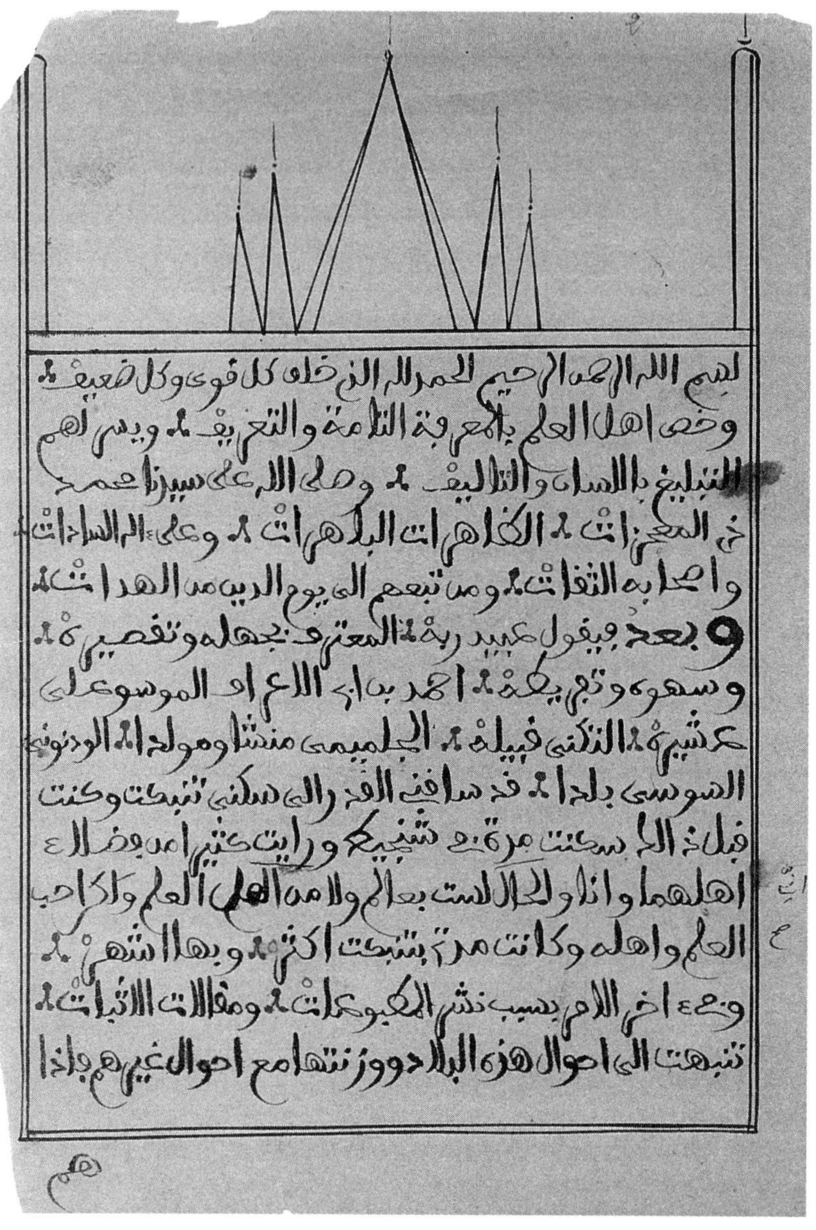

FIG. 14. The first page and index of Ahmad Bularraf's *Izālat al-rayb*, the biographical dictionary that he completed in 1940 in Timbuktu. This is the first appearance of an index in writings from the region. Other copies reveal his working method, and the manuscripts in his collection show how he collected his data for each entry. Both are in his hand. The index page is from a copy on gridline paper. 209 pages; 19 lines per page; text 17 × 13.2 cm; paper 23 × 18 cm. Cedrab 4989. *Image source*: From the archives of the Iheri-Ab (formerly Cedrab), in Timbuktu.

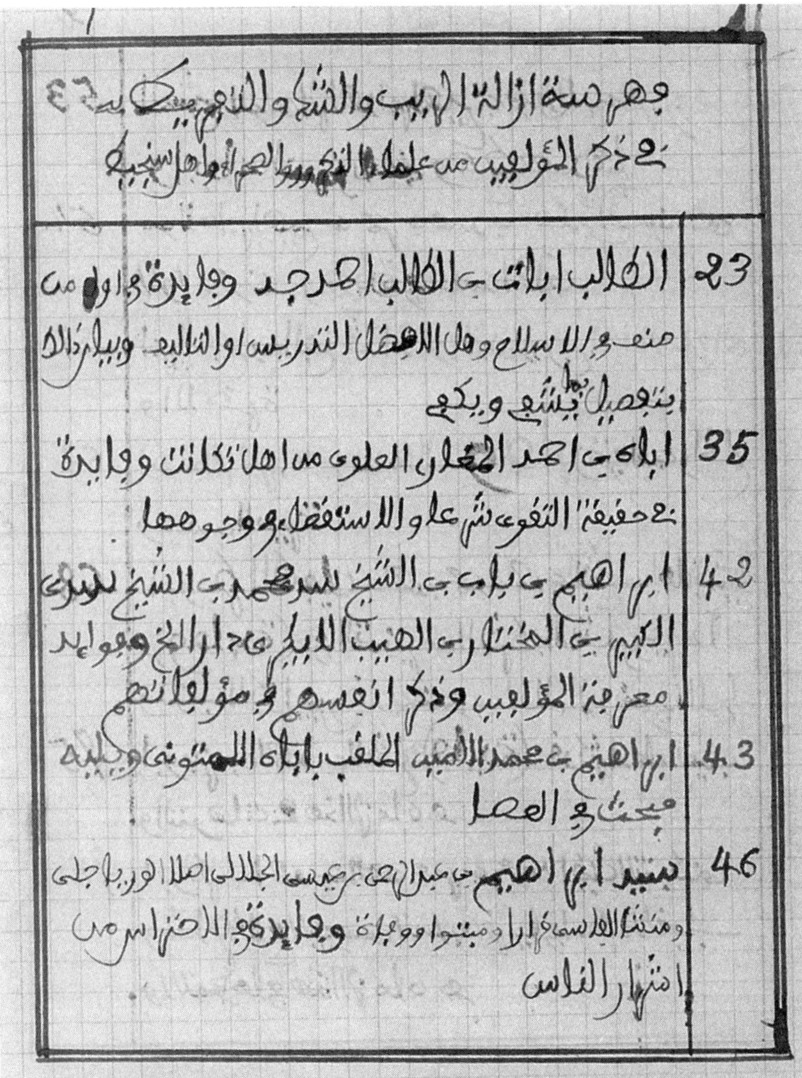

فهرسة ازالة الريب والشك والتفريط
في ذكر المؤلفين من علماء التكرور والصحراء واهل شنقيط

23	الطالب ابات بن الطالب احمد جد وله ايضا في اول من صنف في الاسلام وهل الافضل التدريس او التاليف
35	ابا بن احمد المختار العلوي من اهل تكانت وله ايضا في حقيقة التقوى شرعا والاستغفار ووجوهها
42	ابراهيم بن باب بن الشيخ سيدي محمد بن الشيخ سيدي الكبير بن المختار بن الهيبة الابيري ... وله فوائد معرفة المؤلفين وذكر انفسهم في مؤلفاتهم
43	ابراهيم بن محمد الامين الملقب باباه المحتوشي وله مبحث في العصا
46	سيدي ابراهيم بن عبد الله بن عيسى الجلالي اصلا ... ومنشأ الفاسي ... وله ايضا في الاحتراس من اشرار الناس

FIG. 14. (*continued*)

Bularraf admired men like Wallati. Later, he started to imitate them, probably first by writing out copies of their works. While he was never formally elevated to the status of *ʿalim* or a qadi, he did command respect for his learning. In calling his biographical dictionary his only original work, we are making too strict a distinction between a work that he started and completed, on the one hand, and others that he had himself copied or the copies he had commissioned. The reality was messier and the record of "original" and "copy" rather mixed and intertwined. His hand and mind intervened in the copying process. There is some evidence for this. In a massive text—more than eight hundred folios—that he himself finished copying in August 1937, on the last page he essentially claims that his copy is superior to the copy that he had copied! He writes that he had looked far and wide for the original but when he could look no further, he fell upon a copy and proceeded himself to work with it to produce a second copy. It was his passion for rare nawazil that led him to reproduce the manuscript, despite his initial reluctance due to the poor quality of the copy. The writing was filled with errors (*fasad*). He writes that his copy is the "more correct of the two copies as I carefully searched and reflected on it."[17] Yet he goes on hoping that he may still find the original.

Through copying a text, a new work was produced. We can therefore understand the confusion of catalogers trying to classify Bularraf's materials. This way of working may not have been unfamiliar in Timbuktu. Copies of the same title fill many catalogs and researchers may be missing originality by passing over them as "yet another copy." Timbuktu once had many scholars with their own collections, who were relatively relaxed about lending out their books. A scholar borrowing a copy of a specific work would very often copy it or have a copy made for himself of the borrowed work.

The Bularraf library has been reduced to a modest family collection hardly recognized as a library of significance and barely able to keep going.[18] One estimate is that in 1945 it held 2,076 manuscripts, which had dwindled to 680 by 2002. Many of the items were sold or donated by Bularraf's descendants to the state-run archive in Timbuktu in the late 1970s, with a few to the university library in Niamey, Niger. The Bularraf library is not really known these days, except among a few specialists, and it is seldom included on the circuit of guided visits to the libraries of the town.

Legacy

Ahmad Bularraf died in Timbuktu in September 1955. His family and library remained there, for the most part. Some of his library's holdings were sold and can be found in collections in Niamey, Niger, but most were kept in Timbuktu. When his library was still functioning, it reportedly had a kind of manuscript conservation unit, a place for copyists and for checking copies, and a unit for making covers for the loose leaves of writing (sewn bindings have never been used in Timbuktu). It is remembered as an inspiration for other archival ventures and as an example of an indigenous initiative when the UNESCO General History of Africa experts visited Timbuktu in the late 1960s. Bularraf's activities in the first half of the twentieth century are possibly the best example in West Africa of how an archive was formed. Could Bularraf's work itself be a consequence of an even earlier regional book collecting, archiving, and conservation style? If, for him, a network of copyists and bookmen was crucial, then for his predecessors in Timbuktu it would also have been necessary. In this extensive bibliophilic network, he was a generator of material and a medium for its circulation. In many ways, it is useful to think of him as mediator and middleman in a network.

Bularraf cultivated a network devoted to the reproduction of texts and to growing his personal library and his business. His activity was genuinely transnational. This may not have been unique in the broader narrative of Islamic intellectual or material history, but it was significant work, over many decades, to resuscitate and conserve a way of doing scholarship. There was originality in it, even as it was explicitly concerned with the supposedly unoriginal task of reproduction or copying. Jurisprudence was the field he was keen on—not abstract or classical theories about the subject but the living jurisprudence of Timbuktu and the wider region. This type of jurisprudence was like a living record of his own contemporary society.

The distances his original manuscripts, copies, and new books had to move were enormous. These objects of his passion literally had to travel through a network. The colonial postal service and linked technical innovations came to serve his network well. These means of networking and mobility have been mostly forgotten but they were indispensable tools of communication, especially over the long distances we are considering.

For Africa, studies of book history hardly exist. There is ample material in a number of places on the continent to research the world of writing and reading into which men like Bularraf entered or that they revitalized. Bularraf's work presents us with an opportunity to research, in detail, the formation of a library and archive. Even though the data is most often fragmentary and partial—chronological gaps and missing materials—many material aspects of manuscript and printed book cultures could be studied: cost of paper, size of paper, handwriting styles used, ink colors, which books had leather covers, signatures, copying costs, the politics of the colonial postal service, and so on.

Bularraf's network had a tactile, tangible, and material quality. As a bibliophile, he accumulated works originating great distances from Timbuktu. He bought works and commissioned copies, and so he had to concern himself with prices—of paper, of copying, of the postal service. Content, of course, was important to him; he was not a collector of random materials. He had an interest in specific subjects, and books related to these subjects were the object of his pursuit. However, we want to stress the *object* and the network, the *thing* within a network that stretched thousands of kilometers from Timbuktu in every direction. For instance, he wrote to booksellers as far apart as Fez and Tangier, in the distant west, through to Cairo and Beirut, in the east, to acquire works. The manuscript book and the later printed version are the objects that were made and circulated through a network that he actively stimulated and sustained. His network included writers of works, owners of texts, copyists of books, intermediaries between authors and copyists, middlemen in the movement of the objects from point of origin to him, from point of production to consumption, and ultimately, conservation. When he encountered the printed book, his network embraced booksellers and printers. We cannot say when he first handled printed texts, and whether they struck him as very different to manuscript books, but for the moment we shall keep this distinction between the handwritten and the printed work. The printing press came to Morocco in the early 1860s and took a number of decades to develop into an independent and full-scale commercial sector.[19] The sultan and his government were initially opposed to this technical innovation and it took decades for this technology to gain official recognition. Only by the end of the century did acceptance and then permission lead to the emergence of printed book publishing. However, from quite early on, printed books from elsewhere in the Arabic-speaking world, which had state or private commercial printing businesses such as in Cairo, found their way to the Maghreb. The handwritten work or manuscript, however, remained, for a long time after the introduction of printing—the fundamental means of producing and reproducing books. Scribal transmission of knowledge remained a highly valued activity. Scholars could write their own books but they would also resort to scribes to copy out texts or to make copies for them. These scribes comprised both the literal writers of the texts and a cohort of copyists. How Bularraf first responded to the printed book is unknown. However, he accepted its appearance and took it, alongside the manuscript form of the book, as a means of communicating knowledge.

8

Manuscript, Print, and Memory

DURING THE TIME that Ahmad Bularraf was involved in collecting manuscripts, printed books, newspapers, and printed administrative communications were becoming an integral part of the reading material circulating in French West Africa, even in places far from colonial towns such as Dakar and Bamako. Bularraf accepted the arrival of printed books, and even imported them, while continuing to collect and copy manuscripts. A small number of printed books had arrived in West Africa with explorers such as Clapperton and Barth, who brought them as gifts (see chapter 1). The former brought Arabic printed books that he had purchased in London. Other books, in the Latin script, had been left behind with the luggage of travelers such as Park and Laing when they died in the course of their exploration. These books were merely curiosities to those who had found them.

The spread of print and colonial educational policies went hand in hand.[1] New ways of teaching and learning introduced European languages, blackboards, mass-produced factory-made paper, and printed textbooks. In the French-controlled territories, exercise books, for writing out lessons, and textbooks, initially only to teach French, slowly made their appearance wherever the colonial administration opened new schools. Education was an integral part of the larger project to pacify the colonial territories. The French had come to West Africa where, in large parts of the territory, there was a long and deeply embedded intellectual culture with well-established learning routines and hierarchies, as we saw in previous chapters. The so-called Quranic school, which actually went under a variety of names, was the foundation of this system, followed at higher levels by a type of one-on-one tutorial system. Learning and eventually mastering Arabic was the long-term objective of this system. Arabic gave learners the ability to read and memorize parts or all of the Quran and later, for those who completed the higher levels, the capacity to read classical texts, speak, and write in Arabic. The language also had the potential to connect the learners to a larger Arabic-speaking and Islamic world that stretched far beyond their localities and West Africa. The French, with their colonial empire covering parts of the Muslim world—parts of West Africa, North Africa, and the Levant—were sensitive to the historic connections across this space, enabled by communication through a common language, Arabic. The growing availability of printed texts facilitated this. Manuscripts circulated in much smaller numbers and took much longer to get copied, compared with printed works. Whereas a scholarly manuscript might eventually have no more than a handful of copies, a printed text could be reproduced speedily and hundreds or thousands of copies could easily circulate. Print enabled the formation of new social and political identities. The specter of Pan-Arabism and Pan-Islam preoccupied even the West African colonial officials and their superiors in Paris. Bularraf, as we saw, was interested in getting the books of the Pan-Arabist Syrian intellectual Shakib Arslan, which the French tried to prevent from circulating. The French closely monitored publications moving through their post offices and censored materials they feared would promote solidarities that would undermine their empire.

The indigenous schools that taught Arabic were susceptible to new ideas that would undermine the version of Islam that the French were cultivating. They had to be closely monitored, and the question of how to challenge and impede this system, without stimulating opposition and causing unrest and resistance, was a concern to the administrators. One way of addressing this issue was to introduce a type of school that would teach Arabic and French, that included a certain number of hours of Quranic and religious studies per week but reserved more time for a secular curriculum with an emphasis on French language learning. In 1906, the colonial administration established the first of what they called the *médersa* in Jenne. In 1911, one was opened in Timbuktu, with thirty pupils. These schools—médersa was a version of the Arabic word *madrasa*, meaning school—were fully under French control. Apart from the objective of making inroads into the existing educational landscape so as to weaken it, the eventual aim of these schools was for their pupils to have fluency in French and be capable of working as functionaries in the administration. It was easier to formulate and reformulate in theory than to address the ongoing practical challenges in the areas where they established these schools. There were many twists and turns in practices right into the 1940s and 1950s. The officials engaged in extensive correspondence—between Paris, Dakar, Bamako, and the towns with these schools—and came up with new policy statements about which constituencies to recruit pupils from, how much Arabic to include, things to look out for, and so on.

Secular French schools were also established, offering no Arabic or religious subjects. These were open to pupils, irrespective of religion. Muslim families also sent their children to these schools. However, the Quranic schools that had a long history and were found in every village and also on the move, among the nomads, remained the most common way of educating children. Pupils memorized Quranic texts after writing them on wooden boards. In some families, the children, boys in particular, would be sent to French-language schools but would still be given a basic Islamic education at home or among scholars in the family or neighborhood. The médersa was an attempt to bridge this gap and give students an education in French as well as in some of the basics of what they might learn in the traditional schools. But the longer-term aim was to undermine the older, established, and widespread Quranic schools.

In Timbuktu, the médersa was the subject of debate among policymakers, particularly regarding which groups to recruit for the school, the children of the sedentary population or the children of the nomadic chiefs. Extremely few of the latter ever entered the school. Indeed, the schools did not attract large numbers; more than twenty years after their creation, in 1935, there were only 105 students at the Timbuktu médersa. In the meantime, the Quranic schools continued without colonial support and, of course, their pupils never learned French. Pupils at the Quranic schools continued to learn Arabic grammar and write out their lessons in local styles of calligraphy on wooden boards. They memorized portions of the Quran, the essentials of theology, rules of daily prayer, and so on. Basic education would also entail teaching and learning in local languages such as Songhay, Fulfulde, or Hausa. Thus, some of the primers to teach the essentials of the religion were versified in these languages. The scholars of the town would take under their wing individual pupils whose Arabic reading and writing skills showed promise. These pupils would spend years with one or more teachers, reading texts until they achieved mastery, which meant they could teach the text, in turn. French officials knew the outlines of this system, as they were in contact with some teachers. However, they began to show concern when some of the students traveled to Cairo and Saudi Arabia to study. The Bureau des Affaires Musulman (Muslim Affairs department) followed these developments closely. In 1950, the head of the bureau, Marcel Cadaire, made a tour of a number of Arab capitals and educational institutions where there were students from French West Africa, to gather information on the students.

The Quranic schools were paperless. Pupils relied on wooden boards and their capacity to memorize; they might also write in the sand right where they were sitting on the ground. A wooden board would be a lifetime possession or circulate within a family. Lessons would be written out and washed off, and new lessons written. Paper was reserved for scholars, to write out learned texts and to make talismans when they were requested. The coming of the colonial administration also introduced more and newer types of paper. Numerous manuscripts—from Bularraf's collection, for instance—are written on paper or in writing books that appear to have been brought by the colonial administration for use in their schools. How the scholars acquired this paper is not clear, but one can imagine that there was surplus stock sometimes that found its way to the market—or perhaps paper was gifted by the local administration.

A new educational development started unfolding in the late 1940s, when independent médersas were created by Muslim groups who wanted French and secular subjects to be taught alongside much of what a Quranic school would teach. This initiative began with students returning from studies in the Middle East, who wanted to reform the traditional system of education; they began in Bamako and Segou. The innovation generated much argument among Muslim scholars and leaders. Some of them made a stand for tradition, for wooden boards and memorization, and others for printed textbooks that would be imported from publishers in Rabat, Cairo, or Beirut. Timbuktu was not part of this development; there, the French médersa continued, as well as the older, traditional schools and the scholarly tutorial system for more advanced students.

The lists of books Bularraf imported during this period are intriguing. The quantities and titles show that some could have been for use in these schools. Since he had a long business relationship and a good reputation with publishers in Cairo and Beirut, he could have seen a business opportunity as a distributor in, and from, Timbuktu.

Bularraf's son, Muhammad Abdullahi, went through the local traditional Quranic schools and went from scholar to scholar, mastering texts. He became a noted scholar of Arabic grammar in his own right. The Bularrafs were well-known and were in contact with all the leading scholars of Timbuktu. During Bularraf's time there was, for instance, Ahmad Baber al-Arawani, author of *al-Saʿāda al-abadiyya fīl-taʿrīf bi-ʿulamāʾ Timbuktu* (The eternal bliss in introducing the scholars of Timbuktu).[2] This work was finally completed in 1962, with more than a hundred entries listing scholars from the past and his own era, sixty-five of whom the author knew. The latter number is indicative of whom the author considered scholars. For the earlier periods, the information was taken from the biographical dictionaries by Ahmad Baba, and the chronicles (*Tārīkh al-Sūdān* and *Tārīkh al-fattāsh*). Manuscript copies of these works were still circulating. The printed editions, the ones edited by Octave Houdas and Maurice Delafosse, were also probably brought into the colony, and it is not unlikely that manuscript copies could have been made from the printed editions. The biographical dictionary of Ahmad Baber is much smaller than Bularraf's dictionary and, of course, nothing compared with Ahmad Baba's. The chief departure of Baber's work is that it pays some attention to figures from the small settlements outside of Timbuktu. A copy of the work was completed on the French mass-produced square-lined paper.

Bularraf's death in 1955 did not signal the end of an era of learned writing, copying, and collecting. Conditions had changed, such as with the introduction of new types of schools, but there remained a cohort of students and scholars to reproduce the handwritten book tradition. Local writing continued but nobody took Bularraf's place as a collector; they collected or hoarded works produced within a family. Bularraf had begun his own tradition of collecting when he arrived in Timbuktu. No manuscript in his collection was printed in his lifetime. The biographical dictionary that he compiled was printed only in the 1990s. In his private collection is an undated legal work that was lithographed in Cairo at the Baruniyya Press. Three features reveal the increasing engagement with a wider book culture: the inclusion of a contents page, a copyright statement on the cover page—neither of which are found on manuscripts—and a rubber stamp, in Latin script, with the name "Hamed Boularaf."

The spread of print was also a factor in the growth of ethnic consciousness and the spread of nationalist movements. The French worked at cultivating a literate elite that could work in the administration and would support them. However, there was no certainty that those educated in French would automatically support the French. On the other hand, fortunately for the French, those whose working language was Arabic would not automatically oppose them or instigate rebellion.

Here follow stories of three figures whose writing lives and modes of literary communication crisscrossed manuscript and print technologies, the oral tradition, and book culture; they were all collectors in their own way. All three of them were prominent writers during the colonial period in the territories that became Mali, Niger, and Senegal. Of course, many more writers, or another combination, could be chosen to illustrate these relationships, but these are three outstanding figures whose stories demonstrate issues in the transitions from manuscript to print, with orality playing a prominent role in their work.

The Vocation of a Malian Intellectual: Amadou Hampâté Bâ

Amadou Hampâté Bâ was born in 1900.[3] Bâ was raised and educated first in Bandiagara and Jenne and then in Bamako. His family had ancestral ties to Ahmad Lobbo, the founder of the Hamdallahi-Masina state discussed in chapter 6. His basic education was at a Quranic school, but he did not continue at a higher level to learn to read legal and theological texts. His mother tongue was Fulfulde, and he probably could speak a few of the other languages used in his region; he acquired French through his education at a French-medium school, which was called the "school of the whites" in the community. Having completed the highest level of education possible in the colony, at least in this part of the French Sudan (now Mali), he worked at various levels of the colonial administration in the 1920s. A number of his positions in the administration entailed interpretation and translation work. His religious education and greatest spiritual influence came from the Sufi master and educator Cerno Bokar Salif Tal, from Bandiagara, who had pledged himself to a controversial branch of the Tijani brotherhood called the Hamaliyyah that was founded in Nioro after World War I. In 1933 Bâ "converted," as he put it, and devoted himself to the teachings of Cerno Bokar. The French were, as usual, suspicious of any activity that drew large numbers of followers and of which they were ignorant, and therefore saw a threat in the Hamaliyyah. In 1933, they exiled its founder. For Bâ to have joined the brotherhood, then, was potentially damaging to his career in the colonial administration.

However, with his education in French, his knowledge of the Fulfulde language, and his experience in various parts of the colony, Bâ was appointed to a position as a researcher in Dakar at the newly established Institut fondamental d'Afrique Noire (IFAN) in 1942. The founder and director was the naturalist Théodore Monod, who became a lifelong friend and supporter of Bâ. During Bâ's short sojourn in Dakar, he met many of the important figures in the French administration and the research community concerned with West Africa; in a number of cases, the role of administrator and researcher overlapped, as the officials also had fieldwork interests.

As a researcher, Bâ worked closely with the staff of the IFAN, who relied on his linguistic skills, but he also had his own projects in view. He collected oral narratives and data from locals whose language he spoke, and he saw these as containing the history of his own people. Thus, he came to see the collection of orally transmitted memories as the means of telling the story of those who were thought to live only in the present and to have no past. He did not simply collect raw testimonies but organized them and gave them coherence. In years to come, he became the author of many notable works. His first book, *Kaïdara*, was published in 1943. It was a collection of stories about Fulfulde initiation myths and rituals. In 1955, he published his first major work, *L'empire du Macina*, a history of the movement and state founded by Ahmad Lobbo, who was his ancestor. Bâ never used manuscripts for the book, which was based largely on oral tradition and testimony, but *L'empire du Macina* has since been used by historians drawing on a range of sources, including manuscripts. These historians, even into the present, have shown respect for and skepticism about Bâ's methods and sources. He completed the work with Jacques Daget, who was his supervisor in a hydrology project in the Masina area. IFAN was the publisher and Théodore Monod wrote the preface. Bâ's early significant writing projects were mainly with French collaborators. The exact contribution of each of the collaborators is unknown but Bâ probably used this type of collaboration to ease the publication process. There were many obstacles to a young African in the colony finding an editor or a publisher; there was also the issue of colonial censorship. In 1957, he published *Tierno Bokar le sage de Bandiagara*, with Marcel Cardaire, who was head of the colonial Bureau des affaires Musulman. The colonial administrators were suspicious of Bâ's Sufi master and teacher Cerno Bokar, because of his leadership role in the dissident branch of the Tijani order that the French were monitoring. They feared the order was preparing for some kind of resistance. Possibly only with Cardaire's name on the book could it be published. When Bâ reissued the work in 1980, Cardaire's name no longer appeared on the book's cover and he explained in the preface why Cardaire's name appeared only as coauthor. Bâ was clearly trusted by some of the officials with whom he worked closely. During this period, from the late 1940s, he threw his weight behind an initiative in Bamako to create an independent Muslim school system that would teach schoolchildren to recite the Quran and teach them French, but not the Arabic language; instead, Fulfulde and Bamana would be the languages of instruction. The French feared the Quranic schools that only taught Arabic, and wanted other local languages to be used, so they looked on this initiative favorably, and quietly supported it. Bâ threw his weight behind such a schooling system as an expression of his own identity as a proud Fulfulde-speaker.

Bâ was a strong proponent of the Fulfulde language and the cultural practices of the Fulbe people. He saw no contradiction between most of those practices and beliefs and his deep Islamic commitment. He argued that there is a convergence between Islamic spirituality and African cosmology. Arab and Arabic were not synonymous with Islam for him, and indeed he was at best ambivalent about Arabic, beyond appreciating it as the language of the Quran. However, there is evidence of him writing Arabic and using Arabic script to write Fulfulde (such writing is usually termed "Ajami," used for writing numerous West African languages), and he had a beautiful Arabic signature. The basic lesson of his Sufi master, Cerno Bokar, promoted by Bâ, was an oral teaching in the form of a dialogue between a *marabout* (teacher-cleric) and a new convert. It was originally composed in Fulfulde and visually represented to the initiate by drawing the process of the dialogue, in the sand if need be. It was called *Ma 'd-din* (What is religion?). Bâ transcribed this text and included it in his book on Cerno Bokar and his teaching. He created a diagram—a small artwork, really—of the lesson himself, with the text in Arabic script and signed it in Arabic.

In the 1960s, after Malian independence, and especially in the 1970s, Bâ's book covers did not carry the name of any French administrator as coauthor. These were also years when he was busy as a diplomat for independent Mali. He eventually relocated to neighboring Cote d'Ivoire as ambassador of the Republic of Mali and spent the rest of his years there. During these years, he published his great novel of the colonial experience from the perspective of a colonial functionary-interpreter, which could possibly have an autobiographical element. It appeared in 1973 as *L'étrange destin de Wangrin* (The fortunes of Wangrin) and won the *Grand Prix Littéraire d'Afrique Noire*. His two-part autobiography appeared posthumously. These are some of the highlights of a writing life that saw about twenty books in print, often reprinted, and many of which remain in print (and are gradually being translated into English). He also has countless essays and papers in edited volumes and conference proceedings.

He was active in UNESCO from 1960, as Mali's first representative, and as a member of its Executive Council for two terms from 1966. From 1971, he served on the board of the UNESCO General History of Africa. At UNESCO, he championed the use of African languages at all levels of the national educational systems in West Africa. He wanted to see the development of a common orthography for West African languages, and he envisioned one standard orthography using the Latin alphabet and another the Arabic alphabet. As a board member of the General History of Africa, he ensured that the organization made a commitment to publishing the volumes in African languages: eight volumes appeared in Swahili translation, and two volumes in Fulfulde and Hausa. His essay in volume 1 of the *General History* is titled "The Living Tradition." In it, he shows how oral tradition research is undertaken, and what orality means in an African society. It is a strong statement of his approach. He writes that, "In societies where writing does not exist, there is an intimate bond between Man and the word he utters. A written document is less constraining. Since the word is considered as being the sacred agent of occult forces, it is venerated as such and is handled with caution."[4] The transmitter of oral knowledge has to be of sound character; his knowledge and his action cannot be separated. Oral tradition, for Bâ, is "total knowledge."[5] He writes that he was able to write his book on the empire of Masina because he had received instruction relating to it since childhood and pieced together his narrative from a variety of reliable oral transmitters.

Bâ was invited to the founding conference in Timbuktu, held in 1967, when the UNESCO working group was preparing the establishment of the Ahmed Baba Centre (Cedrab) but he was unable to participate due to ill health. The objective of the meeting was to address the establishment of an institute for collecting and conserving manuscripts from across West Africa. Apart from the distinguished international experts, there were numerous scholars from within West Africa. For instance, the representative from Mali's neighbor Niger was the writer and senior politician Boubou Hama.[6]

The Writer-Politician of Niger: Boubou Hama

Boubou Hama (d. 1982) was born around 1906 in Fonéko, a village in the southwest of Niger. He was educated in the French schools and was sent to the École Normale William Ponty on the island of Gorée, an elite school that supplied the colonial administration with personnel and the schools with teachers. He attended from 1926 until 1929 along with students from throughout Francophone West Africa, many of whom became significant political figures in their countries. On graduation, he joined a school close to home as the first local teacher at a French-medium school. He had not been serving as a teacher long when the education officials started opening cases of insubordination against him. He was finally dismissed, for political activity, in 1947. He then had more time to invest in the emerging nationalist movement. He was elected to serve the Tillabéri region in the National Assembly that had been established in the colony. He was at the founding conference of the leading political party in the nationalist movement at the time, which he represented at the Rassemblement Démocratique Africain—an alliance of West African Francophone political parties—when it was launched in Bamako in 1946. After his party lost badly in local elections, he left politics temporarily and became the director of the IFAN branch in Niamey between 1954 and 1957. His passion for politics and history combined in the 1950s. In this decade, Hama was involved in all the high-level national and regional platforms concerned with independence in Francophone West Africa. At the same time, as director of the IFAN in Niamey, he could conduct research and write, and direct projects that included the collection of manuscripts in Arabic and other languages, held with families and scholars in the region. He also began to plan a museum that would become Niger's national museum. Recovering the histories of the region, starting with his own Songhay- and Zerma-speaking people, was a significant concern for him. Thus, his first book, published in 1954, was *L'empire de Gao: Histoire, coutumes et magie des Sonrai* (The empire of Gao: Songhay history, customs, and magic). Like Amadou Hampâté Bâ, he had a "co-author" for his first book. In his case, Jean Boulnois, a medical doctor who had an interest in the history of the territory. And like Bâ's book on the history of the Hamdallahi-Masina, the preface to Hama's book came from the pen of Théodore Monod. But unlike Bâ, he had to wait for about a decade before the book was published. He submitted it for publication in 1943, when he was still a teacher, but it was only published in the year that he became director of IFAN. His second book, a collection of historical narratives, also had a European name appear on the cover beside his, although he was the actual author.

Hama's books played an important role in communicating ideas about the origins and history of various language groups and states in or close to Niger: the Songhay-Zerma, the Peul, the Tuareg, and Gobir and Sokoto. After independence, in 1965, he wrote a general history of Niger, followed in 1966 by a large volume, nearly six hundred pages long, that plotted out the various levels and expressions of African unity. He wrote of an inner essence in "African civilization" that distinguished it from the West and gave Africans a unique humanism. It was obviously a highly idealized and romanticized image, even at the time. At the political level, there was work to be done to achieve Pan-African unity but he saw the Organization of African Unity (OAU) was a promising start. The book was launched in Dakar at the World Congress of Black Arts. Eleven of Hama's books are works of history. Many of his books were published by the pioneering journal *Présence Africaine* in Paris. His three-volume autobiography, *Kotia Nima*, appeared in 1971, and won the *Grand Prix Littéraire d'Afrique Noire*. The distribution of these books in West Africa, and how and by whom they were read, are questions that deserve investigation.

Hama's former pupil was Diori Hamani, who became Niger's first president, and Hama himself became president of the National Assembly, which made him the most powerful man in the country after the head of state. The post-independence government of Hamani soon became a de facto one-party state and silenced all opposition, often violently. In 1974, the government was overthrown, and Hamani and other politicians close to him, including Hama, were arrested and imprisoned on charges of large-scale embezzlement and fraud. Hama spent three years in prison and was released on the grounds of poor health, age, and, no doubt, his literary reputation. He died in 1982. In the 2000s, his name was rehabilitated and the national museum in the capital, his brainchild, was named in his honor.

Hama's most productive scholarly period was in the 1960s, when he held political office. The projects he had planned or started at IFAN could be implemented, such as the national museum, the center for African languages, and the center for Franco-Nigerian culture. IFAN became the IRSH (L'institut Recherches en Sciences Humaines), with a special Arabic manuscripts library alongside a research library. The manuscript collection is called the Centre for Arabic and Ajami Manuscripts. Hama was in correspondence with Ahmad Bularraf, or with his son Muhammad Abdullahi, about materials for the collection. Among Hama's papers are copies of manuscripts sent from Timbuktu as gifts from the Bularraf collection.

Boubou Hama and Amadou Hampâté Bâ were both at the historic conference of Black writers and artists hosted in Paris in 1956, organized by Alioune Diop, founder of the Pan-African publishing house Présence Africaine. The conference attracted most of the major figures in the world of African and diasporic literature, such as Aimé Césaire, Léopold Sédar Senghor, Cheikh Anta Diop, Richard Wright, and a young Édouard Glissant. In the conference group photograph (fig. 15), Frantz Fanon stands between Bâ, wearing his trademark traditional white boubou, and Hama, in suit and tie. By that time, Fanon had published *Peau noire, masques blancs* (*Black Skin, White Masks*), and was on the verge of joining the Algerian resistance movement. One wonders what they would have discussed while waiting for the photo to be taken; the radical psychiatrist between the gentlemen who were in close contact with senior colonial officials in their regions. Fanon would later travel through Mali for the Algerian National Liberation Front but there is no record of any further contact with Bâ.

The bulk of Hama's and Bâ's publications, and their award-winning works, would only be published in the years following this iconic conference. They were writers who straddled genres, but a golden thread that ran through their work was the African past, as understood by people on the continent. Writing from within the historical experiences of Africans was one of their primary intellectual pursuits. In 1971, both Hama and Bâ joined the board of the General History of Africa, and each has an essay in the first volume. Hama's chapter was titled "The Place of History in African Society" (Bâ's chapter was noted above). Bâ and Hama

FIG. 15. Group photograph of the 1956 Congress of Black Writers and Artists, Paris. Writers (Bâ, Fanon, Hama) mentioned in the book are on left, third row up from the front. Bâ and Hama are positioned on either side of Frantz Fanon. This would be the latter's last visit to Paris. The approach to literature and anti-colonial struggle of Fanon and the two West African writers diverged markedly. In 1960, Fanon traveled through Mali. *Image source*: https://www.aaihs.org/women-and-the-1956-congress-of-black-writers-and-artists-in-paris/. Likely first printed in *Le 1er Congrès international des écrivains et artistes noirs (Paris-Sorbonne-19-22 septembre 1956). Compte-rendu complet, Paris* (Présence Africaine, 1956).

were both renowned proponents for using oral traditions and testimonies in writing history and fiction. In Bâ's *L'empire du Macina*, he lists eighty informants whose memories he used.

In some of Bâ's and Hama's work, genres are blurred. For instance, Bâ's prize-winning novel *L'étrange destin de Wangrin* is sometimes seen as autobiographical. It might seem paradoxical that writers like them—and there are others—who extolled the virtues of orality, and sometimes even made orality seem essentially African, would be so committed to writing and publishing. Bâ did note the impact of global events such as the two world wars on the transmission of oral memory. He never gave up on the value of the human voice, on the spoken word. However, books were just as important to Bâ and Hama. They saw orality as fundamental when collecting their data and believed that it would remain an important means of collecting data. They were pioneers in putting the collection of oral testimonies and performances on the agenda of scholars of and in Africa. Moreover, beyond being sources of historical data, the process of telling stories and historical narratives often had a performative dimension. In both their essays in the *General History of Africa* they present this understanding of how history is lived *and* orally transmitted. Bâ's most famous words are: "In Africa, if an old person dies then a library is burnt."[7] In other words, what is transmitted orally across generations is also an archive.

However, their commitment to orality and performance, as necessary to the transmission of historical knowledge, found expression through the written medium; writing and publishing about these approaches to history was their way of capturing understandings of the past for the future. They could have become models of oral performance and poetry but they opted for writing and publishing instead of having their performances recorded. And Bâ advocated the development of a common orthography for African languages, as he believed in the significance of writing. But the script, he believed, must reflect more closely the actual sounds used by the people at the time. Furthermore, he wanted two parallel systems, one using the Latin script and the other the Arabic script. He was, of course, aware of the texts in his native Fulfulde in the so-called Ajami script.

If we know extremely little about the actual day-to-day practices and habits of writers, as they rose in the morning and wrote, taught and held consultations, then wrote again, we know from Bâ's niece Bintou Sanankoua, who lived in his household, how he literally lived to write. She writes: "He wrote everywhere, under all conditions. One would think that writing came easily to him. While he wrote, if a visitor was announced, often without an appointment, he would receive them on their schedule and return to work immediately thereafter, without complaining." She adds that he would involve her, having her look up words in the dictionary and so on: "It is striking to note how few corrections there are in his manuscripts and how legible they are."[8] He sometimes wrote in Fulfulde but mostly in French.

Bâ and Hama were completely at ease in the world of publishing. They were from what we might call the "late first generation" of writers in French in West Africa. They were, in many ways, self-made men—autodidacts—and had to rely on "sponsors" and "coauthors" to get their first books published. Most of their literary output came late in their lives, when they were active in politics and diplomacy—with books also appearing posthumously, in the case of Bâ. They also participated in an international African and diasporic literary and cultural network. They wrote about their regions and villages but were comfortable in big cities.

Another writer who wrote about his region but remained, for the most part, a writer close to home and to his village was from the middle Senegal River valley. He also connected oral, manuscript, and print but his magnum opus remained a manuscript book, like most of the works discussed in the previous chapters.

The Encyclopedist of Senegal: Musa Kamara

Musa Kamara was born in 1864 in a village of the Futa Toro region, in modern Senegal, which spawned many scholars and teachers going back at least to the early eighteenth century.[9] He was from a Fulfulde-speaking family that did not have a prestigious pedigree and was not wealthy, and although his father was a marabout he did not have a long scholarly lineage. However, he was sent away at a young age to study. He excelled as a student under different scholars in the larger region, with teachers on both sides of the Senegal River, in what is today southern Mauritania and northern Senegal. He would eventually read the major works of law used in the Sahel and receive permission to teach these works. Around 1891, now in his late twenties, he was back in his village as a teacher and scholar. When he was thirty years old, he was given the title of shaykh by a former teacher, Shaykh Saʿd Buh (d. 1917). Saʿd Buh was a scholar and an influential Sufi leader, of the Fadiliyya order, with a network of followers on both sides of the Senegal River. Saʿd Buh sided openly with the French as they were seeking out local allies in territories still restless with resentment and prepared to rebel against colonial control. While other scholars, like his own brother Ma al-ʿAnayn, advocated fighting the French, and called for jihad against them, he, however, argued the case for collaboration. Saʿd Buh was a source of local manuscripts for the French; one set of these manuscripts was translated by Ismaïl Hamet under the title *Chroniques de la Mauritanie sénégalaise: Nacer eddine* (1911) (mentioned in chapter 6). A text that Saʿd Buh wrote in 1906, meant for his brother, counseling him against jihad, was printed by the French administration—but only in 1909—and widely distributed by them among scholars on both sides of the Senegal River. (Figure 16 shows a man with stylus and paper and a writing board in the Senegal Valley in the mid-nineteenth century.)

Musa Kamara would be identified by the French as a potential ally on the other side of the river. As a scholar and leader, he had influence in his community and a presence among other scholars, and this was valuable to the French efforts to

FIG. 16. A mid-nineteenth-century representation of a scholar, here said to be a marabout making an amulet. "Marabout" was a term used by the French to refer to a religious figure who was literate, a holy man. This conception of writing and the writer as someone who makes amulets—secretive objects, not texts to study—was long the dominant way of seeing literacy in West Africa. The setting is close to where the scholar Musa Kamara lived. *Image source*: "Homme et femme toucouleurs: Marabout faisant un grigri," in P. D. Boilat, *Illustrations de esquisses sénégalaises, physionomie du pays, peuplades, commerce, religions, passé et avenir, récits et légendes*, vol. 2 (Paris, 1853), plate 20. This lithograph is attributed to: Jacques-François Llanta (1807–64).

win over local populations. He also agreed with his teacher Saʿd Buh's arguments about not mobilizing communities to take up arms in a jihad against the French. The French cultivated him as a trustworthy friend and a kind of ethnographic informant. Symbolic of his status in his later years, among both the colonial administrators and the Muslim teachers and scholars of French West Africa, was his being chosen to represent the Muslims at the opening of the Cathédrale du Souvenir in Dakar in 1935. His speech focused on the unity of the "religions of the book," in this case Christianity and Islam.[10] His speech was later expanded into a long essay on the subject. However, it was not as a speaker and representative of the scholars on a public stage that he had made his reputation. He was a prolific writer. He wrote around three dozen works that cover the fields of history, law, theology, and ethnographic description.

He completed his magnum opus in 1925, calling it *Zuhūr al-basātīn fī tārīkh al-Sawādīn* (Flowering gardens in the history of the Blacks), a manuscript book in two parts.[11] The book is a sprawling work that covers West Africa, from the middle Niger Valley to the Senegal Valley. There are paragraphs on Ethiopia and East Africa, the impact of European imperialism, and the subsequent division of the continent. He writes of the calendar and measuring system of the Europeans. In places he writes short notes based on well-known narratives and books; in other parts, it is detailed, a kind of micro-history. Early on, he describes the "Kingdoms of Mali and Songhay," and discusses the askiyas and the Saʿdian invasion.[12] The book touches on the early history of Islam, the Sokoto jihad of 1804, and the Hamdallahi-Masina state of Ahmad Lobbo. On Kamara's native region in the middle Senegal River valley, he goes into a great amount of detail, drawing on oral sources, because some of the events covered were only two to three generations before his time. He traces the states that evolved there, the leading historical actors, genealogies, major historical events, and the recent history, organized along the geographical divisions of the Futa Toro region. This regional emphasis occupies most of the work, while the rest is a survey of the broader region and other topics. In a few sections, he introduces documents as a basis for his discussion. He gives extracts of poetry, including his own. The work keeps the Fulbe people firmly in view; he addresses their origins and their language. The founders of the Sokoto state were Fulbe, and he introduces them early on as well. He traveled extensively and probably collected the stories and information that went into this book. When he turns to his own region, the work becomes detailed local history based on oral testimonies and local documents. Clans, families, specialized subgroups, battles, individual leaders, scholars, and teachers are given detailed treatment.

The work is a mine of information, and a record of a curious mind and voracious reader. Giving a brief description of the contents has its challenges, because there is no chronological order or discernible logic to the topics; at times there are many digressions, seemingly arbitrary discussions, only for a historical narrative again to be taken up. For instance, Kamara has a number of pages on *sihr* (sorcery) that seem to have nothing to do with what comes before or after them. He has further digressions, on the Sunjata epic, on the name "Africa," the Hebrew alphabet, and on the Franks and Greeks, to mention a few. He ends with a brief discussion of the Prophet Muhammad's mission and the concept of the Mahdi (the "Expected One," a messianic figure). This idea was behind a number of the movements in West Africa in the preceding century.

By the end of his encyclopedic effort, Kamara had produced a manuscript book—divided into two volumes—of 1,700 pages altogether! Even though it was exhaustive by any estimation, there were themes he did not fully develop in this large work but that he addressed in subsequent books. Kamara used oral informants and written documentation, including the chronicles so closely associated with Timbuktu, *Tārīkh al-Sūdān* and *Tārīkh al-fattāsh*, as well as Ahmad Baba's biographical dictionary *Nayl al-ibtihāj*. He cites Ibn Battuta frequently, has a discussion of Ibn Khaldun's theory about climatic zones, cites Ibn Qutayba, and discusses the *Mu 'jam al-buldān* of Al-Yaqut al-Hamawi, to mention a few. This is an indication of what books he had close at hand, in his own library or the collections of other scholars living close to him.

Kamara had close contact with the French administrators, such as the governor of Mauritania, Henri Gaden, who spoke the Fulfulde dialect of the middle Senegal Valley and wrote on the folklore of Fulfulde speakers. Kamara had met Paul Marty, who was a major figure on the ground in North Africa and wrote a number of books on Islam in West Africa (see chapter 6). Kamara was probably encouraged by Gaden and the Orientalist Maurice Delafosse to finish this large, encyclopedic, writing project. They promised to publish the work, in both its original Arabic and in French. Kamara's inclusion of a contents page is probably a result of his contact with them. Most manuscript books did not have such a basic guide to their contents until this time. During this period, however, such small innovations were beginning to appear in the manuscripts.

Delafosse was in correspondence with Kamara about plans to publish the entire work, but Delafosse died in 1926, and the publication never materialized. The work remained a manuscript, in both senses of the term: a handwritten text and a work on the way to publication. Eventually, copies were made, of which three are extant. Two copies, and many of his other works and papers, were deposited at the IFAN in Dakar. One, the copy that Delafosse had in his collection, reached Timbuktu. It was given to the director of the Ahmed Baba Centre by a descendant of Delafosse. However, the work does not appear in the catalogs of the center. All of Musa Kamara's manuscripts were eventually deposited at IFAN; some of his materials were deposited during his lifetime, the rest after his death in 1945.[13] Amadou Hampâté Bâ, when he was at IFAN, was involved in the organization and archiving of these materials, called the "Fonds Kamara."

As a loyal colonial subject cultivated by French Orientalists and administrators in the colony, five years after completion of his masterpiece Kamara was awarded a prestigious *Legion d'honneur* medal. The promise and possibility of publishing his work was still very much alive then. He was a learned interlocutor with the French but he did not write to defend or promote their colonizing mission. He remained in his village, teaching small groups of students, tending to his land, and writing, surrounded by his family and his collection of books.

Kamara was obviously deeply disappointed that his work did not go into print. Various projects to publish and translate the work began after his death, but only in 1998 did the first volume of a translation appear.[14] That initial project is five hundred pages long. In 2010, a printed edition was published by a literary foundation—in Kuwait! The latter was not produced, however, to the expert philological standards that many scholars expect and that his work deserves.

The Printed Book in a World of Manuscripts and Orality

A biography of Amadou Hampâté Bâ was given a title that translates as "the man of tradition." But this title does not capture him. If anything, he was eminently "modern." He stressed the importance of recovering oral narratives and performance to communicate a sense of the past, but not to recreate any past. He cultivated the use of indigenous languages, such as his own Fulfulde, with contemporary techniques, and used the institutions available to him. The data he collected from informants were conveyed in the native languages of those informants. He did the listening and observation (participant observation, anthropologists might call it), taking notes and turning all the information into narratives in his chosen language of publication, French. He was committed to writing, and to writing primarily in French. Furthermore, he was passionate about seeing his research become books, using the modern codex as a means of capturing "traditions" and giving expression to his own creativity. His most famous words, "In Africa, if an old person dies then a library is burnt," are now proverbial. When he died at the age of ninety-one, he left behind a huge library of books, manuscripts, and private papers. So, his words about old people as libraries were not a rhetorical flourish but had a real referent, except that with his death his books continued to be published and circulated, and his own library later became an archive.

The possibility of transmitting narratives from the past—with more-or-less stable content—is the key argument for using and relying on oral traditions. But it is, in fact, a form of literature and a type of historiography. For the latter, it derives its plausibility from the idea that stories are passed on with good intent over generations, even centuries. The best kind of transmission is when there is little variation between versions or over time, but variation—often by large degrees—is inevitable. The griots (storytellers, called *jelew* in the West African Mande language), or others recognized by a community as relators of narratives, talk among themselves and share stories. Things change over time and from place to place. The fixing of narratives in books, in the regions with literate individuals such as those discussed in the previous chapters, means that the written texts could be potential sources of oral traditions or elements in them. Just as oral traditions were put down on paper by writers such as Bâ and Hama, so that they were saved for posterity, their written works, in turn, would be the sources for further elaboration and representation of narratives. Conversely, the chronicles and other histories written over this vast region were potentially sources for the traditionists' stories. The written and the oral were not two opposite or contradictory positions, but rather they influenced each other and were intertwined. It might seem ironic that the proponents of orality, such as Bâ and Hama, were often the most elegant writers. As the philosopher Souleymane Bachir Diagne has argued, the proponents of orality clearly show tremendous pleasure in their writing. It is in this pleasure that orality is transformed, is given new shape and extended.[15]

Bâ and Hama wrote all their works in French. They published them firstly with IFAN and then with publishers in Paris, and, of course, with Présence Africaine. They worked closely with French collaborators and, in the first phase of their writing careers, published with coauthors attached. Musa Kamara was in close contact with French officials but never copublished anything. If his magnum opus had been published in his lifetime, it is highly unlikely that it would have had a French name, such as Delafosse's, on the cover beside his. But he never had anything printed in his lifetime. His magnum opus has begun to appear in installments, in translation, only since the late 1990s. All three writers were writing in societies experiencing the impact of foreign, colonial rule; things were falling apart, and so was the possibility of knowledge of the past. When Bâ and Hama met Fanon in Paris, he had not yet written that "By a kind of perverted logic, it [colonialism] turns to the past of the oppressed people, and distorts, disfigures and destroys it. The work of devaluing precolonial history takes on a dialectical significance today."[16] What Fanon wrote in his chapter "On National Culture" in *The Wretched of the Earth* was an intuition borne out of his experience of the colonial territories in which he lived and through which he traveled. The three authors discussed in this chapter probably instinctively felt this and reacted, by writing, by working to get the past into print, to make history.

Bularraf wrote an introduction to his biographical dictionary *Izalat al-rayb*. He called the introduction "On the Importance of History" and in it he complained about the neglect of conservation of history in Timbuktu. He did not mean only the conservation of the names and works of scholars, as he was doing, but all aspects of the "cultural life" of the town, its practices, and its folklore. The introduction, in fact, says little about the "high culture" of learned men but concentrates instead on everyday life. Bularraf was of the same generation as Kamara but not of the same rank as a writer; his talents lay elsewhere, in copying and collecting texts vital to the writing of history.

Epilogue

"WRITING," "SCRIPT," "text," "manuscript," and "book" are recurring terms in the foregoing chapters. Each word could be explored at length for its etymology, meanings, and nuances. A thesaurus might give them as synonyms, depending on the context of their use. While "writing," "script," and "text," on the one hand, could lend themselves to an abstract understanding, "manuscript" and "book" can be seen as tangible, as things to hold, handle, and move. The one set stands for substance and content, the other for the container of the content, the support on which writing, a script or text, is inscribed. There is also the term "work," which captures them all, implying intellectual and physical effort and exertion. Working, or work in progress, results in a *work*, which is both an abstraction and an object.

At places in this book, for the sake of variety in the prose, there is some slippage in usage of these terms. However, the manuscript and book—or manuscript as book and vice versa—has been its concern. The phrase "manuscript book" is a way to stress that there was (until recently and even presently, although less so) a culture and economy of codices written by hand in the Sahara-Sahel. Handwriting a text or copying one, even when a copyist or group of them would have to spend a great deal of time to reproduce hundreds of pages to make a single copy, has a long but often forgotten history.[1] While printing technology spread through Europe in the wake of Gutenberg's invention from the mid-fifteenth century, across the Mediterranean Sea, in the interior of West Africa, a tradition of writing books by hand was taking off. And Timbuktu is a symbol of this manuscript book tradition. This book has focused on the Sahara-Sahel. As I have tried to show, Timbuktu was by no means the only or most productive space for writing. It was a small place connected to a number of other small settlements where paper and writing were valued. Going eastward, toward the Red Sea, in the northern Ethiopian highlands there is an even longer tradition of the manuscript book. Ethiopic manuscript books (*mashaf*) represented the epitome of a literate culture in northeast Africa, shaped by the intellectual and cultural trends of south Arabia and Christian Egypt from late antiquity onward.

Christian monks, often high up in the mountains far away from their communities, produced parchment codices for centuries. While there is a long literate tradition, only a handful of the extant manuscripts date to earlier than the twelfth century. Beside this tradition, there are also the Arabic and Harari manuscript cultures of that part of northeast Africa. Thus, spread out across the Sahel belt, manuscript and manuscript book cultures can be found.[2] From the Atlantic Ocean to the Red Sea, manuscripts and books were not alien importations. Coastal East Africa should also be included, although a manuscript culture emerged there somewhat later than the events that begin and are discussed in this book. African manuscript book cultures were diverse and comparing this diversity is yet to be undertaken. It would be simplistic to divide the writing cultures by religious specificity or regional identity.

The book, for most of history, was a handwritten and handmade object, and not only in Europe. In most of the world this was the case, such as in the Far East—in China, Japan, and Korea—with a longer and very different history of printing than Europe's. Writing, as evidenced by the Arabic epigraphy from the eleventh century, has long been part of the cultural life of the Sahara-Sahel. There was literacy among some communities for centuries before the appearance of the Latin script in West Africa. The uses of the Tifinagh script in the Sahara were not addressed in this book. It has a long history and widespread presence in the Sahara, but it was not used for scholarly writing; no manuscript book in this script surfaced during research for this study.

The book before the invention of print is relatively underexplored compared with the field of book history that deals with the printed book. For both the manuscript and the print eras, the invention and spread of paper has been crucial—a precondition for their development. In the Sahara-Sahel, paper has also been the support for most of the manuscripts, but there was no paper production on the continent during the period covered in this book. The importation of paper and the particulars of the economies in which paper was exchanged have hardly been studied. Paper must, however, be seen as an object of value in the communities where there was some literacy. The history of paper before print in Africa is long because print is relatively recent, arriving only with the various contacts with and colonization by European powers. The Christian, especially Protestant, missionaries in the nineteenth century were particularly important in the establishment of presses on the continent. The conflation of the book and print has led to the misrepresentation of the continent as a space without books, except for parts of northern Africa. The manuscript book in Africa, such as those introduced in this work, remained outside the frame of book historians who found no codices to write about because they were looking for printed books. This, then, became a narrative of the arrival and triumph of print in the colonies.[3]

The study of manuscripts has a long scholarly pedigree, for the most part concerned with content, with the text. Manuscript studies was the turf of philologists concerned with establishing authorship when it was doubted, and with producing an authoritative version from several copies of a work. The scholarly discussion about editions of texts was the main object of the field. The complex cultures in which manuscripts were produced, and their materiality, was seldom of significance. Two recent shifts are necessary to note. One is the orientation to "manuscript cultures" that is interdisciplinary and seeks to look beyond one region of the world. (Manuscript studies has mainly focused on European textual output, although there are also philologists in Europe who produced editions of texts from what they called the Orient, for instance.) The increasing accessibility of digital technology has enabled this approach. The second development is the investigation of philological styles and approaches that were practiced outside the dominant canon, as idealized in the major theorists of textual criticism. The initiatives to examine philological practices outside the dominant, inherited standards have enabled newer readings and approaches to manuscript cultures. Thus, the works discussed in this book are no longer viewed as being without a tradition worthy of attention. The purpose of philology is no longer to produce a standard edition but to pay attention to a larger set of practices, interventions, copies, and conventions of conserving texts.[4] In the case of many of the works introduced in this book, there are no colophons, and copies without dates abound. Yet there are traces of local approaches to texts.

In the Sahara-Sahel, the works discussed are all considered to be books. The term "manuscript"—*makhtuta*—is never used in the period that this book covers. The word "book" (kitab) is used even for what we might consider to be small essays. "Manuscript" is a term that has been applied by scholars who study the collections. Indeed, they are manuscripts, in the sense that they are *manus scriptus* (handwritten). But they are also codices, handwritten volumes kept between covers, meant to be read, shared, copied, circulated. They never achieved the number of copies that a printed book would, but that does not disqualify them as books. Thus, the expression "manuscript book" points to their form and allows a discussion of several fields.

The manuscript books introduced here are a handful from a vast body of manuscripts and books that were written, copied, and made in the Sahara-Sahel. From the stirrings of African history as a professional field during the years of decolonization in the late 1950s and 1960s, there was some attention paid to retrieving primary sources. Then began the collection of manuscripts for conservation and for the writing of histories. Only recently have there been attempts at quantification.[5] Counting them has not been without its challenges, one reason being that collections have never been stable entities and most of them are privately owned. The manuscript cultures of the region are not artifacts from the past but living archives. In counting them, there are many questions: What is a manuscript or a book? What is an original work and what is a copy? Then there is the question of forgery. These issues cannot yet be addressed to make any easy generalization. The longest-running attempt to quantify literary output suggests a total of just under seventy thousand titles at a minimum. (This number does not include texts in Ajami—non-Arabic languages in Arabic script. There has been a recent increase in attention to Ajami and its present uses in West Africa.) Out of this number, certain trends have been identified—for instance, the Islamic literary culture that was in place in the nineteenth century. Most works counted were written in that period, fewer before then. The growth of manuscript output in the nineteenth century does not mean a much longer tradition did not exist. Only a small number of manuscripts—from any era but especially the earlier periods—have been studied comprehensively. But there have been many advances—the quantification effort itself is significant—and importantly, there is some recognition in diverse scholarly communities of the manuscript and book cultures of Africa.

In this book, the manuscript books were shown to cover a variety of subjects. Their contents reflect local and regional intellectual concerns and trends. Evaluations of the "originality" or "quality" of the thought would be anachronistic and a misreading of the contexts of their articulation. It would also feed into the questionable, and outmoded, binary discourse of a "Great Tradition" of Islamic thought against a small tradition, with writers discussed in this book all falling into the latter category. The manuscript book form, and its ideas, should be understood in their contexts and appreciated as products of a long tradition that persisted through great challenges and across many generations.

NOTES

Introduction: Books and Rebels in the Desert

1. For the history of ethno-nationalist politics and insurgencies in northern Mali, see Jean Sebastian Lecocq, *Disputed Desert Decolonisation, Competing Nationalisms and Tuareg Rebellions in Northern Mali*, Afrika-Studiecentrum 19 (Leiden: Brill, 2010), and essays in Michel Galy and Bertrand Badie, eds., *La guerre au Mali* (Paris: La Découverte, 2013). On the larger complexities of Malian politics around this time, see Baz Lecocq et al., "One Hippopotamus and Eight Blind Analysts: A Multivocal Analysis of the 2012 Political Crisis in the Divided Republic of Mali," *Review of African Political Economy* 40, no. 137 (2013): 343–57. See also Roman Loimeier, *Islamic Reform in Twentieth-Century Africa* (Edinburgh: Edinburgh University Press, 2016), chapter 3, on the rise of Islamism in northern Mali. Two journalists published books about the capture and then liberation of Timbuktu: Joshua Hammer, *The Bad-Ass Librarians of Timbuktu: And Their Race to Save the World's Most Precious Manuscripts* (New York: Simon & Schuster, 2016); and Charlie English, *The Book Smugglers of Timbuktu: The Quest for This Storied City and the Race to Save Its Treasures* (London: William Collins, 2017). See the former for a taste of sensationalist writing based on hearsay at best. I offer some reflection regarding the reporting on the book burning that never happened in Shamil Jeppie, "Schaurmärchen über Timbuktu," *Zeithschrift für Ideengeshichte* 16, no. 1 (2022): 48–56. The latest work to survey the issues of book burning and library destruction in European and American history is Richard Ovenden, *Burning the Books: A History of the Deliberate Destruction of Knowledge* (Cambridge, MA: Belknap Press of Harvard University Press, 2020).

2. A comprehensive introduction to northwest African ecology, geography, and history is Raymond Mauny, *Tableau géographique de l'ouest africain au Moyen Age* (Dakar: Institut Francais d'Afrique Noire, 1961). This work is a good place to get an impression of the history, geography, and commerce of the region, and the range of sources available at the time. See also Timothy Insoll, *The Archaeology of Islam in Sub-Saharan Africa* (Cambridge: Cambridge University Press, 2003), chapter 5. For a deeper historical introduction based on recent archaeological work in an important market town in the region, see the essays in Sam Nixon, ed., *Essouk-Tadmekka: An Early Islamic Trans-Saharan Market Town* (Leiden: Brill, 2017). Lydon studies the long-distance trade networks and the role of written documents in the nineteenth century in Ghislaine Lydon, *On Trans-Saharan Trails: Islamic Law, Trade Networks, and Cross-Cultural Exchange in Nineteenth-Century Western Africa* (Cambridge: Cambridge University Press, 2009). In most studies on the economies of the region, the sources used have allowed more to be said about long-distance exchange than productive processes

or technologies. In the recent writing, attention to sources has evolved away from attempts in the 1980s to produce concepts and theories to understand the political economies of the larger region. There are attempts to theorize the economies or political economies of the Sahara going back to the 1980s; see, for example, the work of E. Ann McDougall in her "The View from Awdaghust: War, Trade and Social Change in the Southwestern Sahara, from the Eighth to the Fifteenth Century," *Journal of African History* 26, no. 1 (1985); and E. Ann McDougall, "Conceptualising the Sahara: The World of Nineteenth-Century Beyrouk Commerce," *Journal of North African Studies* 10, nos. 3–4 (2005).

3. This chapter refers to the Ahmed Baba Centre. At its founding in the early 1970s, it was named Centre de Documentation et de Recherche Ahmed-Baba (Cedrab); in the 2000s, this changed to L'Institut des Hautes Etudes et de Recherches Islamiques Ahmed-Baba (Iheri-Ahmed Baba). On the library initiatives, see the descriptions on the websites of the Institute for the Study of Islamic Thought in Africa (Northwestern University, Evanston, Illinois), the Centre for the Study of Manuscript Cultures—Understanding Written Artefacts (University of Hamburg), and the Hill Museum and Manuscript Library in Minnesota. The Vecmas (Valorisation et Édition Critique des Manuscrits Arabes Sub-sahariens) project at the École Normale Supérieure de Lyon) has published editions of manuscripts from West Africa. A record of the South African building project is titled *Building an African Partnership: The Ahmed Baba Institute's New Library Archive in Timbuktu* (Midrand: South Africa-Mali Timbuktu Manuscripts Trust, Development Bank of South Africa, 2011).

4. The traditions of study and associated manuscript collections are discussed in Graziano Krätli and Ghislaine Lydon, eds., *The Trans-Saharan Book Trade: Manuscript Culture, Arabic Literacy and Intellectual History in Muslim Africa*, The Manuscript World 3 (Leiden: Brill, 2011). See also essays and descriptions by collection owners in Shamil Jeppie and Souleymane Bachir Diagne, eds., *The Meanings of Timbuktu* (Cape Town: HSRC Press, 2008). Ousmane Kane, in *Beyond Timbuktu: An Intellectual History of Muslim West Africa* (Cambridge, MA: Harvard University Press, 2016), focuses on learning and teaching and goes far beyond Timbuktu in his coverage. The specialist journal *Sudanic Africa*, rebranded in 2010 as the online journal *Islamic Africa* (Brill Online), carries discussions of individual scholars and texts, among other things. Similarly, *Islam et Société au Sud du Sahara*, between 1986 and 2004, is a necessary journal to search for articles on the scholars and intellectual trends in the region.

5. On political formations—from states to larger formations—in the region, see Nehemia Levtzion, *Ancient Ghana and Mali* (London: Methuen, 1973); John O. Hunwick's introduction in ʿAbd al-Raḥmān ibn ʿAbd Allāh al-Saʿdī, *Timbuktu and the Songhay Empire: Al-Saʿdi's Tarikh al-Sudan down to 1613 and other Contemporary Documents* (Leiden: Brill, 1999); and Michael A. Gomez, *African Dominion: A New History of Empire in Early and Medieval West Africa* (Princeton, NJ: Princeton University Press, 2018). See also Lansiné Kaba, "The Pen, the Sword, and the Crown: Islam and Revolution in Songhay Reconsidered, 1464–1493," *Journal of African History* 25, no. 3 (1984); and John O. Hunwick, "Gao and the Almoravids Revisited: Ethnicity, Political Change and the Limits of Interpretation," *Journal of African History* 35, no. 2 (1994). The writing on power and politics has, in most cases, opted for descriptions of events and powerful political personalities. Problems with the sources are one reason for this.

6. On book borrowing, there is a letter from the Saharan scholar-politician M. Ould-Cheikh to A. Bularraf (MS 6101, MS 8846, Bularraf Collection, Cedrab, Timbuktu). For more

about the latter, see chapter 7. On book-buying trips, see Shamil Jeppie, "Examples of Sahelian Book Collectors Over Two Centuries," in *Landscapes, Sources and Intellectual Projects of the West African Past: Essays in Honour of Paulo Fernando de Moraes Farias*, ed. Toby Green and Benedetta Rossi (Leiden: Brill, 2018).

7. A work that takes into account the continuing importance of manuscripts and handwriting on paper deep into modern times, and clearly makes the point that the manuscript is in fact an integral part of "print culture" is Lothar Müller, *White Magic: The Age of Paper*, trans. Jessica Spengler (Malden, MA: Polity Press, 2014), a translation of *Weisse Magie: Die Epoche des Papiers* (Munich: Hanser, 2012).

8. On the inscriptions in the region, see the work of P. F. de Moraes Farias, *Arabic Medieval Inscriptions from the Republic of Mali* (Oxford: Oxford University Press, 2003); as well as, most recently, his "Arabic and Tifinagh Inscriptions," in *Essouk-Tadmekka*, ed. Nixon. Much more attention should be given to the epigraphy, and de Moraes Farias's work is the starting point.

9. Umberto Eco, *Serendipities: Language and Lunacy* (New York: Columbia University Press, 1998).

10. John Hunwick and Fatima Harrak, eds. and trans. *Mi'rāj al-su'ūd: Ahmad Baba's Replies on Slavery* (Rabat: University Mohammed V. Souissi, 2000), 22.

11. Michel de Certeau, *The Writing of History* (New York: Columbia University Press, 1992).

12. See Jack Goody, ed., *Literacy in Traditional Societies* (Cambridge: Cambridge University Press, 1968).

Chapter 1. Discovering Books in the Desert

1. On French imperialism in West Africa, there are many works, and one that pays close attention to the military aspects is A. S. Kanya-Forstner, *The Conquest of the Western Sudan: A Study in French Military Imperialism* (London: Cambridge University Press, 1969), 22, from where the quote comes. See also Christopher Harrison, *France and Islam in West Africa, 1860–1960* (Cambridge: Cambridge University Press, 1988).

2. For selections from the Arabic texts cited in this chapter, describing parts of the continent, see Salah al-Din Munajjid, ed., *Mamlakat Mālī 'inda al-jughrāfiyyīn al-Muslimīn*, vol. 1 (Beirut: Dar al-Kitab al-Jadid, 1963) for the Arabic texts; Joseph Cuoq, *Recueil des sources arabes concernant l'Afrique occidentale du VIIIe au XVIe siècle (Bilād Al-Sūdān)* (Paris: Éditions du Centre National de la Recherche Scientifique, 1975) for French translations; and J.F.P. Hopkins and Nehemia Levtzion, *Corpus of Early Arabic Sources* (Cambridge: Cambridge University Press, 1981) for English versions. Munajjid did not publish a second volume. Since these collections are now between forty and sixty years old and new editions of many of the sources used in these works have appeared, it might be time to reread the original sources.

3. The Cresques map can be seen online on numerous sites, and a dedicated website gives closer views of various sections of the map (see https://caravans.library.northwestern.edu/works/26/; and https://images.cnrs.fr/en/video/6862, accessed December 1, 2022). An edition of the map has been published as *Der katalanische Weltatlas vom Jahre 1375: Nach dem in der Bibliothèque Nationale, Paris, verwahrten Original farbig wiedergegeben*, translated and with an introduction by Hans-Christian Freiesleben (Stuttgart: Brockhaus, Abt. Antiquarium, 1977).

4. On Leo Africanus, there is a large body of work, from textual editions to speculative history, a novel, and at least one documentary. For an attempt at a biography, see Natalie Zemon-Davis, *Trickster Travels: A Sixteenth-Century Muslim between Worlds* (London: Faber and Faber, 2007). The textual history of the works of Leo Africanus is a complicated subject. The English translation is *The History and Description of Africa and of the Notable Things Therein Contained Written by Al-Hassan Ibn Mohammed Al-Wezan Al-Fasi a Moor Baptised As Giovanni Leone but Better Known As Leo Africana* (1869). A more recent German edition and translation of the portions dealing with Africa is Dietrich Rauchenberger, *Johannes Leo der Afrikaner und seine Beschreibung des Raumes zwischen Nil und Niger nach dem Urtext* (Wiesbaden: Harrassowitz, 1999). A new Italian edition is by Gabriele Amadori, *Giovanni Leone Africano, La cosmographia de l'Affrica* (Rome: Aracne Editrice, 2014).

5. Leo Africanus, *Cosmographia de l'Affrica (Ms. V.E. 953 - Biblioteca Nazionale Centrale Di Roma—1526)*, ed. Gabriele Amadori (Roma: Aracne, 2014), 515–19. The German translation is by Dietrich Rauchenberger: *Johannes Leo der Afrikaner und seine Beschreibung des Raumes zwischen Nil und Niger nach dem Urtext* (Wiesbaden: Harrassowitz, 1999), 239–328.

6. Leo Africanus, *Cosmographia de l'Affrica*, ed. Amadori, 515–19; in Rauchenberger's translation *Johannes Leo der Afrikaner*, 239–328.

7. On the Portuguese in the Sahara, see Michał Tymowski, *Europeans and Africans: Mutual Discoveries and First Encounters* (Leiden: Brill, 2020). European travelers in Africa have fascinated Western readers, and there are numerous reissues of their works and collections with extracts, such as G. R. Crone, *The Voyages of Cadamosto and Other Documents on Western Africa in the Second Half of the Fifteenth Century* (London: Printed for the Hakluyt Society, 1937).

8. The European travelers left a large body of writing. Those who went to West Africa in the late eighteenth and early nineteenth centuries discussed in this chapter are Mungo Park, *Travels in the Interior Districts of Africa: Performed under the Direction and Patronage of the African Association in the Years 1795, 1796, and 1797* (Cambridge: Cambridge University Press, 2011); and René Caillié, *Travels through Central Africa to Timbuctoo: And across the Great Desert, to Morocco, Performed in the Years 1824–1828* (London: Henry Colburn and Richard Bentley, 1830).

9. The observations of James Grey Jackson are in his *An Account of the Empire of Marocco and the Districts of Suse and Tafilelt Compiled from Miscellaneous Observations Made during a Long Residence* (London, 1814), 252.

10. Alfred Lord Tennyson, *Timbouctoo, a Poem* (Cambridge: Cambridge University Press, 1829), 63.

11. For selections from Barth on parts of the regions covered here, see Heinrich Barth, *Barth's Travels in Nigeria: Extracts from the Journal of Heinrich Barth's Travels in Nigeria, 1850–1855*, ed. A.H.M. Kirk-Greene (London: Oxford University Press, 1962). Essays on Barth's work are in Mamadou Diawara et al., eds., *Heinrich Barth et l'Afrique* (Cologne: Rüdiger Köppe Verlag, 2006). For a project making available Barth's correspondence, see https://heinrich-barth.ub.uni-due.de/. The most recent biography of Barth is by Christoph Marx, who has also created a major archive of his materials. See his *Von Berlin nach Timbuktu der afrikaforscher Heinrich Barth: Biographie* (Göttingen: Wallstein Verlag, 2021).

12. Heinrich Barth, *Reisen und Entdeckungen in nord- und central-Afrika in den Jahren 1849 bis 1855: Tagebuch seiner im Auftrag der brittischen Regierung unternommenen Reise* (Gotha:

Justus Perthes, 1857). In 1860, a US edition appeared in a single volume as *Travels and Discoveries in North and Central Africa.*

13. There are translated extracts from the manuscripts that Clapperton collected in Hugh Clapperton, *Journal of a Second Expedition into the Interior of Africa from the Bight of Benin to Soccatoo: To Which Is Added, the Journal of Richard Lander from Kano to the Sea-Coast* (Cambridge: Cambridge University Press, 2015 [1829]).

14. For one estimate of books in Sokoto, see Murray Last, "The Book in the Sokoto Caliphate," in *The Meanings of Timbuktu*, ed. Jeppie and Diagne.

15. Felix Du Bois, *Timbuctoo the Mysterious*, trans. Diana White (London: Heinemann, 1897), 80–89.

16. Felix Du Bois, *Tombouctou la mystérieuse* (Paris: E. Flammarion, 1897). The English translation appeared also in 1897, translated by Diana White as *Timbuctoo the Mysterious* (London: Heinemann, 1897).

17. Du Bois, *Timbuctoo the Mysterious*, 80–89.

18. For his diatribes against Barth, see Du Bois, *Timbuctoo the Mysterious*, 321–51.

19. Du Bois, *Timbuctoo the Mysterious*, 267.

20. Du Bois, *Timbuctoo the Mysterious*, 344.

21. Du Bois, *Timbuctoo the Mysterious*, inside cover.

22. There is a vast literature on the representation of Africa in European thought, which is not the focus of this chapter. On Timbuktu in this discourse, see Isabelle Surun, "La décourverte de Tombouctou: Déconstruction et reconstruction d'un mythe geographique," *L'Espace géographique* 31, no. 2 (2002). Also on the travelers, see Gerd Spittler, "European Explorers as Caravan Travellers in the West Sudan: Some Thoughts on the Methodology of Journeys of Exploration," *Paideuma* 33 (1987): 391–406; and Gerd Spittler, "Explorers in Transit: Travels to Timbuktu and Agades in the Nineteenth Century," *History & Anthropology* 9, no. 2/3 (1996).

23. See Georges de Gironcourt, *Missions de Gironcourt en Afrique occidentale, 1908–1909, 1911–1912: Documents scientifiques, publiés avec le concours de l'Académie des sciences (Fonds Bonaparte), de l'Académie des inscriptions et belles-lettres et de la Société de Géographie* (Paris: Société de Géographie, 1920). See also Mauro Nobili, *Catalogue des manuscrits arabes du fonds de Gironcourt (Afrique de l'ouest) de L'institut de France* (Rome: Istituto per l'Oriente C. A. Nallino, 2013).

Chapter 2. The Education of Ahmad Baba, 1556–91

1. The place to start on Baba's life and works—which remains the only attempt at a biography—is Mahmoud Zouber, *Ahmad Baba de Tombouctou: Sa vie et son oeuvre* (Paris: G. P. Maisonneuve et Larose, 1977). This is the Sorbonne doctoral dissertation of the first official director of the Ahmed Baba Centre in Timbuktu, who had unparalleled access to manuscripts of Baba. The two biographical dictionaries of Baba are basic sources: *Nayl al-ibtihāj* (manuscript original, 1596) was edited and published in 1999; and *Kifāyat al-muḥtāj* (1603) was edited for a PhD thesis in Rabat in 1986 and published in 2000. In Algiers, the Arabist J-A Cherbonneau (1813–82), brought attention to Baba when he offered a short summary of the *Nayl al-ibtihāj* in the 1850s. The statements by Baba about his father come from the *Kifāyat al-muḥtāj*; his memory of his teacher al-Wangari is from the same source. Sections of it were

incorporated into the *Tārīkh al-Sūdān*; see chapters 9 and 10, with entries on Baba's father and al-Wangari in chapter 10; translated by Hunwick in Sa'dī, *Timbuktu and the Songhay Empire.*

2. Ahmad Baba, *Nayl al-ibtihāj bi-taṭrīz al-dībāj* (Tripoli: Kulliya al-dawah al-Islamiyyah, 1989), p. 141.

3. Ahmad Baba, *Nayl al-ibtihaj*, p .600.

4. The *Jalb al-ni'ma* was completed in Timbuktu in October 1588/89 (*Dhū l-ḥijja* 997) and is one of the earliest *dated* writings of Baba. Zouber, *Ahmad Baba de Tombouctou*, 156–62, found five copies of the manuscript. There are seven extant copies of the manuscript according to the catalog by Hunwick, *Arabic Literature of Africa*, vol. 4, *The Writings of Western Sudanic Africa* (Leiden: Brill, 2003), 22. There is a single published version by Muhammad bin Azuz (Casablanca: Dar ibn Hazm, 2011) based on three manuscripts in Rabat libraries. Hunwick dated the work to Baba's Marrakesh exile "Aḥmad Bābā and the Moroccan Invasion of the Sudan (1591)," *Journal of the Historical Society of Nigeria* 2, no. 3 (1962): 311–28.

5. On the politics of the period, see the source from closest to the period, Sa'dī, *Tarikh al-Sudan*, in *Timbuktu and the Songhay Empire*, and Hunwick's introduction to the region and era.

6. Sa'dī, *Timbuktu and the Songhay Empire*, 91.

Chapter 3. Exile in Marrakesh

1. The conquest of Goa and Timbuktu are covered in numerous works. See, for instance, Lansiné Kaba, "Archers, Musketeers, and Mosquitoes: The Moroccan Invasion of the Sudan and the Songhay Resistance (1591–1612)," *Journal of African History*, 22, no. 4 (1981): 457–75; Stephen Cory, "The Man Who Would Be Caliph: A Sixteenth-Century Sultan's Bid for an African Empire," *International Journal of African Historical Studies* 42, no. 2 (2009): 179–200; Sa'dī, *Tarīkh al-Sudan*; and Chouki El Hamel, *Black Morocco* (Cambridge: Cambridge University Press, 2013).

2. Sa'dī, *Timbuktu and the Songhay Empire*, 186.

3. Sa'dī, *Timbuktu and the Songhay Empire*, 190.

4. On the early reports about gold, see Yāqūt al-Ḥamawī (d. 1228) in Munajjid, *Mamlakat Mālī 'inda al-jughrāfiyyīn al-Muslimīn*, 15; Cuoq, *Recueil des sources arabes concernant l'Afrique occidentale du VIIIe au XVIe siècle (Bilād Al-Sūdān)*, 182; and Hopkins and Levtzion, *Corpus of Early Arabic Sources*. See also the discussion in chapter 1.

5. The reports and later historical commentary differ on the issue of what was taken back to Marrakesh. See Sa'dī, *Timbuktu and the Songhay Empire*, 190–97, on the battle and the immediate aftermath; in the same volume, see Ifrānī's account (309–17) and Hunwick's introduction. 'Abd Allāh Laroui ['Abd Allāh 'Arawī], *L'histoire du Maghreb: Un essai de synthèse* (Casablanca: Centre Cultural Arabe, 2011), 229–43, covers succinctly all the main regional political entities in play that probably forced the rulers in Marrakesh to undertake the conquest. See also Mohammed Kably, ed., *History of Morocco: A Work of Synthesis and Update* (Rabat: Royal Institute for Research on the History of Morocco, 2015). Additional background on Morocco in the late sixteenth century and particularly good on al-Mansur is Mercedes García-Arenal, *Ahmad Al-Mansur: The Beginnings of Modern Morocco* (London: Oneworld Books, 2009). See also Nabil Mouline, *Le califat imaginaire d'Ahmad Al-Mansūr* (Paris: Presses Universitaires de France, 2009).

6. From García-Arenal, *Ahmad Al-Mansur*, 76.

7. From Elias N. Saad, *Social History of Timbuktu: The Role of Muslim Scholars and Notables, 1400–1900* (Cambridge: Cambridge University Press, 1983), 180.

8. Saʿdī, *Timbuktu and the Songhay Empire*, 225.

9. After the withdrawal of the leadership of the occupation, the mercenaries and foot-soldiers were largely leaderless and the local populations suffered in the following decades of internecine fighting and growing disorder. See Michel Abitbol, *Tombouctou et les Arma de la conquête marocaine du Soudan nigérien en 1591 à l'hégémonie de l'Empire Peul du Maçina en 1833* (Paris: Maisonneuve et Larose, 1979), 89–116; Muḥammad al-Ṣaghīr ibn Muḥammad Ifrānī, *Nuzhat al-ḥādī bi-akhbār mulūk al-qarn al-ḥādī*, ed. Octave Victor Houdas (Paris: Leroux, 1888). Extracts related to the invasion in Saʿdī, *Timbuktu and the Songhay Empire*, 309–17. Al-Fishtali is discussed in all the writings on the Saʿdian dynasty. In relation to the invasion, he is discussed in various papers of the Rabat colloquium (1995)—for example, by Abdelmajid Kaddouri, "L'expedtion d'Aḥmad al-Manṣūr au Soudan historiographie et discours," in *Le Maroc et l'Afrique subsaharienne aux débuts des temps modernes: Les Saʿadiens et l'empire Songhay* (Rabat: Institut des Etudes Africaines, 1995), 207–18.

10. From *Tārīkh al-Sūdān*, 186–99.

11. Baba's statement is reported in Ifrānī, *Nuzhat al-ḥādī* (translation by Hunwick in Saʿdī, *Timbuktu and the Songhay Empire*, 315); M. Hajji, *al-Ḥarakat al-fikrīyah bi-l-Maghrib fī ʿahd al-Saʿdiyyīn*, vol. 2 (Rabat: Dar al-Maghrib, 1978), 375; Kably, *History of Morocco*, 395.

12. From *Tārīkh al-Sūdān*, 205.

13. *Tuḥfat al-fuḍalā* has been edited and translated; edition prepared by Saʿīd Sāmī, with French translation by Mohamed Zniber. On *Ghāyat al-amal*, see Zouber, *Ahmad Baba de Tombouctou*, 179–84, 199.

14. Ahmad Baba, *Tuḥfat al-fuḍalā*, p. 38.

Chapter 4. Ahmad Baba's Later Years in Timbuktu, 1608–27

1. Aḥmad ibn Qāsim ibn al-Ḥajarī, *Kitāb Nasir Al-Dīn ʿalā 'l-Qawm Al-Kāfirīn = The Supporter of Religion against the Infidels*, ed. P. Sj. van Koningsveld, Qāsim Sāmarrāʾī, and Gerard Albert Wiegers (Madrid: Consejo Superior de Investigaciones Científicas, 2015), 271.

2. Zouber, in *Ahmad Baba de Tombouctou*, 31–34, notes Baba's return; he mentions Baba's students in Marrakesh (56–57) and discusses the question of his descendants (34–37).

3. The description of Baba's departure from Marrakesh is in Ifrānī, *Nuzhat al-ḥādī*. On Ifrani, see Évariste Lévi-Provençal, ed., *Les historiens des Chorfa: Essai sur la littérature historique et biographique au Maroc du XVIe au XXe siècle* (Paris: Larose, 1922), 122–31. The relevant portion of *Nuzhat al-ḥādī* is translated by Hunwick in Saʿdī, *Timbuktu and the Songhay Empire*, 309–19.

4. On Tamgrout, see Hajji, *al-Ḥarakat al-fikrīyah bi-l-Maghrib fī ʿahd al-Saʿdiyyīn*, 549. The tobacco fatwa is titled *al-Lamʿ fīl'ishāra*. See Zouber, *Ahmad Baba de Tombouctou*, 184–87. The fatwa is translated in Abdal-Aziz Batran, *Tobacco Smoking under Islamic Law: Controversy over Its Introduction* (Beltsville, MD: Amana Publications, 2003). Baba's note on the calendar is in *al-Lumʿa fī ajwibat al-asʾilat al-arbaʿ*. See also Abdallah Hammoudi, "Sainteté, pouvoir et société: Tamgrout aux XVIIe et XVIIIe siècles," *Annales: Histoire, Sciences Sociales* 35, no. 3/4 (1980): 615–41. On the Nasiriyya, see David Gutelius, "The Path Is Easy and the Benefits Large: The Nāṣiriyya, Social Networks and Economic Change in Morocco, 1640–1830," *Journal of*

African history 43, no. 1 (2002): 27–49. Tobacco consumption generated a long debate that continued into the nineteenth century (see chapter 6). See also Dorrit van Dalen, *Doubt, Scholarship and Society in 17th-Century Central Sudanic Africa* (Leiden: Brill, 2016).

5. On the Arma, see Abitbol, *Tombouctou et les arma*; and Saad, *Social History of Timbuktu.*

6. Quoted in Sa'dī, *Timbuktu and the Songhay Empire*, 193.

7. Aḥmad ibn Aḥmad Bābā, *Mi'rāj al-ṣu'ūd: ajwibat Aḥmad Bābā ḥawla al-istirqāq*, ed. and trans. John O. Hunwick and Fatima Harrak (Rabat: Al-Mamlakah al-Maghribīyah, Jāmi'at Muḥammad al-Khāmis, Ma'had al-Dirasāt al-Afrīqīyah bi-al-Rabāṭ, 2000), 22.

8. Bābā, *Mi'rāj al-su'ūd*, 21.

9. For the translation of *Mi'rāj al-ṣu'ūd*, see Bābā, *Mi'rāj al-ṣu'ūd*, ed. and trans. Hunwick and Harrak. See also Zouber, *Ahmad Baba de Tombouctou*, 77–78, 110, 129–46; Timothy Cleaveland, "Ahmad Baba Al-Timbukti and His Islamic Critique of Racial Slavery in the Maghrib," *Journal of North African Studies* 20, no. 1 (2015): 42–64.

10. Bābā, *Mi'rāj al-ṣu'ūd*, 13.

11. Bābā, *Mi'rāj al-ṣu'ūd*, 14.

12. From Bābā, *Mi'rāj al-ṣu'ūd*, 21–22.

13. Bābā, *Mi'rāj al-ṣu'ūd*, 22.

14. Bābā, *Mi'rāj al-ṣu'ūd*, 38.

15. Bābā, *Mi'rāj al-ṣu'ūd*, 35.

16. On Baba's students, see Zouber, *Ahmad Baba de Tombouctou*, 57–70. His students' works include: Abu l'Abbas Aḥmad bin Yaḥya al-Tilmisānī al-Maqqarī, *Rawdat al ās al-'aṭirati al anfās fī dhikr man laqiytuhu min a'lām al-ḥadratayn Marrākush wa Fās* (Rabat: al-Maṭb'at l'malikiyyah, 1964 [1383]). For al-Maqqari's description of Baba, see 303–15. See also 'Abdullah Muḥammad bin Ya'qūb al-Isī al-'Adīb al-Marrakushī's extract, in Ahmad Baba, *Kifāyat al-muḥtāj li ma'rifa man laysa fi al-dībāj*, ed. Muhammad Mutī', vol. 2 (Rabat: Wizarat al-Awqaf wa al-Shu'un al-Islamiyyah a, 2000), 282–84. On al-Marrakushi, see also Hajji, *al-Ḥarakat al-fikrīyah bi-l-Maghrib fī 'ahd al-Sa'diyyīn*, 396. On Tamanartī, see Lévi-Provençal, *Les historiens des Chorfa*, 257–58.

17. Abu l'Abbas Ahmad bin Yahya al-Tilmisani al-Maqqari, *Rawdat al ās al-'aṭirati al anfās fī dhikr man laqiytuhu min a'lām al-ḥadratayn Marrākush wa Fās* (Rabat: Al-matba't al-malikiyya, 1964), 303–14.

18. Sa'dī, *Timbuktu and the Songhay Empire*, 2.

19. Sa'dī, *Timbuktu and the Songhay Empire*, 269.

20. Sa'dī, *Timbuktu and the Songhay Empire*, 269.

Chapter 5. The Rise of Shinqit

1. On the name Shinqit, see the entry "Shinkīt" in the *Encyclopedia of Islam*, vol. 9 (Leiden, Brill: 1997), 445. Khalil al-Nahwi, *Bilād Shinqīṭ, al-manārah wal-ribāṭ: 'Arḍ lil-ḥayāh al-'ilmīyah wal-ish'ā' al-thaqāfī wal-jihād al-dīnī min khilāli al-jāmi'āt al-badawīyah al-mutanaqqilah (al-maḥāḍir)* (Tunis: Al-Munaẓẓamah al-'Arabīyah lil-Tarbiyah wa-al-Thaqāfah wa-al-'Ulūm, 1987) is a good place to start for the intellectual history.

2. From Charles Stewart's introduction to *Arabic Literature of Africa*, vol. 5, *The Writings of Mauritania and the Western Sahara* (Leiden: Brill, 2015) part 1, 1–17.

3. H. T. Norris's writings cover various aspects of the intellectual life of the region, often with generous extracts from the texts. See his books and articles in the bibliography.

4. On education and the Mahadra, see the article by M. Nouhi (with Stewart) in *Arabic Literature of Africa*, vol. 5, *The Writings of Mauritania and the Western Sahara*, part 1, 18–48. See also Chouki El Hamel, "The Transmission of Islamic Knowledge in the Moorish Society from the Rise of the Almoravids to the 19th Century," *Journal of Religion in Africa* 29, no. 1 (1999): 62–87; and articles by C. Fortier in *Islam et Societés au Sud du Sahara*, no. 11 (1997), and in *Cahiers d'Études africaines* 43, nos. 1–2 (2003).

5. Mohamed El Mokhtar Ould Bah, "Introduction à la poésie mauritanienne (1650–1900)," *Arabica* 18, no. 1 (1971): 1–48.

6. For the woman scholar Khadija bint al-Aqil, see Stewart in *Arabic Literature of Africa*, vol. 5, *The Writings of Mauritania and the Western Sahara*, part 1, 451.

7. On al-Mukhtār bin Būna al-Jakanī (d. 1805), who described his use of the back of camels as teaching lecterns, see Mohamed Lahbib Nouhi's article, "The Mahazra Education Institution," in *Arabic Literature of Africa*, vol. 5, 18–48.

8. On Wuld Raziqa, see Nahwi, *Bilād Shinqīṭ*, 506, 557, for list of his works; on his poetry, see Ould Bah, "Introduction à la poésie mauritanienne (1650–1900)," 37.

9. Ould Bah, "Introduction à la poésie mauritanienne (1650-1900)," 37.

10. On Yadali, see H. T. Norris, "Znaga Islam during the Seventeenth and Eighteenth Centuries," *Bulletin of the School of Oriental and African Studies* 32, no. 3 (1969): 507. For a detailed discussion of Yadali's text on Sufism, see Mohamed Lahbib Nouhi, "Religion and society in a Saharan tribal setting: Authority and Power in the Zwâya Religious Culture" (PhD diss., University of Alberta, 2009), 180–93.

11. Ghislaine Lydon, "A Thirst for Knowledge: Arabic Literacy, Writing Paper and Saharan Bibliphiles in the Southwestern Sahara," in *The Trans-Saharan Book Trade*, ed. Krätli and Lydon, 53.

12. Norris, "Znaga Islam," 507.

13. Norris, "Znaga Islam," 507.

14. On Walid Daymani: see Norris, "Znaga Islam," 123 (for summaries of some of the stories), 153 (on his works), and 78 (characterizing the genres, the language, etc.). See also H. T. Norris, *Shinqiti Folk Literature* (Oxford: Clarendon Press, 1968), 153, with a list of his works.

15. On Nabigha al-Ghallawi, see Nahwi, *Bilad Shinqīt*, 614, for list of his works.

16. On Bartili, see Chouki El Hamel, *La vie intellectuelle islamique dans le Sahel ouest-africain* (Paris: L'Harmattan, 2002), 29–34. See also John O. Hunwick, "A New Source for the Biography of Aḥmad Bābā Al-Tinbuktī (1556–1627)," *Bulletin of the School of Oriental and African Studies, University of London* 27, no. 3 (1964): 568–93. The work of Al-Bartili, *Fath al-Shakūr*, was edited and translated by El Hamel in *La vie intellectuelle islamique dans le Sahel ouest-africain*.

17. On the term "Takrur," see 'Umar Al-Naqar, "Takrur: The History of a Name," *Journal of African History* 10, no. 3 (1969): 365–74. See also Stewart's first note in the introduction to *Arabic Literature of Africa*, vol. 5, *The Writings of Mauritania and the Western Sahara*, part 1. A major anthropological study of the region is Abdel Wedoud Ould Cheikh's *La société maure: Éléments d'anthropogie historique* (Rabat: Centre des Etudes Sahariennes, 2017). See also Cheikh's other studies, including a basic history of Mauritania. See the concise introductory essay in Ulrich Rebstock, *Maurische Literaturgeschichte*, vol. 1 (Würzburg: Ergon, 2001), although as a reference catalog it is not user-friendly. The volumes of Stewart also, in many

ways, surpass this work. Rainer Oßwald, *Die Handelsstädte der Westsahara* (Berlin: D. Reimer, 1986) is dense, and filled with historical detail and references to supporting manuscripts.

18. On Walata, see Rahal Boubrik, "Anthropologique historique d'une cité saharienne: Walata, parenté et pouvoir," *Hespéris Tamuda* 50 (2015): 133–53.

19. A brief note on Ahmad al-Shinqiti and his *al-Wasīṭ* is in the entry on him ("al-Shinkitī (Sid) Ahmad bin al-Amin"), in *The Encyclopaedia of Islam*, vol. 9 (Leiden: Brill, 1997), 445–46.

20. Al-Nahwi, *Bilād Shinqīṭ, al-manārah wal-ribāṭ*, 504.

21. Edmund Burke III, *The Ethnographic State: France and the Invention of Moroccan Islam* (Oakland: University of California Press, 2014) is useful for the larger context of scholarship of the colonial administrators.

Chapter 6. The Kunta Writers: From Tuwat to Timbuktu and Beyond

1. On the Kunta as leaders of the Qadiriyya in the Sahara, see Yahya Ould el-Bara, "The Life of Shaykh Sidi al-Mukhtar al-Kunti," in *The Meanings of Timbuktu*, ed. Jeppie and Diagne, 193–211.

2. Abdel Wedoud Ould Cheikh, "A Man of Letters in Timbuktu: Shaykh Sidi al-Mukhtar al-Kunti," in *The Meanings of Timbuktu*, ed. Jeppie and Diagne, 236.

3. From *al-Ṭarā'if wa'l-talā'id*, cited in Abdal-Aziz Batran, *The Qadiriyya Brotherhood in West Africa and the Western Sahara: The Life and Times of Shaykh Al-Mukhtar Al-Kunti (1729–1811)* (Rabat: Institut des Etudes Africaines, 2001), 163.

4. See Caillié, *Travels through Central Africa to Timbuctoo*, vol. 2, 261–27, for his description of Arawan in 1830.

5. For necessary historical background, see H. T. Norris, *The Arab Conquest of the Western Sahara: Studies of the Historical Events, Religious Beliefs and Social Customs Which Made the Remotest Sahara a Part of the Arab World* (Harlow, UK: Longman, 1986), especially parts 1 and 2. On the Kunta specifically, see Batran, *The Qadiriyya Brotherhood in West Africa and the Western Sahara.*

6. MS no. 7880, translated in Ebrahim Moos, "The Literary Works of Shaykh Sīdī Al-Mukhtār Al-Kuntī (d. 1811): A Study of the Concept and Role of 'Miracles' in Al-Minna fī i'tiqād ahl al-Sunna" (MA thesis, University of Cape Town, 2011), 36.

7. Hunwick, *Arabic Literature of Africa*, vol. 4, *The Writings of Western Sudanic Africa*, 70.

8. For Sīdī Mukhtar's tafsir (exegesis), see Batran, *The Qadiriyya Brotherhood*, 6.

9. On the work *Al-minna*, see Moos, "The Literary Works of Shaykh Sīdī Al-Mukhtār Al-Kuntī (d. 1811)."

10. On al-Maghili, see 'Abd-Al-'Azīz 'Abd-Allah Batrān, "A Contribution to the Biography of Shaikh Muḥammad ibn 'Abd-Al-Karīm ibn Muḥammad ('Umar A'mar) Al-Maghīlī, Al-Tilimsānī," *Journal of African History* 14, no. 3 (1973): 381–94.

11. On Ibn Buna, see Al-Bartili's entry in *Fatḥ al-Shakūr*, 321–23. See also Abdel Wedoud Ould Cheikh, "La grande figure de l'aš'arisme ouest saharien de l'époque" in *L'esprit ou le lettre de soufisme* (unpublished), 9; and Stewart, *Arabic Literature of Africa*, vol. 5, *The Writings of Mauritania and the Western Sahara*, part 1, 21, 28; vol. 2., 973–75.

12. The Shehu's daughter, Nana Asmau, was also a prolific writer famous especially for her poetry. See Beverly B. Mack and Jean Boyd, *One Woman's Jihad: Nana Asma'u, Scholar and Scribe* (Bloomington: Indiana University Press, 2000).

13. Sidi Muhammad to Muhammad Bello, in Cheikh, "A Man of Letters in Timbuktu: Shaykh Sidi al-Mukhtar al-Kunti," 243.

14. Bello, in Cheikh, "A Man of Letters in Timbuktu."

15. On the Kunta-Hamdullahi-Sokoto history, see Abdelkadir Zebadia, "The Career and Correspondence of Ahmad al-Bakkayi of Timbuktu" (PhD diss., University of London, 1974); Mauro Nobili, *Sultan, Caliph, and the Renewer of the Faith: Ahmad Lobbo, the Tarikh al-Fattash and the Making of an Islamic State in West Africa* (Cambridge: Cambridge University Press, 2020), esp. chapters 6 and 7. On Bakkay, see Zebadia, "The Career and Correspondence of Ahmad al-Bakkayi of Timbuktu."

16. On Barth and Bakkay meeting, see Aḥmad Bularraf al-Taknī, *Izālat al-rayb wal-shakk wal-tafrīṭ fī dhikr al-mu'allifīn min ahl al-Takrūr wal-saḥrā' wa ahl Shinqīṭ*, ed. Al-Hādī al-Mabrūk Al-Dālī (n.d. [Tripoli, 2000]), 47–48; Barth, *Travels and Discoveries in North and Central Africa: Being a Journal of an Expedition Undertaken under the Auspices of H.B.M.'s Government, in the Years 1849–1855*, vol. 2 (Cambridge: Cambridge University Press, 2011), 308. See also Stewart, *Arabic Literature of Africa*, vol. 5, *The Writings of Mauritania and the Western Sahara*, part 1, 118.

17. From Barth, *Travels and Discoveries in North and Central Africa*, vol. 2, 471.

18. On Al-Hajj 'Umar work, see Bernd Radtke, "Studies on the Sources of the Kitāb Rimāḥ Ḥizb al-Raḥīm of al-ḥājj 'Umar," *Sudanic Africa* 6 (1995): 73–113.

19. From David Robinson, "Reflections on Legitimation and Pedagogy in the 'Islamic Revolutions' of West Africa on the Frontiers of the Islamic World," *Journal of West African History* 1, no. 1 (2015): 119–32.

20. The most recent and convincing interpretations of the *Tārīkh al-fattāsh* are found in Shahid Mathee and Mauro Nobili, "Towards a New Study of the So-Called Tārīkh al-fattāsh," *History in Africa* 42 (2015): 37–73; and Nobili, *Sultan, Caliph, and the Renewer of the Faith.* See also articles in "Le califat de Hamdallāhi: Une histoie de l'interieur," special issue, *Afriques* 12 (2021).

21. On Sokoto scholars, see Paul Naylor, *From Rebels to Rulers: Writing Legitimacy in the Early Sokoto State* (Martlesham, UK: Boydell & Brewer, 2021). See also Last, "The Book in the Sokoto Caliphate."

Chapter 7. The Collector of Timbuktu: Ahmad Bularraf

1. Biographical details on Bularraf are from Mahmud bin Muhammad Dadab, "Ma'lūmāt an khizānah usrah Bularrāf wa jami'ahu" (undated manuscript). The author of this manuscript was a student of Bularraf's son, and this twenty-page eulogistic essay was given "authorization" by the son. See my essay "Making Book History in Timbuktu," in *The Book in Africa: Critical Debates*, ed. Caroline Davis and David Johnson (Basingstoke, UK: Palgrave Macmillan, 2015).

2. On the diaspora from southern Morocco, see Yahia Abou el-Farah et al., *La présence Marocaine en Afrique de l'ouest: Cas du Sénégal, du Mali, et de la Côte d'Ivoire* (Rabat: Instiut des Etudes Africaines, 1997), 163–69. See also Daniel J. Schroeter, *Merchants of Essaouira: Urban*

Society and Imperialism in Southwestern Morocco, 1844–1886 (Cambridge: Cambridge University Press, 1988).

3. On learning and teaching in the area, see El Hamel, "The Transmission of Islamic Knowledge in Moorish Society." See also Ghislaine Lydon, "The Thirst for Knowledge: Arabic Literacy, Writing Paper and Saharan bibliophiles in the Southwestern Sahara," in *The Trans-Saharan Book Trade*, ed. Krätli and Lydon, esp. 63–70.

4. The biographical dictionary of Bularraf was published as Aḥmad Bularraf al-Taknī, *Izālat al-rayb wal-shakk wal-tafrīṭ fī dhikr al-mu'allifīn min ahl al-Takrūr wal-saḥrā' wa ahl Shinqīṭ.*

5. This letter and those in the following paragraphs are cited and quoted in Abou el-Farah et al., *La présence Marocaine en Afrique de l'ouest*, 163–74. Copies of the letters can be consulted at the manuscripts section of the Bibliothèque Nationale du Royaume du Maroc, Rabat.

6. The letters used in this chapter are held as part of the Bularraf Collection of manuscripts at the Cedrab, Timbuktu. There are also copies in the manuscripts section of the Bibliothèque Nationale du Royaume du Maroc in Rabat.

7. Letter of September 30, 1936, Bularraf Collection.

8. On communications, see Du Bois, *Timbuctoo the Mysterious*, 70. Details and figures in: Direction des Archives du Senegal, series J, Postes et telecommunications; versement no.3 1911/1950; Bularraf letter, Timbuktu, MS no. 8195 (Cedrab collections); Archives Nationales—Senegal, Sous serie 2 G, Soudan Français, 1929: 2G 29–52; Postes et Telegraphies, Annee 1929, Rapport ensemble; Manuscript no. 1145, Timbuktu (Cedrab collections).

9. Letter dated "15 Jumādā al-'Ūlā 1344" (1926).

10. Letter dated "15 Jumādā al-'Ūlā 1344" (1926).

11. The Akansus referred to was a well-known scholar himself, born in the Sus in 1796. He went to Fez by the time he was twenty, where presumably he joined the Tijaniyya brotherhood. See Hunwick, *Arabic Literature of Africa*, vol. 4, *The Writings of the Western Sudanic Africa*, 120, item 6. On the Tijaniyya, see the essays in two volumes coedited by Jean-Louis Triaud and David Robinson: *Le temps des Marabouts: Itineraires et strategies islamiques en Afrique occidentale française* (Paris: Karthala, 1997); and *La Tijâniyya: Une confrérie musulmane à la conquête de l'Afrique* (Paris: Karthala, 2000).

12. See mss nos. 5064, 4903, and 5054 (Cedrab collections). See also Mohamed Shaid Mathee, "Muftīs and the Women of Timbuktu: History through Timbuktu's Fatwās, 1907–1960" (PhD diss., University of Cape Town, 2011), 136–77.

13. On issues raised here, see mss nos. 5064, 4903, and 5054 (Cedrab collections). See also Mathee, "Muftīs and the Women of Timbuktu," 136–77.

14. Bularraf, *Izālat al-rayb wal-shakk wal-tafrīṭ fī dhikr al-mu'allifīn min ahl al-Takrūr wal-saḥrā' wa ahl Shinqīṭ.* It is based on three manuscripts: the main manuscript is from the copy made by Mahmoud Dadab (176 pages), manuscript copy 2 (Cedrab collection), and manuscript 3 (archives in Libya). An edition of the *Izālat al-rayb* is by Dālī; see the introduction to the work by Bularraf, 14. The published edition of the classical Arabic grammarian Sibawayhi's work in Bularraf's library was possibly from the edition of Sibawayh: H. Derenbourg, ed., *Le livre de Sibawaih* (Paris, 1881–89). There is no indication of how Bularraf acquired this work. The scholar who wrote in praise of Bularraf, Mahmoud Dadab, has yet to convert to print. All his works are handwritten and circulated in this form. His most recent extant work is a 355-page handwritten work, *Kashf al-hā'il.* He had it digitally scanned for my use.

15. On biographical dictionaries, see Wadad al-Qadi, "Biographical Dictionaries as the Scholars' Alternative History of the Muslim Community," in *Organizing Knowledge: Encyclopaedic Activities in the Pre-eighteenth Century Islamic World*, ed. Gerhard Endress (Leiden: Brill, 2006).

16. On Muhammad Yahya Salim (1936), see Bularraf, *Izālat al-rayb*, 131–41. Manuscripts mentioned: *al-'Amal al-mashkūr fi jam' nawāzil al-Takrūr*, ms no. 1031; Bul'araf letter, ms 8195, Timbuktu (Cedrab collections). Information about the origins of Cedrab are based on oral information from Mahmoud Zouber, first head of the Cedrab (Interviewed in Bamako, August 2013).

17. See MS 1145, Bularraf Collection, Timbuktu, Shawwal 21 1364/ 21 September 1945.

18. On one family collection, see Ismael Diadie Haidara and Haoua Taore, "The Private Libraries of Timbuktu," in *The Meanings of Timbuktu*, ed. Jeppie and Diagne, 271–275.

19. On the history of printing in Morocco, see F. A. Abdulrazak, "The Kingdom of the Book: The History of Printing in Morocco" (PhD diss., Boston University, 1990). Mathee, "Muftīs and the Women of Timbuktu," 221–23.

Chapter 8. Manuscript, Print, and Memory

1. On the education policies in colonial Mali, see the comprehensive work of Louis Brenner, *Controlling Knowledge: Religion, Power and Schooling in a West African Muslim Society* (London: Hurst & Co, 2000). See also essays on West Africa in Robert Launay, ed., *Islamic Education in Africa: Writing Boards and Blackboards* (Bloomington: Indiana University Press, 2016).

2. On Ahmad Baber al-Arawani (d. 1997), see his *al-Sa'āda al-abadiyya fīl-ta'rīf bi-'ulamā' Timbuktu* (completed in 1962; edited and published in 2020).

3. On Amadou Hampâté Bâ, see the short biography by Muriel Devey, *Hampate Bâ: L'homme de la tradition* (Senegal: LivreSud, 1993). More details on him are in the essays by Louis Brenner and by Bintou Sanankoua in Triaud and Robinson, *Le temps des Marabouts*. The journal *Islamic Africa* devoted a section to him in its winter 2010 special issue titled "Amadou Hampâté Bâ's Life and Work Reconsidered: Critical and Historical Perspectives." See especially the essays of Louis Brenner, "A Living Library"; and Bintou Sanankoua, "Amadou Hampâté Bâ: A Testimony." Images of Bâ's writing in the Arabic script—expressing both Arabic and Peul—are from photographs from his archives by Philippe Dupuich in Bernard Magnier and Philippe Dupuich, *Sur les traces d'Amkoullel, l'enfant peul* (Arles: Actes Sud, 1998).

4. Amadou Hampâté Bâ, "The Living Traditon," in *UNESCO General History of Africa*, vol. 1, *Methodology and Prehistory* (Berkeley: University of California Press, 2003), 71.

5. Bâ, "The Living Traditon," 62.

6. Despite his extensive body of writing and his political roles in colonial and post-colonial Niger, Boubou Hama has had far less scholarship devoted to him; a short biography of him is hard to find. The basics of his writing and public life can be found in the obituary by Robert Cornevin, "Hommage à Boubou Hama," *Présence Africaine* (1982): 278–80. A more diverse set of perspectives is presented in Diouldé Laya et al., eds., *Boubou Hama: Un homme de culture nigerien* (Paris: Editions L'Harmattan, 2012). On his role in the establishment of the national museum in Niamey, see Amanda Gilvin, "Boubou Hama: Africa's Duty to Save Humanity," *Nka: Journal of Contemporary African Art* 42 (2018): 250–62.

7. Amadou Hampâté Bâ, in *UNESCO Courier*, December 1960.

8. Bintou Sanankoua, "Amadou Hampâté Bâ: A Testimony," *Islamic Africa*, June 2010, 143–67.

9. On Kamara, the best place to start is the article by David Robinson, "Un historien et anthropologue sénégalais: Shaikh Musa Kamara," *Cahiers d'Études Africaines* 28, no. 109 (1988): 89–116. For the colonial background and context to the Senegal River Valley region in which Kamara was educated, wrote, and taught, see David Robinson, *Paths of Accommodation: Muslim Societies and French Colonial Authorities in Senegal and Mauritania, 1880–1920* (Athens: Ohio University Press, 2000).

10. The speech of Kamara on the occasion of the opening of the cathedral was translated by Amr Samb and published as "L'Islam et le Christianisme," *Bulletin de l' I.F.A.N.* 35, series B, no. 2 (1973), 269–322.

11. There is, at present, no scholarly edition of Kamara's magnum opus. An apparently complete version of the Arabic text was published in Kuwait, without an indication of which copy or copies of the text were used. In the absence of a scholarly or critical edition, this is the only printed version in circulation at the moment. See Musa Kamara, *Zuhūr al-basātīn fī tārīkh al-sawādīn*, prepared and presented by Nasr al-Din Sa ʿīdūni and Muʾawiyah Sa ʿīdūni (Kuwait: Muʾasasah Jaʾizah Abd al-aziz Saud al-Babtain lil-ibdaʾa al-shiʾir, 2010). I was unable to access any manuscript of the work.

12. Kamara, *Zuhūr al-basātīn*, 168, 171.

13. A recent article on another of Kamara's works is Marsh Wendell, "Reading with the Colonial in the Life of Shaykh Musa Kamara a Muslim Scholar-Saint," *Africa: The Journal of the International African Institute* 90, no. 3 (2020): 604–24.

14. The first volume of the project to translate Kamara's work into French appeared in 1998: Kamarā Mūsa, with Jean Schmitz, *Florilège au jardin de l'histoire des Noirs: 1 l' aristocratie peule et la révolution des clercs musulmans (vallée du Sénégal)* (Paris: CNRS Éditions, 1998).

15. Souleymane Bachir Diagne, *L'Encre des Savants* (Dakar: Codesria, 2013), 69–81.

16. For more on the gathering of writers in Paris from the perspective of Fanon's participation, see David Macey, *Frantz Fanon: A Biography*, 2nd ed. (London: Verso, 2012), 283–89. The quote from Fanon is in the chapter "On National Culture," in *The Wretched of the Earth*, trans. Constance Farrington (New York: Grove Press, 1963), 210. While traveling through newly independent Mali in 1960, Fanon records in his notebook: "In Kidal I plunge into some books on the history of Sudan [meaning here western Soudan]. I relive with the intensity the circumstances and the place confer upon them, the old empires of Ghana, of Mali, of Gao, and the impressive Odyssey of the Moroccan troops with the famous Djouder." Frantz Fanon, *Toward the African Revolution* (Harmondsworth, UK: Penguin, 1970), 183–85.

Epilogue

1. For one influential approach to the text and writing, ultimately concerned with forms of reading or interpretation, see Paul Ricoeur, "What Is a Text: Explanation and Understanding," in his *Hermeneutics and the Human Sciences*, ed. John B. Thompson (Cambridge: Cambridge University Press, 1981). Book history scholarship is extensive: one useful collection is Simon Eliot and Jonathan Rose, eds., *A Companion to the History of the Book* (Chichester, UK:

Wiley-Blackwell, 2020); for a discussion of Japan, see Peter Kornicki, *The Book in Japan: A Cultural History from the Beginnings to the Nineteenth Century* (Leiden: Brill, 1998); on India, see Abhijit Gupta and Swapan Chakravorty, eds., *Founts of Knowledge: Book History in India* (New Delhi: Orient Blackswan, 2016).

2. On Manuscript cultures, see Jörg B. Quenzer, Dmitry Bondarev, and Jan-Ulrich Sobisch, eds., *Manuscript Cultures: Mapping the Field*, Studies in Manuscript Cultures 1 (Berlin: De Gruyter, 2014). See especially the Alessandro Bausi essay "Writing, Copying, Translating: Ethiopia as a Manuscript Culture." There are now more than forty volumes in the Studies in Manuscript Cultures series, the outcomes of work at the Centre of the Study of Manuscript Cultures (Understanding Written Artefacts) at the University of Hamburg. See https://www.degruyter.com.

3. For reflections on the study of the book in Africa, see the introduction to Caroline Davis and David Johnson, eds., *The Book in Africa: Critical Debates* (Basingstoke, UK: Palgrave Macmillan, 2015). For some recent scholarship on Arabic Islamic manuscripts and book history that covers many of the issues alluded to in this chapter, see work by Beatrice Gruendler, Konrad Hirschler, Marina Rustow, and Ahmad El-Shamsy, among others. See the bibliography for details of their recent work.

4. See Sebastiano Timpanaro, *The Genesis of Lachmann's Method*, ed. and trans. Glenn W. Most (Chicago: University of Chicago Press, 2005), for a presentation and critique of philology's task of producing an edition that reflects what the author might have intended. The call to "return to philology" has been repeated for the last few decades. For more recent articulations, see Sheldon Pollock, "Future Philology?: The Fate of a Soft Science in a Hard World," *Critical Inquiry* 35, no. 4 (2009): 931–61. See also Sheldon Pollock, Benjamin A. Elman, and Ku-ming Kevin Chang, eds., *World Philology* (Cambridge, MA: Harvard University Press, 2015); and Islam Dayeh, "The Potential of World Philology," *Philological Encounters* 1, nos. 1–4 (2016): 396–418.

5. For the most recent summary of the attempts to quantity the manuscripts, see Charles Stewart, "Literary Authority in West African Islam," in *Manuscripts and Arabic-script writing in Africa*, ed. Charles Stewart and Ahmed Chaouki Binebine (Al-Iskandarīyah, Miṣr: Hay'at al-Makhṭūṭāt al-Islāmīyah bi-al-ta'āwun ma'a Maktabat al-Iskandarīyah, 2023). The database that forms the basis of the quantification is the West Africa Arabic Manuscript Database (WAAMD) available at: https://waamd.lib.berkeley.edu/home.

BIBLIOGRAPHY

Abdulrazak, F. A. "The Kingdom of the Book: The History of Printing in Morocco." PhD diss., Boston University, 1990.

Abitbol, Michel. *Tombouctou et les Arma de la conquête marocaine du Soudan nigérien en 1591 à l'hégémonie de l'Empire Peul du Macina en 1833*. Paris: G.-P. Maisonneuve et Larose, 1979.

Abou el-Farah, Yahia, et al. *La présence Marocaine en Afrique de l'ouest: Cas du Sénégal, du Mali, et de la Côte d'Ivoire*. Rabat: Instiut des Etudes Africaines, 1997.

Africanus, Leo. *The History and Description of Africa and of the Notable Things Therein Contained*. Edited by Robert Brown. Translated by John Pory. London: Hakluyt Society, 1896.

al-Nahwi, Khalil. *Bilād Shinqīṭ, al-manārah—wa-al-ribāṭ: 'Arḍ lil-ḥayāh al-'ilmīyah wa-al-ish'ā' al-thaqāfī wa-al-jihād al-dīnī min khilāli al-jāmi'āt al-badawīyah al-mutanaqqilah (al-maḥāḍir)*. Tunis: Al-Munaẓẓamah al-'Arabīyah lil-Tarbiyah wa-al-Thaqāfah wa-al-'Ulūm, 1987.

Al-Naqar, 'Umar. "Takrur: The History of a Name." *Journal of African History* 10, no. 3 (1969): 365–74.

Amadori, Gabriele. *Giovanni Leone Africano, La cosmographia de l'Affrica*. Rome: Aracne Editrice, 2014.

"Amadou Hampâté Bâ's Life and Work Reconsidered: Critical and Historical Perspectives." Special issue, *Islamic Africa* 1, no. 2 (winter 2010).

Azuz, Muhammad bin, ed. *Jalb al-ni'ma wa daf' al-niqma*. Casablanca: Dar ibn Hazm, 2011.

Bâ, Amadou Hampâté. *Amkoullel, l'enfant peul: Mémoires*. Paris: Éditions J'ai lu, 2000.

———. *Vie et enseignement de Tierno Bokar: Le sage de Bandiagara*. Points, Sagesses 23. Paris: Seuil, 1980.

Bâ, Amadou Hampâté, and J. Daget. *L'empire peul du Macina*. Paris: Mouton, 1962.

Bâ, Amadou Hampâté, and Roger Gaetani. *A Spirit of Tolerance: The Inspiring Life of Tierno Bokar*. Bloomington, IN: World Wisdom, 2008.

Baba, Ahmad. *Kifāyat al-muḥtāj li ma'rifa man laysa fi al-dībāj*. Edited by Muhammad Mutī'. Rabat: Wizarat al-Awqaf wa al-Shu'un al-Islamiyyah a, 2000.

———. *Nayl al-ibtihāj bi-taṭrīz al-dībāj*. Tripoli: Kulliya al-dawah al-Islamiyyah, 1989.

———. *Tuḥfatu-l-Fuḍalā (Des mérites des 'ulama)*. Edited by Saïd Sami and Moahmed Zniber. Textes et Documents. Rabat: Institut des Etudes Africaines, Universite Mohammed V, 1992.

Bābā, Aḥmad ibn Aḥmad. *Mi'rāj al-ṣu'ūd: ajwibat Aḥmad Bābā ḥawla al-istirqāq*. Edited and translated by John O. Hunwick and Fatima Harrak. Rabat: Al-Mamlakah al-Maghribīyah, Jāmi`at Muḥammad al-Khāmis, Ma`had al-Dirasāt al-Afrīqīyah bi-al-Rabāṭ, 2000.

Barth, Heinrich. *Barth's Travels in Nigeria: Extracts from the Journal of Heinrich Barth's Travels in Nigeria, 1850–1855*. Edited by A.H.M. Kirk-Greene. London: Oxford University Press, 1962.

———. *Reisen und Entdeckungen in nord- und central-Afrika in den Jahren 1849 bis 1855: Tagebuch seiner im Auftrag der brittischen Regierung unternommenen Reise*. Gotha: Justus Perthes, 1857.

———. *Travels and Discoveries in North and Central Africa: Being a Journal of an Expedition Undertaken under the Auspices of H.B.M.'s Government, in the Years 1849–1855*. Cambridge: Cambridge University Press, 2011.

———. *Travels and Discoveries in North and Central Arica: Including Accounts of Tripoli, the Sahara, the Remarkable Kingdom of Bornu, and the Countries Round Lake Chad*. London: Ward, Lock, 1890.

Batran, Abdal-Aziz [Batrān, 'Abd-Al-'Azīz 'Abd-Allah]. "A Contribution to the Biography of Shaikh Muḥammad ibn 'Abd-Al-Karīm ibn Muḥammad ('Umar-A 'Mar) Al-Maghīlī, Al-Tilimsānī." *Journal of African History* 14, no. 3 (1973): 381–94.

———. "An Introductory Note on the Impact of Sidi al-Mukhtar al-Kunti (1729–1811) on West African Islam in the 18th and 19th Centuries." *Journal of the Historical Society of Nigeria* 6, no. 4 (1973): 347–52.

———. *The Qadiriyya Brotherhood in West Africa and the Western Sahara: The Life and Times of Shaykh Al-Mukhtar Al-Kunti (1729–1811)*. Rabat: Institut des Etudes Africaines, 2001.

———. *Tobacco Smoking under Islamic Law: Controversy over Its Introduction*. Beltsville, MD: Amana Publications, 2003.

Bivar, A.D.H., and M. Hiskett. "The Arabic Literature of Nigeria to 1804: A Provisional Account." *Bulletin of the School of Oriental and African Studies* 25, no. 1 (1962).

Boubrik, Rahal. "Anthropologique historique dúne cité saharienne: Walata, parenté et pouvoir." *Hespéris Tamuda* 50 (2015): 133–53.

Brenner, Louis. *Controlling Knowledge: Religion, Power and Schooling in a West African Muslim Society*. London: Hurst & Co, 2000.

———. *West African Sufi: The Religious Heritage and Spiritual Search of Cerno Bokar Saalif Taal*. London: C. Hurst, 1984.

Bularraf al-Takni, Ahmad. *Izālat al-rayb wal-shakk wal-tafrīṭ fī dhikr al-mu'allifīn min ahl al-Takrūr wal-saḥrā' wa ahl Shinqīṭ*. Edited by Al-Hādī al-Mabrūk Al-Dālī. Tripoli, Al-Sharika al-āma lil-waraq wa al-tiba'a, 2000.

Burke, Edmund, III. *The Ethnographic State: France and the Invention of Moroccan Islam*. Oakland: University of California Press, 2014.

Caillié, René. *Travels through Central Africa to Timbuctoo: And across the Great Desert, to Morocco, Performed in the Years 1824–1828*. London: Henry Colburn and Richard Bentley, 1830.

Cheikh, Abdel Wedoud Ould. *La société maure: Éléments d'anthropologie historique*. Rabat: Centres des Etudes Sahariennes, 2017.

Clapperton, Hugh. *Journal of a Second Expedition into the Interior of Africa from the Bight of Benin to Soccatoo: To Which Is Added, the Journal of Richard Lander from Kano to the Sea-Coast*. Cambridge: Cambridge University Press, 2015 [1829].

Cleaveland, Timothy. "Ahmad Baba Al-Timbukti and His Islamic Critique of Racial Slavery in the Maghrib." *Journal of North African Studies* 20, no. 1 (2015): 42–64.

Cornevin, Robert. "Hommage à Boubou Hama." *Présence Africaine* (1982): 278–80.

Cory, Stephen. "The Man Who Would Be Caliph: A Sixteenth-Century Sultan's Bid for an African Empire." *International Journal of African Historical Studies* 42, no. 2 (2009): 179–200.

Crone, G. R. *The Voyages of Cadamosto and Other Documents on Western Africa in the Second Half of the Fifteenth Century*. London: Printed for the Hakluyt Society, 1937.

Cuoq, Joseph. *Recueil des sources arabes concernant l'Afrique occidentale du VIIIe au XVIe siècle (Bilād Al-Sūdān)*. Paris: Éditions du Centre national de la recherche scientifique, 1975.

Davis, Caroline, and David Johnson, eds. *The Book in Africa: Critical Debates*. Basingstoke, UK: Palgrave Macmillan, 2015.

Davis, Natalie Zemon. *Trickster Travels: A Sixteenth-Century Muslim between Worlds*. London: Faber and Faber, 2007.

Dayeh, Islam. "The Potential of World Philology." *Philological Encounters* 1, nos. 1–4 (2016): 396–418.

de Certeau, Michel. *The Writing of History*. New York: Columbia University Press, 1992.

de Gironcourt, Georges. *Missions de Gironcourt en Afrique occidentale, 1908–1909, 1911–1912: Documents scientifiques, publiés avec le concours de l'Académie des sciences (Fonds Bonaparte), de l'Académie des inscriptions et belles-lettres et de la Société de Géographie*. Paris: Société de Géographie, 1920.

Denham, Dixon, and Hugh Clapperton. *Narrative of Travels and Discoveries in Northern and Central Africa, in the Years 1822, 1823, and 1824*. Cambridge: Cambridge University Press, 2011.

Derenbourg, H., ed. *Le livre de Sibawaih*. Paris, 1881–89.

Der katalanische Weltatlas vom Jahre 1375: Nach dem in der Bibliothèque Nationale, Paris, verwahrten Original farbig wiedergegeben. Translated and with an introduction by Hans-Christian Freiesleben. Stuttgart: Brockhaus, Abt. Antiquarium, 1977.

Devey, Muriel. *Hampaté Bâ: L'homme de la tradition*. Senegal: LivreSud, 1993.

Diagne, Souleymane Bachir. *L'encre des savants*. Paris: Présence Africaine, 2013.

Diawara, Mamadou, et al., eds. *Heinrich Barth et l'Afrique*. Studien Zur Kulturkunde 125. Cologne: Rüdiger Köppe Verlag, 2006.

Du Bois, Felix. *Timbuctoo the Mysterious*. Translated by Diana White. London: Heinemann, 1897.

———. *Tombouctou la mystérieuse*. Paris: E. Flammarion, 1897.

Eco, Umberto. *Serendipities: Language and Lunacy*. New York: Columbia University Press, 1998.

Eliot, Simon, and Jonathan Rose, eds. *A Companion to the History of the Book*. Chichester, UK: Wiley-Blackwell, 2020.

El Moudden, Abderrahmane. "Sharifs and Padishahs: Moroccan-Ottoman Relations from the 16th through the 18th Centuries; Contribution to the Study of a Diplomatic Culture." PhD diss., Princeton University, 1992.

El Shamsy, Ahmed. *Rediscovering the Islamic Classics: How Editors and Print Culture Transformed an Intellectual Tradition*. Princeton, NJ: Princeton University Press, 2020.

Endress, Gerhard, ed. *Organizing Knowledge: Encyclopaedic Activities in the Pre-Eighteenth Century Islamic World*. Leiden: Brill, 2006.

English, Charlie. *The Book Smugglers of Timbuktu: The Quest for This Storied City and the Race to Save Its Treasures.* London: William Collins, 2017.

Fanon, Frantz. *Toward the African Revolution.* Harmondsworth, UK: Penguin, 1970.

———. *The Wretched of the Earth.* Translated by Constance Farrington. New York: Grove Press, 1963.

Ficquet, Éloi, and A. Mbodj-Pouye. "Cultures de l'écrit en Afrique: Anciens débats, nouveaux objets." *Annales, Histoire, Sciences Sociales* 64, no. 4 (2009): 751–64.

Galy, Michel, and Bertrand Badie, eds. *La guerre au Mali.* Paris: La Découverte, 2013.

García-Arenal, Mercedes. *Ahmad Al-Mansur: The Beginnings of Modern Morocco.* London: Oneworld Books, 2009.

Ghali, Noureddine, Sidi Mohamed Mahibou, and Louis Brenner. *Inventaire de la bibliothèque 'umarienne de Ségou, conservée à la Bibliothèque nationale, Paris.* Paris: Editions du Centre National de la Recherche Scientifique, 1985.

Gilvin, Amanda. "Boubou Hama: Africa's Duty to Save Humanity." *Nka: Journal of Contemporary African Art* 42 (2018): 250–62.

Gomez, Michael A. *African Dominion: A New History of Empire in Early and Medieval West Africa.* Princeton, NJ: Princeton University Press, 2018.

Goody, Jack, ed. *Literacy in Traditional Societies.* Cambridge: Cambridge University Press, 1968.

Goody, Jack, and Ian Watt. "The Consequences of Literacy." *Comparative Studies in Society and History* 5, no. 3 (1963): 304–45.

Gruendler, Beatrice. *The Rise of the Arabic Book.* Cambridge, MA: Harvard University Press, 2020.

Gupta, Abhijit, and Swapan Chakravorty, eds. *Founts of Knowledge: Book History in India.* New Delhi: Orient Blackswan, 2016.

Gutelius, David. "The Path Is Easy and the Benefits Large: The Nāṣiriyya, Social Networks and Economic Change in Morocco, 1640–1830." *Journal of African History* 43, no. 1 (2002): 27–49.

Hajji, M. *al-Ḥarakah al-fikrīyah bil-Maghrib fī 'ahd al-Sa'dīyīn.* Rabat: Dar al-Maghrib, 1978.

Hall, Bruce S. *A History of Race in Muslim West Africa, 1600–1960.* Cambridge: Cambridge University Press, 2011.

Hamel, Chouki El. *Black Morocco: A History of Slavery, Race and Islam.* Cambridge: Cambridge University Press, 2014.

———. *La vie intellectuelle islamique dans le Sahel ouest africain.* Paris: L'Harmattan, 2002.

———. "The Transmission of Islamic Knowledge in the Moorish Society from the Rise of the Almoravids to the 19th Century." *Journal of Religion in Africa* 29, no. 1 (1999): 62–87.

Hammer, Joshua. *The Bad-Ass Librarians of Timbuktu: And Their Race to Save the World's Most Precious Manuscripts.* New York: Simon & Schuster, 2016.

Hammoudi, Abdallah. "Sainteté, pouvoir et société: Tamgrout aux XVIIe et XVIIIe siècles." *Annales: Histoire, Sciences Sociales* 35, no. 3/4 (1980): 615–41.

Harrison, Christopher. *France and Islam in West Africa, 1860–1960.* Cambridge: Cambridge University Press, 1988.

Hirschler, Konrad. *The Written Word in the Medieval Arabic Lands: A Social and Cultural History of Reading Practices.* Edinburgh: Edinburgh University Press, 2012.

Hiskett, M. *The Sword of Truth: The Life and Times of the Shehu Usuman Dan Fodio.* New York: Oxford University Press, 1973.

Hopkins, J.F.P., and Nehemia Levtzion. *Corpus of Early Arabic Sources.* Cambridge: Cambridge University Press, 1981.

Hunwick, John O. "Aḥmad Bābā and the Moroccan Invasion of the Sudan (1591)." *Journal of the Historical Society of Nigeria* 2, no. 3 (1962): 311–28.

———. "Al-Tinbukti's Nayl Al-Ibtihāj." *Sudanic Africa* 3 (1992).

———, comp. *Arabic Literature of Africa.* Vol. 4, *The Writings of Western Sudanic Africa.* Leiden: Brill, 2003.

———. "Gao and the Almoravids Revisited: Ethnicity, Political Change and the Limits of Interpretation." *Journal of African History* 35, no. 2 (1994).

———. "A New Source for the Biography of Aḥmad Bābā Al-Tinbuktī (1556–1627)." *Bulletin of the School of Oriental and African Studies, University of London* 27, no. 3 (1964): 568–93.

———. "A Region of the Mind: Medieval Arab Views of African Geography and Ethnography and Their Legacy." *Sudanic Africa* 16 (2005): 103–36.

———. "Timbuktu: A Bibliography." *Sudanic Africa* 12 (2001): 115–29.

———. "Timbuktu: A Refuge of Scholarly and Righteous Folk." *Sudanic Africa* 14 (2003): 13–20.

Hunwick, John O., and Fatima Harrak, eds. and trans. *Mi'raj Al-Su'ud: Ahmad Baba's Replies on Slavery.* Rabat: University Mohammed V. Souissi, 2000.

Ifrānī, Muḥammad al-Ṣaghīr ibn Muḥammad. *Nuzhat al-ḥādī bi-akhbār mulūk al-qarn al-ḥādī.* Edited by Octave Victor Houdas. Paris: Leroux, 1888.

Insoll, Timothy. *The Archaeology of Islam in Sub-Saharan Africa.* Cambridge: Cambridge University Press, 2003.

Jackson, James Grey. *An Account of the Empire of Marocco and the Districts of Suse and Tafilelt Compiled from Miscellaneous Observations Made during a Long Residence.* London, 1814.

Jeppie, Shamil. "About a Manuscript on Tea Found in Timbuktu, Mali: Mamma Haidara Collection, MS 125, Tārīkh Al-Shāy Fī 'l-Maghrib." In *Exploring Written Artefacts,* edited by Jörg B. Quenzer, 333–43. Berlin: De Gruyter, 2021.

———. "Examples of Sahelian Book Collectors Over Two Centuries." In *Landscapes, Sources and Intellectual Projects of the West African Past: Essays in Honour of Paulo Fernando de Moraes Farias,* edited by Toby Green and Benedetta Rossi. Leiden: Brill, 2018.

——— "Schaurmärchen über Timbuktu." *Zeithschrift für Ideengeshichte* 16, no. 1 (2022): 48–56.

Jeppie, Shamil, and Souleymane Bachir Diagne, eds. *The Meanings of Timbuktu.* Cape Town: HSRC Press, 2008.

Johansen, Julian, Abd al-Muhsin Abbas, and Sīdī 'Umar ibn 'Alī. *Handlist of Manuscripts in the Centre de Documentation et de Recherches Historiques Ahmed Baba, Timbuktu.* London: Al-Furqan Islamic Heritage Foundation, 1995.

Kaba, Lansiné. "Archers, Musketeers, and Mosquitoes: The Moroccan Invasion of the Sudan and the Songhay Resistance (1591–1612)." *Journal of African History* 22, no. 4 (1981): 457–75.

———. "The Pen, the Sword, and the Crown: Islam and Revolution in Songhay Reconsidered, 1464–1493." *Journal of African History* 25, no. 3 (1984).

Kably, Mohammed, ed. *History of Morocco: A Work of Synthesis and Update.* Rabat: Royal Institute for Research on the History of Morocco, 2015.

Kamara, Musa. *Zuhūr al-basātīn fī tārīkh al-sawādīn.* Prepared and presented by Nasr al-Din Sa ʿīdūni and Muʾawiyah Sa ʿīdūni. Kuwait: Muʾasasah Jaʾizah Abd al-aziz Saud al-Babtain lil-ibdaʾa al-shiʾir, 2010.

Kamarā, Mūsa, with Jean Schmitz. *Florilège au jardin de l'histoire des Noirs: 1 l' aristocratie peule et la révolution des clercs musulmans (vallée du Sénégal).* Paris: CNRS Éditions, 1998.

Kane, Ousmane. *Beyond Timbuktu: An Intellectual History of Muslim West Africa.* Cambridge, MA: Harvard University Press, 2016.

———. *Intellectuels non europhones.* Dakar: Codesria, 2003.

———, ed. *Islamic Scholarship in Africa: New Directions and Global Contexts.* Woodbridge, UK: Boydell & Brewer, 2021.

Kanya-Forstner, A. S. *The Conquest of the Western Sudan: A Study in French Military Imperialism.* London: Cambridge University Press, 1969.

Kornicki, Peter. *The Book in Japan: A Cultural History from the Beginnings to the Nineteenth Century.* Leiden: Brill, 1998.

Krätli, Graziano, and Ghislaine Lydon. *The Trans-Saharan Book Trade: Manuscript Culture, Arabic Literacy and Intellectual History in Muslim Africa.* The Manuscript World 3. Leiden: Brill, 2011.

Laroui, ʿAbd Allāh [ʿAbd Allāh ʿArawī]. *L'histoire du Maghreb: Un essai de synthèse.* Casablanca: Centre Cultural Arabe, 2011.

Last, Murray. "Text and Authority in Nineteenth Century Nigeria." *Journal of African History* 63, no. 2 (2022): 252–53.

Launay, Robert, ed. *Islamic Education in Africa: Writing Boards and Blackboards.* Bloomington: Indiana University Press, 2016.

Laya, Diouldé, et al., eds. *Boubou Hama: Un homme de culture nigerien.* Paris: Editions L'Harmattan, 2012.

Le Maroc et l'Afrique subsaharienne aux débuts des temps modernes: Les Saʿadiens et l'empire Songhay. Rabat: Institut des Etudes Africaines, 1995.

Lecocq, Baz, et al. "One Hippopotamus and Eight Blind Analysts: A Multivocal Analysis of the 2012 Political Crisis in the Divided Republic of Mali." *Review of African Political Economy* 40, no. 137 (2013): 343–57.

Lecocq, Jean Sebastian. *Disputed Desert Decolonisation, Competing Nationalisms and Tuareg Rebellions in Northern Mali.* Afrika-Studiecentrum 19. Leiden: Brill, 2010.

Lévi-Provençal, Évariste, ed. *Les historiens des Chorfa: Essai sur la littérature historique et biographique au Maroc du XVIe au XXe siècle.* Paris: Larose, 1922.

Levtzion, Nehemia. *Ancient Ghana and Mali.* London: Methuen, 1973.

Loimeier, Roman. *Islamic Reform in Twentieth-Century Africa.* Edinburgh: Edinburgh University Press, 2016.

Lothar, Müller. *White Magic: The Age of Paper.* Translated by Jessica Spengler. Cambridge: Polity Press, 2014.

Lydon, Ghislaine. *On Trans-Saharan Trails: Islamic Law, Trade Networks, and Cross-Cultural Exchange in Nineteenth-Century Western Africa.* Cambridge: Cambridge University Press, 2009.

Macey, David. *Frantz Fanon: A Biography*. 2nd ed. London: Verso, 2012.

Mack, Beverly B., and Jean Boyd. *One Woman's Jihad: Nana Asma'u, Scholar and Scribe*. Bloomington: Indiana University Press, 2000.

Maghīlī, Muḥammad ibn 'Abd al-Karīm. *Sharī'a in Songhay: The Replies of Al-Maghīlī to the Questions of Askia Al-Ḥājj Muḥammad*. Edited and translated by John O. Hunwick. London: Published for the British Academy by Oxford University Press, 1985.

Magnier, Bernard, and Philippe Dupuich. *Sur les traces d'Amkoullel, l'enfant peul*. Arles: Actes Sud, 1998.

Marsh, Wendell. "Reading with the Colonial in the Life of Shaykh Musa Kamara, a Muslim Scholar-Saint." *Africa: The Journal of the International African Institute* 90, no. 3 (2020): 604–24.

Marx, Christoph. *Von Berlin nach Timbuktu der Afrikaforscher Heinrich Barth: Biographie*. Göttingen: Wallstein Verlag, 2021.

Mathee, Mohamed Shaid. "Muftīs and the Women of Timbuktu: History through Timbuktu's Fatwās, 1907–1960." PhD diss., University of Cape Town, 2011.

Mathee, Mohamed Shahid, and Nobili, Mauro. "Towards a New Study of the So-Called Tārīkh Al-Fattāsh." *History in Africa* 42 (2015): 37–73.

Mauny, Raymond. *Tableau géographique de l'ouest africain au Moyen Age*. Dakar: Institut Francais d'Afrique Noire, 1961.

McDougall, E. Ann. "Conceptualising the Sahara: The World of Nineteenth-Century Beyrouk Commerce." *Journal of North African Studies* 10, nos. 3–4 (2005).

———. "The View from Awdaghust: War, Trade and Social Change in the Southwestern Sahara, from the Eighth to the Fifteenth Century." *Journal of African History* 26, no. 1 (1985).

Minna, M. T. "Sultan Muhammad Bello and His Intellectual Contribution." PhD diss., University of London (SOAS), 1982.

Moos, Ebrahim. "The Literary Works of Shaykh Sīdī Al-Mukhtār Al-Kuntī (d. 1811): A Study of the Concept and Role of 'Miracles' in Al-Minna fī i'tiqād ahl al-Sunna." MA thesis, University of Cape Town, 2011.

Moraes Farias, Paulo Fernando de. *Arabic Medieval Inscriptions from the Republic of Mali: Epigraphy, Chronicles and Songhay-Tuareg History*. Fontes Historiae Africanae 4. Oxford: Oxford University Press, 2003.

———. "Arabic and Tifinagh Inscriptions." *Journal of African Archaeology Monograph* 12 (2017).

Mouline, Nabil. *Le califat imaginaire d'Ahmad Al-Mansūr*. Paris: Presses Universitaires de France, 2009.

———. "Sens et puissance: L'idéologie califale du Sultan Aḥmad al-Manṣûr al-Dhahabî (1578–1603)." *Studia Islamica*, no. 102 (2006): 91–156.

Müller, Lothar. *White Magic: The Age of Paper*. Translated by Jessica Spengler. Malden, MA: Polity Press, 2014.

Munajjid, Salah al-Din, ed. *Mamlakat Mālī 'inda al-jughrāfīyūn al-Muslimīn*. Vol. 1. Beirut: Dar al-Kitab al-Jadid, 1963.

Naylor, Paul. *From Rebels to Rulers: Writing Legitimacy in the Early Sokoto State*. Martlesham, UK: Boydell & Brewer, 2021.

Nixon, Sam, ed. *Essouk-Tadmekka: An Early Islamic Trans-Saharan Market Town.* Leiden: Brill, 2017.

———. *A New Cultural History of Essouk-Tadmekka.* Journal of African Archaeology Monograph Series 12. Leiden: Brill, 2017.

Nobili, Mauro. *Catalogue des manuscrits arabes du fonds de Gironcourt (Afrique de l'ouest) de L'institut de France.* Rome: Istituto per l'Oriente C. A. Nallino, 2013.

———. *Sultan, Caliph, and the Renewer of the Faith: Ahmad Lobbo, the Tarikh al-Fattash and the Making of an Islamic State in West Africa.* Cambridge: Cambridge University Press, 2020.

Norris, H. T. *The Arab Conquest of the Western Sahara: Studies of the Historical Events, Religious Beliefs and Social Customs Which Made the Remotest Sahara a Part of the Arab World.* Harlow, UK: Longman, 1986.

———. "Ṣanhājah Scholars of Timbuctoo." *Bulletin of the School of Oriental and African Studies, University of London* 30, no. 3 (1967): 634–40.

———. *Shinqiti Folk Literature and Song.* Oxford: Clarendon Press, 1968.

———. *The Tuaregs: Their Islamic Legacy and Its Diffusion in the Sahel.* Warminster, UK: Aris & Phillips, 1975.

———. "Znaga Islam during the Seventeenth and Eighteenth Centuries." *Bulletin of the School of Oriental and African Studies* 32, no. 3 (1969): 496–526.

Nouhi, Mohamed Lahbib. "Religion and Society in a Saharan Tribal Setting: Authority and Power in the Zwâya Religious Culture." PhD diss., University of Alberta, 2011.

Oßwald, Rainer. *Die Handelsstädte der Westsahara.* Berlin: D. Reimer, 1986.

Ould Bah, Mohamed El Mokhtar. "Introduction à la poésie mauritanienne (1650–1900)." *Arabica* 18, no. 1 (1971): 1–48.

Ovenden, Richard. *Burning the Books: A History of the Deliberate Destruction of Knowledge.* Cambridge, MA: Belknap Press of Harvard University Press, 2020.

Park, Mungo. *The Journal of a Mission to the Interior of Africa, in the Year 1805.* Cambridge: Cambridge University Press, 2011.

———. *Travels in the Interior Districts of Africa: Performed under the Direction and Patronage of the African Association in the Years 1795, 1796, and 1797.* Cambridge: Cambridge University Press, 2011.

Petrucci, Armando. *Prima lezione di paleografia.* Roma: Editori Laterza, 2002.

Polastron, Lucien X. *Livres en feu.* Paris: Gallimard, 2009.

Pollock, Sheldon. "Future Philology?: The Fate of a Soft Science in a Hard World." *Critical Inquiry* 35, no. 4 (2009): 931–61.

Pollock, Sheldon, Benjamin A. Elman, and Ku-ming Kevin Chang, eds. *World Philology.* Cambridge, MA: Harvard University Press, 2015.

Quenzer, Jörg B. *Exploring Written Artefacts.* Studies in Manuscript Cultures 25. Berlin: De Gruyter, 2021.

Quenzer, Jörg B., Dmitry Bondarev, and Jan-Ulrich Sobisch, eds. *Manuscript Cultures: Mapping the Field.* Studies in Manuscript Cultures 1. Berlin: De Gruyter, 2014.

Radtke, Bernd. "Studies on the Sources of the Kitāb Rimāḥ Ḥizb al-Raḥīm of al-ḥājj 'Umar." *Sudanic Africa* 6 (1995): 73–113.

Rauchenberger, Dietrich. *Johannes Leo der Afrikaner und seine Beschreibung des Raumes zwischen Nil und Niger nach dem Urtext.* Wiesbaden: Harrassowitz, 1999.

Rebstock, Ulrich. *Maurische Literaturgeschichte.* Vol. 1. Würzburg: Ergon, 2001.

Ricoeur, Paul. *Hermeneutics and the Human Sciences.* Edited by John B. Thompson. Cambridge: Cambridge University Press, 1981.

Robinson, David. *Paths of Accommodation: Muslim Societies and French Colonial Authorities in Senegal and Mauritania, 1880–1920.* Athens: Ohio University Press, 2000.

———. "Reflections on Legitimation and Pedagogy in the 'Islamic Revolutions' of West Africa on the Frontiers of the Islamic World." *Journal of West African History* 1, no. 1 (2015): 119–32.

———. "Un historien et anthropologue sénégalais: Shaikh Musa Kamara." *Cahiers d'Études Africaines* 28, no. 109 (1988): 89–116.

Robinson, David, and Jean-Louis Triaud, eds. *Le temps des marabouts: Itinéraires et stratégies islamiques en Afrique occidentale française v.1880–1960.* Paris: Karthala, 1997.

Rustow, Marina. *The Lost Archive: Traces of a Caliphate in a Cairo Synagogue.* Princeton, NJ: Princeton University Press, 2020.

Saad, Elias N. *Social History of Timbuktu: The Role of Muslim Scholars and Notables, 1400–1900.* Cambridge: Cambridge University Press, 1983.

Saʿdī, ʿAbd al-Raḥmān ibn ʿAbd Allāh. *Timbuktu and the Songhay Empire: Al-Saʿdi's Taʾrikh Al-Sudan down to 1613 and Other Contemporary Documents.* Edited by John O. Hunwick. Leiden: Brill, 1999.

Sadki, Hassan. *Makhtuṭāt Aḥmad Bābā al-Tinbuktī fi al-khazāʾin al-Maghribiyya.* Rabat: Royaume du Maroc Université Mohammed V, Institut des Etudes Africaines, 1996.

Schroeter, Daniel J. *Merchants of Essaouira: Urban Society and Imperialism in Southwestern Morocco, 1844–1886.* Cambridge: Cambridge University Press, 1988.

Shinqīṭī, Aḥmad ibn al-Amīn. *Al-wasīṭ fī tarājim udabāʾ Shinqīṭ.* Cairo: Muḥammad Amīn al-Khanjī, Miṣr, 1911.

Somogyi, Joseph de. "A History of the Caliphate in the 'Ḥayāt Al-Ḥayawān' of Ad-Damīrī." *Bulletin of the School of Oriental Studies, University of London* 8, no. 1 (1935): 143–55.

Spittler, Gerd. "European Explorers as Caravan Travellers in the West Sudan: Some Thoughts on the Methodology of Journeys of Exploration." *Paideuma* 33 (1987): 391–406.

———. "Explorers in Transit: Travels to Timbuktu and Agades in the Nineteenth Century." *History & Anthropology* 9, no. 2/3 (1996).

Stewart, Charles C. "Frontier Disputes and Problems of Legitimation: Sokoto-Masina Relations, 1817–1837." *Journal of African History* 17, no. 4 (1976): 497–514.

———. "A New Source on the Book Market in Morocco in 1830 and Islamic Scholarship in West Africa." *Hespéris Tamuda* 9 (1970): 209–46.

———. "Southern Saharan Scholarship and the Bilad Al-Sudan." *Journal of African History* 17, no. 1 (1976): 73–93.

Stewart, Charles C., and Ahmed Chaouki Binebine, eds. *Manuscripts and Arabic-Script Writing in Africa.* Alexandria: Hayʾat al-Makhṭūṭāt al-Islāmīyah bi-al-taʿāwun maʿa Maktabat al-Iskandarīyah, 2023.

Stewart, Charles C., comp. *Arabic Literature of Africa.* Vol. 5, *The Writings of Mauritania and the Western Sahara.* Leiden: Brill, 2015.

Stewart, Charles C., and E. K. Stewart. *Islam and Social Order in Mauritania: A Case Study from the Nineteenth Century.* Oxford: Clarendon Press, 1973.

Surun, Isabelle. "La décourverte de Tombouctou: Déconstruction et reconstruction d'un mythe geographique." *L'Espace géographique* 31, no. 2 (2002).

Tamari, Tal, and Dmitry Bondarev. "Introduction and Annotated Bibliography / مقدمة وثبت المراجع." *Journal of Qur'anic Studies* 15, no. 3 (2013): 1–55.

Timpanaro, Sebastiano. *The Genesis of Lachmann's Method.* Edited and translated by Glenn W. Most. Chicago: University of Chicago Press, 2005.

Touati, Houari. *L'armoire à Sagesse.* Paris: Aubier, 2003.

Triaud, Jean-Louis, and David Robinson, eds. *La Tijâniyya: Une confrérie musulmane à la conquête de l'Afrique.* Paris: Karthala, 2000.

———. *Le temps des Marabouts: Itineraires et strategies islamiques en Afrique occidentale française.* Paris: Karthala, 1997.

Tymowski, Michał. *Europeans and Africans: Mutual Discoveries and First Encounters.* Leiden: Brill, 2020.

van Dalen, Dorrit. *Doubt, Scholarship and Society in 17th-Century Central Sudanic Africa.* Leiden: Brill, 2016.

Ware, Rudolph T., III. *The Walking Qur'an: Islamic Education, Embodied Knowledge and History in West Africa.* Chapel Hill: University of North Carolina Press, 2014.

Warscheid, Ismail. *Droit musulman et société au Sahara prémoderne : La justice islamique dans les oasis du Grand Touat (Algérie) aux xviie–xixe siècles.* Leiden: Brill, 2017.

Yahya, Dahiru. *Morocco in the Sixteenth Century: Problems and Patterns in African Foreign Policy.* Atlantic Highlands, NJ: Humanities Press, 1981.

Zebadia, Abdelkadir. "The Career and Correspondence of Ahmad Al-Bakkayi of Timbuktu." PhD diss., University of London, 1974.

Zouber, Mahmoud. *Ahmad Baba de Tombouctou: Sa vie et son oeuvre.* Paris: G. P. Maisonneuve et Larose, 1977.

INDEX

Page numbers in italics indicate illustrations.

Abdullahi, Muhammad, 158, 165
Abdullahi, Sidi, 37–8
Adrar, 99
Africanus, Johannes Leo, xix, xxiii, 22, 32–33, 37, 41–42, 69
Aḥmad bin Aḥmad bin 'Umar bin Muḥammad 'Umar bin 'Ali bin Yaḥyā, xxiii, 51. *See also* Ahmad Senior
Ahmad Senior (Ahmad Baba's father), 51–53
Ahmed Baba Centre, 4, 7, 17, 19, 172. *See also* Cedrab
Ajami (a local language written in Arabic script), 22, 118, 162, 165, 167, 178
Ali, Sonni, xix, 52, 61–63, 100
Amr al-wali nasir al-Din, 107
al-'Anayn, Ma, 105, 111–12
Ansar Dine, xxvii, 3–4
Aqits, xix, 49–50, 52, 60–61, 74, 76, 88, 93–94, 109
Arab Spring, 1–3
Arabic Medieval Inscriptions of the Republic of Mali, 14
Arabicization, 100–101
Arawan, 37, 46, 86, 115–17, 122, 135, 138
al-Arawani, Ahmad Baber, xxiii, 158
archive-library, 3–6, 8
Arma rulers, xx, 87, 89, 96, 98
arshif (archive), xxvii, 21
Association for Promoting the Discovery of the Interior Parts of Africa (Africa Association), 35
Bâ, Amadou Hampâté, xxiii, 160–65, *166*, 167, 172–73
Baba, Ahmad, vii, ix, xi, xvii, xxi, xxiii, xxv, 4, 7, 10, *11*, 18, 20, 22, 24, 39, 41–42, 47, 56, *77*, *80*, 82, 108, 127, 130; advice to scholars, 54, 59, 128; ancestors, 22, 43, 61–62, 100, 109; arrest and exile, xx, 42, 53–54, 60, 65, 69–71, *72*, 73–74, 86–88, 98, 119; biographical dictionaries, 41, 60, 78–79, 127, 159, 171; birth, xx, 50, 62; death, 93, 97; education of, 49, 53, 117; family, 51–53, 83, 94; later years in Timbuktu, xx, 85, 87, 89, 91–93; leaving Marrakesh, 83–85; legacy, 93; role as teacher, 75–76, 94–96; scholarship of, 48, 141; writings of, 52, 55, 57–58, 60–61, 63, 69–70, 74–75, 79–82, 85–86, 90, 93
al-Bakkay, Ahmad, xx, xxiii, 46, 129–31, 144
al-Bakkay, Shaykh Sidi Ahmad, 38, 114, 118, 121, 129
al-Bakri, Abu 'Ubayd 'Abd Allah, 28, 30, 42, 93, 100
al-Bakri, Muhammad Tawfiq, 103, 110
Bamako, xvi, xxi, 2, 6–8, *11*, 12, 21, 138, 155–56, 158, 160–61, 163
Banu Hasan, 101–2
Banu Maghfar, 100
Barth, Heinrich (Abd al-Kerim), xi, xx, xxiv, 37–39, *40*, 42, 46–47, 96, *116*, 127, 130–31, 134, 155

al-Bartili Al-Walati, Al-Talib Muhammad Abu Bakr al-Siddiq, 97, 104, 108–9, 111
Bello, Muhammad, 38, 126–28, 130–31, 136
Berber, xxvii, xxviii, 3, 34, 47, 49, 100–101, 108, 114, 121, 135
Bilad al-Sudan (Land of the Blacks), xix, 28, 65–66, 120, 138
Bilad Shinqit (Land of Shinqit), 97, 99, 101, 104, 108–9, 114, 137, 139
Bin Raziqa, Abd Allah bin Muhammad, 106–7
book culture, 8–9, 18, 22–23, 25, 59, 153, 159, 176, 178
book tradition, 21, 25, 159, 175
Buh, Sa'd, 112, 168, 170
Bularraf, Ahmad, xx, xxviii, 10, *11*, 18, 20, 25, 46, 108, 112, 137–49, *150*, 151–55, 165

Cadamosto, Alvise, 34, 37, 42
Caillié, René, xi, xx, xxiv, 36–37, 42, 46, *116*
Catalan Atlas, xix, *31*, 33, 114
Cedrab, xxi, xxviii, 4, 6, 8, 56, 77, 80, 123–25, 150, 163
Centre d'Etudes et documentation et Recherche Ahmed Baba. *See* Cedrab
Clapperton, Hugh, 38, 127, 131, 136, 155
codices, 9, 175–77; of Timbuktu, 17
Collection of vocabularies of Central African languages, 39
Congress of Black Writers and Artists, xi, *166*
conquest of Timbuktu, 16, 44, 99
Cresques, Abraham, xix, 30–33, 114

Damiri, 57–58
Dan Fodio, Abdullahi, 126–27
Dan Fodio, Usman Shehu, 126–29
database of scholars, 76
Dawud, Askiya, 52, 62
al-Daymani, Muhammad bin al-Mukhtar al-Sa'id al-Yadali, 107
al-Daymani, Walid, 108
de Certeau, Michel, 24
de Gironcourt, Georges, xi, 47, *48*
"Déchiffrement de manuscrits chez les puels de say," xi, *48*
Delafosse, Maurice, xxi, 134–35, 159, 171–73
discovering books in the desert, 27, 29
Dīwān al-mulūk fī salāṭīn al-Sūdān, xxv, 98
Du Bois, Felix, xx, xxiv, 40–43, *44*, 46–48, 93, 96, 134, 139, 143

El Badi Palace, xi, 72
encyclopedist of Senegal, 168
exile in Marrakesh, 64–65, 119

Fatḥ al-Shakūr fī ma'rifat a'yān 'ulamā al-Takrūr, xxvi, 108
fatwa (legal opinion), xxvii, 91, 93, 145–49
Francophone West Africa, 163–64
Fulfulde, 47, 50, 126, 157, 160–62, 167–8, 171–72

Gaddafi, Muammar Muhammad Abu Minyar, 1–2
al-Ghallawi, Nabigha, 107–8, 111
Ghāyat al-amal fi tafdil al-niyya 'alal 'amal, xxvi, 70
Gibla, 101, 106
Goody, Jack, 25

hagiographer, 122
al-Hajari, Ahmad ibn Qasim, xxiii, 85, 93
Al-Ḥājj 'Umar Tāl, xxiii, 131
Hama, Boubou, xxiii, 163–65, *166*, 167, 173
Hamaliyyah, 169
Hamani, Diori, 164–65
Hamdallahi-Masina state, 130–31, 133, 160, 164, 170
Haratin (freed slaves), 101–2
Hasan tribes, 102
Hasani warriors, 102
Hasaniyya, 19, 74, 100, 103, 108, 112
Hassani Maghfar Arabs, 101
History of the Tatars, 38

"Homme et femme toucouleurs: Marabout faisant un grigri," xi, *169*
Hunwick, John, xiv, xxi, 61

Ibn Battuta, Abu 'Abdullah, xix, 29–30, 42, 100, 114, 171
IFAN, 160–65, 172–73
ijaza, xxviii, 53, 75, 95, 118
Institut fundamental d'Afrique Noir. *See* IFAN
Izālat al-rayb, xi, xxvi, 149, *150*, 174, 189–91

Jackson, James Grey, 36
Jalb al-ni'ma, xi, xxvi, 55, *56*, 59–64, 73, 76, 86
Jawāhir al-ma'ānī, xxvi, 132, 140
Jenne (Djenne), xvi, *11*, 12–13, 28, 36–37, 40–43, 87, 96–97, *116*
Jirari, 91–92

Kabara, 5, 144
Kamara, Musa, xxiii, 168–74, 192
Kanya-Forstner, A. S., 27
Kel Tamasheq, xix, xxvii, 2
al-Khalifa, Sidi Muhammad, xxiii, 122
khizana (store/storehouse), xxvii, 21
Kifāyat al-muḥtāj li ma'rifa man laysa fi al-Dībāj, xi, xxvi, 76, *77*, 79, 94, 97
kitab (book), xxvii, 21, 177
Kunta, xx, xxvii, 115, 121, 129, 133
Kunta clan, xxvii, 118
Kunta family, 38, 42, 109, 112–13
Kunta leadership, 130
Kunta scholars, 116–17, 130
Kunta writers, 114, 126
al-Kunti, Sidi Muhammad, xx, xi, 119, *123–25*, 128

al-La'ālī al-sundusiyya fīl-faḍā'il al-sanūsiyya, xxv, 74
Laing, Alexander Gordon, xx, 36, 38, 155
al-Lam' fīl'ishāra li-ḥukm al-tibgh, xxv, 86
al-Luma' fī ajwibat al-as'ilat al-arba'a, 90
L'empire de Gao: Histoire, coutumes et magie des Sonrai, 164
L'empire du Macina, 161, 166

Mā rawāhu al-ruwāt, xxvi, 64, 76
al-Maghili, Abd al-Karim, 114, 120, 128
Maghribi, xxvii, 17, 23
Mahadra, 103–5, 110, 117
mahfuthat (lit. a place of protection), 21
makhtuta (manuscript), xxviii, 21, 177
maktaba (library), xxviii, 21
Malfante, Antonio, 35, 114
Maliki law school, 53, 55, 57, 59, 75–76, 90–91, 100, 102, 128, 149
Mansa Musa, xix, 28–31, 51, 62
al-Mansur, Ahmad, xx, 67, 71, 83, 95
manuscript books, 6–7, 9, *11*, 20, 22, 24, 26, 51, 106, 110, 138, 154, 171, 178; Ethiopic (*mashaf*), 176; European, 17; main places, *11*
manuscript collections, 4–5, 7, 10, 12, 17, 21, 61
al-Maqqari, Abu l'Abbas Ahmad bin Yahya al-Tilmisani, 73, 75, 94–95
Marrakesh, image of, xi, 72
al-Marrakushi, Abu Abdullah Muhammad bin Ya'qub al-Isi al-'Adib, 73, 75, 94–95
Marty, Paul, 47, 135–36, 171
Masina, xx, xxv, 49, 96, 130, 132–35, 161, 163–64, 170
Matham, Adriaen, xi, *72*
Mauritania, 8, 11, 99, 104, 106; literary history of, 109–11
Miner, Horace Mitchell, 46
al-Minna fī i'tiqād ahl al-sunna, xxv, 119–20
Missions de Gironcourt en Afrique occidentale, xi, *48*
MNLA (Le Mouvement national pour la Liberation de l'Azawad, or the National Movement for the Liberation of Azawad), 2

Moriscos, 65, 85, 90
Morocco, 4, 11–2, 17, 22, 33, 61, 67, 78, 132–3, 135, 137, 154 ; conquest of Timbuktu by, 16
Mudawwana, 53, 57, 93
mufti, xxvii, 53, 95, 145
Muhammad, Askiya, xix, 32, 52, 62–63
Mukhtar al-Kunti, Sidi, 46, 99, 122, 135
al-Mukhtar al-Kunti, Sidi, xx, xxiii, 105, 115, 117–22
Mukhtar bin Buna al-Jakani, 104–5, 121

Nasir al-Din, 102–3, 107, 112
Naskhi, xxviii,17
Nayl al-ibtihāj, xxvi, 76, 79, 95, 127, 171
Niger River, xiii, 2, 5–6, *11*, 12, 28, 35–6, 40–1, 47, 52, 65–7, 87
Norris, H. T., 103, 108

omnishambles, 2
Ould Bah, Mokhtar, 104
Overweg, Adolf, 37, 39

Paris Societé de Geographie, 36
Park, Mungo, 35–37, 42, 155
pilgrimage to Mecca, xix, 51, 127
Primitive City of Timbuctoo, The, 46
private libraries, xxi, 5, 61, 191
Prophet Muhammad, 55, 70–71, 82, 92, 103–4, 107, 120, 129, 171

qadi (judge), 50, 88
Qadiriyya, xx, 114–15, 117–18, 121–22, 128–33, 147
Qadiriyya Sufi order, 117, 130, 147
Quran, 3, 37–38, 55, 79, 104–5, 107, 117–19, 127–28, 156–57, 161–62; exegesis of, 53, 59; verses of, *12*, 103
Quranic schools, 155, 157–58, 160–61

Rawḍat al-ās, 95
Republic of Mali, xxi, xxvii, 6, 162, 179
Richardson, James, 37, 39
Rimāḥ ḥizb al-Raḥīm'alā nuḥūr ḥizb al-rajīm, xxvi, 132
al-Risāla al-ghallāwiyya, xi, xxvi, 122, *124*
Risāla fī taṣawwuf, 90
rise of Shinqit, 98–99

al-Sa'āda al-abadiyya fīl-ta'rīf bi-'ulamā' Timbuktu, 158
al-Sa'di, Abd al-Rahman, xx, xxiii, 42, 61, 68, 88, 96, 98
Sa'dian dynasty, 16, 54, 60, 62, 69
al-Saghir, Mukhtar, 129–30
Sahara-Sahel, 25, 133, 135, 175–78
Sahel, xiv, xxi, xxviii, 8, 20, 25, 94, 129–30, 133, 135–36, 138, 148, 168, 175–78
al-Sahili, Ibrahim Abu Ishaq, xix, 51
Sahnun bin Said, 57, 59, 93
Sámbo, Fáki, 38
Sanhaja, 49, 100
Sankoré Mosque, xix, xxi, 3–4, 68, 93, 96
al-Shaykh, Sidi A'mar, 114, 120
Shinqit, 11, 99–103, 105–13, 137–38; rise of, 98–99. *See also* Bilad Shinqit
Shinqiti: scholars, 105, 139; society, 101–3, 106; statement, 107; writers, 109, 111
al-Shinqiti, Ahmad bin al-Amin, 109–11
Shurr Bubba War, 101–3, 106–7, 111–12
Sidi al-Mukhtar, 115
Sina, Ibn (Avicenna), 38, 52
Sīrāj al-mulūk, 58, 60
Sokoto, xx, *11*, 38–39, 126, 128, 130–32, 135–36, 164, 170
Songhay, xix, xx, 42, 67, 74, 89, 96–97, 134, 170; dialect of, 39, 47, 50, 98, 118, 157, 164
Songhay rulers, 52, 54, 56, 61, 65–66, 69
Souleymane Bachir Diagne, xiv, 173
Stewart, Charles C., xiv, xxv, 101
Strait of Gibraltar, 32–33
Sufi orders, 114, 126, 129, 147

Tadhkirat al-nisyān fī akhbār mulūk al-Sūdān, xxvi, 98

Takrur, xxvi, 28, 49, 108, 112, 127
al-Tamanarti, Abu Zayd bin Muhammad al-Jazuli, 94–6
Tamasheq, 2, 3, 50
Tamgrout (Tamegroute), *11*, 61, 86, 89–90
Taoudeni, 50, 69, 86, 115
al-Ṭarāʾif waʾl-talāʾid min karāmāt al-shaykhayn al-wālida wal-wālid, xi, xxv, 122, *123*, 126
Tārīkh al-fattāsh, xxi, 99, 133–35, 159, 171
Tārīkh al-Sūdān, xx, 17, 39, 42–43, 47, 61, 70, 88, 96–97, 108, 134, 159, 171
Tijaniyya, 129, 131–32, 144, 147
Tikna, xxviii, 138–40
Timbuktu: collections in, 12, 24, 26, 52; collector of, 137; conquest of, 16, 44, 99; fall of, 2–3, 99; history of, 23, 48, 146; occupation of, xxvii, 23, 24, 71, 89; saints in, 3
Tombouctou la mystérieuse, xi, xx, 41, 44
tombstones, 10, *12*, 47
Touré, Amadou Toumani, 2
Travels and discoveries in North and Central Africa, 39
Tuareg nationalists, 2, 3
Tuḥfat al-fuḍalā bi baʿḍ fadāʾil al-ʿulamā, xxvi, 79, *80*
Ṭurṭushi, Abu Bakr Muhammad, 58, 60, 128
Tuwat, *11*, 34–35, 91–92, 114–18, 128

al-Umari, Ibn Fadlallah, 28–30
Ummul Barahin, 104
UNESCO, xxi, 3, 21, 153, 162, 163
UNESCO General History of Africa, 153, 162
UNESCO World Heritage Site, 3, 21
Usodimire, Antoniotto, 34

view of Timbuktu, xi, *40*, *116*

Walata, *11*, 28–30, 49, 52, 61, 69, 97, 99–100, 108, 117–18, 121
al-Wallātī al-Yūnusī Muḥammad Yaḥya Sālim, xxiii, 149
al-Wangari, Muhammad Baghayogho, xxiii, 53, 88, 96, 109
West African Arabic calligraphy, 17
wooden tablet (*lawh*), 104, 107

al-Yadali, Muhammad, 105–8

al-Zarqun, Mahmud, 68, 70
Znaga, 34, 101, 108
Zwaya, 101–4, 107–8